Arthur Schnitzler

Biography

Arthur Schnitzler

Biography

Max Haberich

Arthur Schnitzler | Biography
By Max Haberich

Originally published by Kremayr & Sheriau
Arthur Schnitzler: Anatom des Fin de Siècle
English translation by Patricia Lawson
reprinted with kind permission by the author

Front cover image:
Arthur Schnitzler, circa 1912.
Photograph by Ferdinand Schmutzer (1870–1928).

Publishers Cataloging in Publication Data

Names: Haberich, Max, author.
Title: Arthur Schnitzler : biography / by Max Haberich.
Series: Studies in Austrian Literature, Culture and Thought
Description: Includes bibliographical references. | First English Edition. | Riverside, CA: Ariadne Press, 2021.
Identifiers: LCCN: 2021906879 | ISBN: 978-1-5724-121-4-9 (paperback) | 978-1-5724-121-5-6 (ebook)
Subjects: LCSH Schnitzler, Arthur, 1862-1931. | Dramatists--Austria--Vienna--Biography. | Authors, Austrian--Austria--Vienna--Biography. | BISAC BIOGRAPHY & AUTOBIOGRAPHY / Literary Figures | BIOGRAPHY & AUTOBIOGRAPHY / Jewish | HISTORY / Europe / Austria & Hungary | HISTORY / Modern / 20th Century
Classification: LCC PT2638.N5 H33 2021| DDC 832/.809--dc23

TABLE OF CONTENTS

INTRODUCTION

Arthur Schnitzler was one of the greatest authors that Austria produced in the 20th century. In his versatility, he stood out as a playwright as well as a writer of prose. The first Hollywood silent films, such as *Anatol* (1893) and *Daybreak* (1931), were based on his plays. His books were translated into English, French, Swedish, Italian, and Russian, and were read in those countries by a broad public. Thus, in the 1920's, he could be considered one of the best-known German-language authors world-wide. As a contemporary of Freud, he followed with great interest the early findings of psychoanalysis, and introduced psychological character development into German literature. Twenty years before James Joyce, he began to use the interior monologue, or stream-of-consciousness, as a literary technique to render the unconscious currents and associations of the human psyche. These fascinating, direct insights into the behaviour of his masculine and feminine characters have secured Schnitzler's relevance even up to the present. It was not long ago that Stanley Kubrick based his final film *Eyes Wide Shut* (1999) on Schnitzler's *Traumnovelle* (1926).

With this in mind, it seems odd that even today, Schnitzler is not included in official city tours of his native city, whereas there are several different tours, having to do with Carol Reed's film, *The Third Man* (1949). Neither can one find, at the house of his birth nor at his last residence, one of the City of Vienna's official plaques, with its characteristic four red-and-white flags. This, even though his birth house in today's Praterstrasse is only a few minutes away by foot from the city center. And what a contrast to Freud's former apartment, before which huge flags, impossible to overlook, indicate the presence of a museum! The proverbial Viennese cult of memory proves itself here to be unfairly selective. No other author has identified with Vienna to the same extent as Schnitzler has, nor made Vienna society, in all its facets, the theme of his work.

Fortunately, the several-year-long campaign of Michael Schnitzler, the author's grandson, finally bore fruit: The space in front of the Volkstheater, in which a number of Schnitzler's plays were premiered, in Vienna's seventh district, was named Arthur-Schnitzler-Platz in May 2017.

In contrast to the literary naturalists, Schnitzler is considered to be apolitical, or even indifferent to the deeper social problems of his day. The circle of naturalists around Karl Kraus and Alfred Polgar, who met in the Café Central, thought of themselves as concept-oriented as opposed to the "aestheticists," to which Schnitzler, Hugo von Hofmannsthal, Richard Beer-Hofmann and Hermann Bahr belonged. This group gathered at the Café Griensteidl.

But even if Schnitzler's social criticism is not as readily discernible as that of the naturalist Emile Zola, one cannot jump to the conclusion that it did not exist. It is true that Schnitzler did not, in fact, make the lot of the working classes one of his common themes. Rather, his milieu was the bourgeoisie, from whose upper layers he had sprung. It was here, in a world that he knew well, that he applied his social criticism. In particular, it was the women of the middle classes and their fates that engaged his interest. As a young man, he had an unusual number of female acquaintances and lovers, from the better-off daughters of his neighborhood to the girls from the outskirts. With their meager incomes, they could barely make ends meet, and still had brothers and sisters to provide for. He knew, therefore, what he was talking about, when he made a woman's life his theme. He could sympathize as readily with the manufacturer's daughter who was forced into marriage, as with the seamstress for whom it was completely impossible to break out of her lower middle-class existence. Many of his novellas, such as *Frau Berta Garlan* (1900), *Frau Beate and Her Son* (1913) and *Fräulein Else* (1924) bear witness to Schnitzler's being thoroughly aware of the social grievances of his times. And to his ever more clearly castigating this injustice: at first subtly, and later to the point of the overt social criticism of *Therese* (1928).

Schnitzler had a faithfulness to detail that was not reflected solely in his literary creations. With an exactitude bordering on pedantry, Schnitzler collected and filed away materials and documents about himself and his work. For 52 years, from age 17 to age 69, he kept a diary with daily entries. In the same way, he had his secretary type folders full of his correspondence, which was conducted over decades with literary colleagues. He also set up entire binders with reviews of his dramas and novellas. Students of his life and times have available a wealth of material that, for the most part, is stored in the Cambridge University Library (primarily manuscripts and correspondence with Samuel Fischer) and in the Deutsches Literaturarchiv at Marbach (diaries and correspondence with Olga Schnitzler). Another center of Schnitzler research is at the University of Freiburg, where the Schnitzler Archive has available most of the primary sources. Censorship documents forbidding the staging of the drama *Professor Bernhardi* can be viewed in the Niederösterreichisches Staatsarchiv of St. Pölten. In Vienna itself, there remain, and only by chance, some isolated letters in the Österreichische Nationalbibliothek. But it is essential to mention at this point the collection of 21,000 newspaper clippings in the library of the University of Exeter (GB), which Schnitzler had press clipping agencies compile in order to keep current on the critical response to his works. The earliest reviews are from 1891, the latest from 1937.

Why is half of the Schnitzler estate in Great Britain? That is the dramatic story of a rescue that took place through the intervention of a British doctoral student, Eric A. Blackall, who was studying in Vienna in 1938. He helped Olga Schnitzler, through the British ambassador, turn over her husband's papers as a donation to the Cambridge University Library. Doing so enabled this huge amount of personal and literary material to escape destruction by Hitler's stormtroopers.[1]

Research interest in Schnitzler has increased greatly in recent years. It was only in 2014 that a "new" novella, *Später Ruhm* [Late Fame], was published. Because the last critical edition of the collected works was published in the 1960's, since 2009, the University of Vienna has been publishing a new historical-critical edition of the early works from 1880

1 More detail in: Lorenzo Bellettini and Christian Staufenbiel: The Schnitzler 'Nachlass'. Saved by a Cambridge Student. In: *Schnitzler's Hidden Manuscripts*. ed. by Lorenzo Bellettini and Peter Hutchinson. New York: Peter Lang 2011, pp. 11–21.

to 1904. The University of Cambridge is working at present on a digital historical-critical edition of the works from 1905 to 1913. In tandem, the Bergische Universität Wuppertal is focusing on the later works from 1914 to 1931. When this joint international research project is finally completed, literary science will have at its disposal a well-grounded, up-to-date edition of Schnitzler's complete works.[2]

Drawing on hitherto unpublished sources from the Marbach and Cambridge literary archives, this biography intends to revise the traditional depiction of Schnitzler as an author indifferent to social issues. This book may also be used as a companion volume to the collected works. To the extent possible, for each prose work and each play, the historical context, the inspiration, and the possible real-life individuals on whom characters were based, can be identified in it. The focus, however, must be on Schnitzler's Austrian-Jewish identity. With this in mind, the author hopes not only to do critical justice to this great novelist and dramatist, but to help expand Schnitzler's readership once more to the large audience that he deserves.

Max Haberich
Vienna, March 2019

---

2 The websites of the projects: http://www.arthur-schnitzler.at/historisch-kritische-ausgabe/ (Vienna) and http://www.arthur-schnitzler.de/ (Cambridge and Wuppertal).

"VIENNA — PRESENT"

The Jewish Community of Vienna in the Late 19th Century

"It was the best of times, it was the worst of times, it was the age of wisdom, it was the age of foolishness, [...] it was the season of Light, it was the season of Darkness, it was the spring of hope, it was the winter of despair." The famous opening lines of *A Tale of Two Cities* by Charles Dickens, which describes Paris before the outbreak of the revolution, is equally appropriate to turn-of-the-century Vienna. The multinational capital of the Habsburg Empire was, together with Berlin, Paris, Munich and Prague, an epicenter of modernism. It was the city of Klimt and Kokoschka, of Mahler and Schönberg, of Hofmannsthal and Musil, and of Freud. Vienna brimmed over with a multi-ethnic mix of Germans, Hungarians, Czechs, Croats, Slovenes, Poles, Ruthenians, Italians, and, of course, Jews.

From the assassination of the reformist Czar Alexander II in 1881 onwards, waves of pogroms rocked the settlements of Russian Jews in what is now the Ukraine. Thousands upon thousands of refugees streamed over the border into Germany and Austria. These Orthodox Jews were visibly foreign, with their caftans, their long curls and their Yiddish language. By 1910, 2,259,685 citizens of the Jewish faith lived in Austria-Hungary, or 4,4% of the total population of both halves of the empire.[3] In comparison, 615,000 Jews lived in Germany in the same year, of whom 79,000 came from the East.[4] This was equivalent to just barely 1% of the total German population.

But in view of the overall increasing numbers, in 1879, the reputable German historian Heinrich von Treitschke launched, with a contribution to the *Preussische Jahrbücher*, the so-called "Antisemitismusstreit" [Debate on anti-Semitism]. He argued that Jews were a threat to national integrity. He called for their expulsion in order to preserve the purity of the German

---

3 Rudolf Rothaus: *Geographischer Atlas zur Vaterlandskunde an den österreichischen Mittelschulen.* Vienna: Kartographische Anstalt Freytag und Berndt 1911, Table 3.

4 Ernest Hamburger: *Juden im öffentlichen Leben Deutschlands.* Tübingen: Mohr Siebeck, 1968, p. 6.

people.[5] Treitschke lent anti-Semitism a middle-class and academic tone that the phenomenon had never before possessed. His opponent in this debate was the classical philologist Theodor Mommsen, editor of the multi-volume *Römische Geschichte*.[6] In 1881, Chancellor Bismarck was handed an "anti-Semitic petition," which requested a revocation of the constitutional clause guaranteeing Jewish citizens equality before the law. Bismarck rejected this. With their caricatures of these "Eastern" Jewish immigrants, the anti-Semites created a stereotype that they then applied to assimilated members of the middle-class. But these middle-class Jews had, for the most part, little connection to the Jewish religion. They had much more in common with their German or Austrian social equals than with the impoverished refugees from the East. A friend of Schnitzler's, the Jewish author Jakob Wassermann, who had come to Vienna from the Nuremberg area, admitted in his autobiographical work, *Mein Weg als Deutscher und Jude* (1921):

> When I saw a Polish or Galician Jew, when I spoke to him, [...] he might well move me to sadness and pity, but there was no sense of brotherhood, nor even of any relationship. He was entirely foreign to me, in his opinions, in every respect, and if there was no individual sympathy, he even repelled me.[7]

The Western Jews had been, on the whole, happily integrated. They had embraced and internalised German (and Austrian) customs, mores, literature and culture; i.e., everything that could be subsumed under the term "Bildung." Now, through the refugees from Russia and the Eastern areas of the Habsburg Empire, their cultural identity was suddenly being called into question. To cite Wassermann once more: "In all innocence, I had been convinced until then that not only did I belong to the German

---

5 Ibid., p. 59.

6 For a more thorough treatment of the Debate on Anti-Semitism, see: *Der Berliner Antisemitismusstreit.* Hg. von Walter Böhlich. Frankfurt/Main: Insel 1988.

7 Jakob Wassermann: Mein Weg als Deutscher und Jude. In: *Jakob Wassermann – Deutscher und Jude*. ed. by Dierk Rodewald. Heidelberg: Schneider 1984, p. 115.

way of life and the German people, but that I had a right to this by birth."[8]

Toward the end of the 19th century, assimilated Jews now found themselves forced to accept a heritage they had been estranged from for generations. The anti-Semitic press depicted this heritage with the stereotype of the uncultured, uneducated and generally primitive "Eastern" Jew. It was not uncommon for assimilated Jews to turn on these Eastern Jews themselves, in a desperate attempt to prove their adherence to German culture. Prominent examples include the author of *Geschlecht und Charakter* (1903), Otto Weininger, who committed suicide at the age of 23. Another case in point is the editor of the satirical magazine, *Fackel*, Karl Kraus, who indulged in anti-Semitic rants and secretly converted to Catholicism, only to leave the Church several years later.[9]

One response to the acceleration of modern urban life and continuing industrialization was a glorification of rural life. In his *Deutsche Schriften* (1878), Paul de Lagarde called for a revitalization of German traditions and the German national character. This would only be possible with a distinct distancing from German Jews, who, as Lagarde maintained, had no appreciation for the German need for a national identity. Lagarde was the first to expand the theories of such conservative thinkers as Walter Riehl, for whom the modern city was the catalyst of social inequality, to include clearly anti-Semitic components. Riehl argued that the peasantry, thanks to its traditional connection to the soil, provided the natural counterweight to modern urban existence.[10]

In 1890, Julius Langbehn, who lived in Munich, depicted in his oft-reprinted book *Rembrandt als Erzieher*, the way real art only springs from a close association with the soil and the people, not out of the anonymous, decadent, big cities. Langbehn, whose work was viewed as one of the seminal texts of the "Heimatkunst-"movement, wrote that the farmers not only made up the "foundation of the state," but, rather, were also indispensable for the "Aryan renewal" of society. "The power of the blood [...] is stronger than anything," according to Langbehn. For him, the Germans enjoyed

8 Ibid., pp. 67–68.

9 The most comprehensive biography on Karl Kraus is Edward Timms: *Karl Kraus, Apocalyptic Satirist*. New Haven: Yale University Press 1986.

10 Thomas Kraft: *Jakob Wassermann*. Munich: DTV 2008, pp. 52–53.

a God-given right, because of their highly developed sense of virtue and the "purity of their blood," to rule over other peoples. In other words, "The Germans have been selected to be the nobility of the world."[11] If Lagarde added anti-Semitism to Riehl's promotion of a natural life on the land, Langbehn supplied the additional theme of imperialism.[12]

These ideas were circulating in German and Austrian cities in the last decades of the 19th century. Even when the temptation is great to label these ideas reactionary from the contemporary viewpoint, it should not be forgotten that in their time they were considered highly modern. Equally modern was Charles Darwin's Theory of Evolution, as well as pseudo-scientific racial theories, such as those from Houston Stewart Chamberlain or Arthur de Gobineau. In his essay *Sur l'inegalite des races humaines* (1853), the latter further developed the already existing hypothesis of a white, Aryan race, one superior to all others, which should not mingle with other races. Chamberlain embraced this concept, and emphasized in his writings the dominant position of the German people in terms of Aryanism. He also contributed an anti-Semitic element that Gobineau lacked. One-hundred thousand copies of Chamberlain's major work *Die Grundlagen des Neunzehnten Jahrhunderts* (1899) had been sold by 1914.[13]

Vienna — Multinational Capital of the Dual Monarchy

As the central cultural melting pot of the Habsburg Empire, Vienna reflected the ethnic conflicts of the entire Monarchy in concentrated form. The convergence of Germans, Czechs, Hungarians, Poles, Italians and other peoples made for an astounding ferment of cultural creativity. At the same

11 Kraft, p. 55.

12 cf. Fritz Stern: *The Politics of Cultural Despair: A Study in the Rise of the Germanic Ideology*. Berkeley: University of California Press 1974.

13 William L. Shirer: *The Rise and Fall of the Third Reich*. London: Bookclub Associates Edition 1985, p. 107.
More detail on Chamberlain's theories of race can be found in Geoffrey G. Fields: *Evangelist of Race: the Germanic Vision of Houston Stewart Chamberlain*. New York: Columbia University Press 1981.

time, the early 20th century was an era of nationalism and national states. How aggressively the people of the Monarchy quarreled with each other is illustrated by the decisions of the minister president Count Badeni in 1897. The new rules that Bohemian civil servants' official correspondence from then on had to be composed both in German and Czech led respectable citizens to take to the streets by the hundreds and peaked in a genuine rebellion. Czech and German representatives in the Austrian Parliament even physically assaulted each other.[14]

Even if these major differences were by no means primarily motivated by a desire for independence from Habsburg rule, they were conducive to a widespread atmosphere of decline and disintegration. After Hungary, in 1867, was elevated to the status of a half-autonomous kingdom, other minorities began to demand similar rights. The Serbs were the most militant – all the more so since an independent Serbian state came into being in 1878 on the other side of the southeastern border. The Italian population around Trieste saw themselves in a similar situation.

Only a small minority of the German "Staatsvolk," who were among the most loyal supporters of the dynasty, rallied to the "Pan-German" movement of Georg von Schönerer. Schönerer was a convinced anti-Semite and very much admired by the young Hitler. He demanded that Austria-Hungary be completely broken up and that the German-speaking areas be united with the neighboring German Empire. In 1889, however, his Alldeutsche Vereinigung [Pan-German Union] numbered only 1,200 members. Furthermore, in 1907, only three German separatists were elected to Parliament. At this point, the movement was already in decline.[15] Nevertheless, in spite of its meagre numbers, this group would not allow itself to be ignored, thereby contributing to social tensions in Vienna during mayor Karl Lueger's term of office.

In 1890, the Jewish community made up 5% of the Viennese population. Twenty years later, the number had practically doubled, from 99,441

14 Gunther E. Rothenburg: *The Army of Francis Joseph.* West Lafayette: Purdue University Press 1976, p. 128.

15 Robert S. Wistrich: *The Jews of Vienna in the Age of Francis Joseph.* Oxford: Oxford University Press 1989, p. 192.

to 175,318, or 8.6% of a total population of somewhat over 2 million.[16] Theoretically, since the Emancipation of 1867, the Jews had the same rights as all other citizens. In practice, things looked very different. Jews could only rise to a certain rank in the administration, judiciary, army, or higher education system. Then, they hit a glass ceiling.

Robert Wistrich cites Hans Tietze's *Die Juden Wiens* (1933), in which a German nationalist named Türk announced in Parliament that there were "55 Jewish professors of Medicine and Law in Vienna." Rabbi Joseph Bloch held, however, that "21 of these professors are converts and only two of them are invested as full professors."[17] These restrictions explain why many Viennese Jews concentrated on trade and finance. A number of Jews were also in the professions: 15% of employable male Jews were lawyers, 6% were doctors and 8% were novelists or journalists.[18]

A third of the Jews of Vienna (34%) lived in the traditional Jewish quarter on the other bank of the Danube Canal, the Leopoldstadt. The center and the district immediately north of it, the Alsergrund, housed, respectively, 20%. The rest of the Jewish population distributed itself among the Brigittenau, Mariahilf and Neubau districts.

In light of the relentless national quarrels that paralysed Parliament during the last decades of Austria-Hungary, the Jews could be characterised as the Kaiser's most loyal subjects. They were cognizant of being under the special protection of Franz Joseph to the point that the nationalist press labeled him the "Judenkaiser" or Jews' Emperor.[19] Because he was a guarantor of emancipation within the framework of the "Ausgleich" of 1867, higher Austrian civil servants could not permit themselves to discriminate openly against Jews. If they did so, they were acting in clear opposition to one of the Habsburgs' central principles of government.

If a latent anti-Semitic posture in the higher state administration was nevertheless widespread, this can be traced to the centuries'-old marriage of church and state, in a country that saw itself as a bastion of the counter

16 Ibid., p. 42.

17 cited in ibid., p. 173.

18 Hans-Otto Horch: *Judentum, Antisemitismus und europäische Kultur*. Tübingen: Francke 1988. pp. 211–12.

19 Wistrich, p. 179.

reformation. The alliance of clerical and political interests was also, for example, responsible for the banning of Schnitzler's drama, *Professor Bernhardi*. During the term of mayor Karl Lueger, anti-Semitism was tolerated by the highest city authorities. Under his aegis, the anti-Semitic press indulged in increasingly daring attacks on the Jewish community.

Franz Joseph had withheld the acknowledgment of Lueger's election as mayor four times, precisely because he feared official discrimination against his Jewish subjects. When Lueger won the election for the fifth time, the Kaiser gave in. Lueger held the office of Mayor from 1897 until his death in 1910. Although he habitually ranted against Jews in his political speeches, Lueger had Jewish supporters and friends in finance, industry, and the liberal press. There were "good" Jews under his protection, and "bad" ones, whose reputations he was willing to sacrifice for his political ends.

Already at this time, anti-Semitism was no longer a hallmark of the lower social classes. Only a few decades before, it had been considered a characteristic of the small tradesman, who had possibly become indebted to a Jewish bank, or who resented his Jewish competitors. Now, anti-Semitism was also gaining ground among the students and professors of the University. In 1896, student fraternities proclaimed the "Waidhofener Beschluss," which denied Jews the right to defend their honor with the sword.[20] Having a chance to defend one's honor with a sword in a duel was, for students of this era, extraordinarily important. The Waidhofen Decree states: "Every son of a Jewish mother, every person with Jewish blood in his veins is born without honor, and incapable of finer feeling. [...] In ethical terms, he stands on a lower level. Interacting with Jews slights one's own honor, and Jewish company should be avoided. By this definition, a Jew is incapable of being offended; therefore he cannot demand satisfaction for the insults he suffers."[21] After this proclamation, purely Jewish fraternities were established (among which the Kadimah should, in particular, be noted) that demonstratively upheld the traditions of fencing.[22] Nor did they avoid confrontation with nationalistic fraternities. Among the professors, a

20 Ibid., p. 367.

21 Arthur Schnitzler: *Jugend in Wien*. Wien: Molden 1968, S. 156. Abbreviated as JiW.

22 Marsha Rozenblit: *The Jews of Vienna 1867–1914: Assimilation and Identity*. Albany, NY: State of New York University Press 1983, p. 161.

reputable surgeon, Dr. Theodor Billroth, publicly voiced his worries over the growing numbers of "Eastern" Jewish students at the University. He feared that this trend would unavoidably lower academic standards: For one, because of their allegedly imperfect mastery of the German language; and for another, because of the "insurmountable differences between the German and the Jewish races."[23]

Anti-Semitism and Zionism in Austria and France

Anti-Semitism was by no means restricted to the German-speaking world. In France, the Dreyfus Affair raged for a full twelve years. The young army captain Alfred Dreyfus was convicted of treason in November of 1894, for having allegedly sold military secrets to the Germans. He was sent to the penal colony on Devil's Island, off the coast of French Guyana, where he was placed in solitary confinement for five years. Two years later, evidence emerged pointing to the real culprit, Ferdinand Esterhazy. The military officials suppressed this evidence, however, and acquitted Esterhazy on the second day of his trial. They intended to re-convict Dreyfus, based on additional charges drawn from forged documents. As rumours about the framing of Dreyfus by the military court began to spread, Émile Zola published his fiery letter *J'accuse* (1898). The government finally conceded to pressure from liberal circles to re-open the case. In 1899, a new trial resulted in a ten-year sentence, but Dreyfus was pardoned and set free. It was not until 1906, however, that all accusations against him were officially proven groundless, and he was reinstated in the French army. He continued to serve throughout the length of the First World War.[24]

The trial split the entire country. Dreyfus' supporters and opponents engaged in bitter debates in the French press. In France, as well, anti-Semitism was not restricted to the petite bourgeoisie, but could also

---

23 Theodor Billroth: *Über das Lehren und Lernen der medizinischen Wissenschaften an den Universitäten deutscher Nation*. Wien: C. Gerold 1876, pp. 152-54.

24 A more detailed account of the Dreyfus Scandals may be found in George R. Whyte: *Die Dreyfus-Affäre — die Macht des Vorurteils*. Frankfurt/Main: Peter Lang, 2010.

be found in intellectual circles. In essence, the Dreyfus Affair was an ideological struggle between those who believed in the glory of France's cultural achievements, which they saw embodied in the army, and those who held the individual rights of man higher than any specific political program. It was a clash between the political right and left and their sympathizers. When it was revealed that Dreyfus had been convicted twice on the basis of forged evidence, after he had already spent five years on Devil's Island, the French anti-Semites suffered a defeat their German counterparts never underwent. Neither Germany nor Austria ever saw the triumph of republican values over political intrigue, as happened in France with such a decisive, reverberating victory on the part of the opponents of anti-Semitism.

The affair was followed with great interest in Vienna. For its duration, Theodor Herzl was correspondent in Paris of the *Neue Freie Presse*, the flagship newspaper of the liberal middle-class. Paul Goldmann, a friend of Schnitzler's, demanded the resumption of the trial several times between September and November of 1896, when it came to light that Dreyfus had been convicted on the basis of forged evidence. Lucien Millevoie, a former member of Parliament, called Goldmann a "lâche coquin," or a coward, in a newspaper article, whereupon Goldmann challenged him to a duel. Schnitzler thus felt these reverberations of the Dreyfus Affair in his immediate environment. After the positive outcome, he wrote a telegram to Goldmann, "And for this, I write plays against duelling."[25] This Dreyfus Affair proved how firmly entrenched anti-Semitism was at high levels of the French administration and the army, and that, before Dreyfus' ultimate exoneration and reinstatement, it had come to be perfectly acceptable among the middle and upper classes of society,

The most disturbing feature of the contemporary anti-Semitism was that conversion was no longer an adequate solution to the problem. According to the theories of Gobineau and Chamberlain, Jewishness was no longer considered a religious, but a racial category. At the same time, European Jews saw themselves confronted with two opposing stereotypes. No longer was the distinction primarily between the "good" assimilated

25 Arthur Schnitzler: Briefe 1875–1912. ed. by Therese Nickl und Heinrich Schnitzler. Frankfurt/Main: S. Fischer 1981, p. 307.

Western Jews and the "bad" orthodox Eastern Jews. On an industrialised continent, Jews were considered to be capitalist exploiters in the socialist press, as exemplified by such successful bankers as the Rothschilds or the Ephrussis. At the same time, conservative papers never tired of reminding their readers that not only Karl Marx, but also Viktor Adler, the founder of the Austrian Social Democratic Party, were of Jewish origin. Since other Social Democratic politicians also had Jewish backgrounds, some journalists in these papers suggested that in reality it was the Jews who were the driving force behind the "communist world revolution." The assimilated Jews of the middle classes could not win against this double-edged sword. These theories of a Jewish world conspiracy, conducted by either capitalist or revolutionary means, were summarised in the highly influential – and fraudulent – *Protocols of the Elders of Zion.* It appeared first in Russian in 1903, but was soon translated into all major languages.[26]

In the imperial capital, Jewish responses to this new form of anti-Semitism were highly varied. Although Theodor Herzl is generally considered the "Father of Zionism," similar theories did, in fact exist before him. Herzl's energy and ambition organised these tendencies and brought them onto the world stage. The first Zionist congress took place in August, 1897, with the stated goal of establishing a state for the Jewish people in Palestine. The Zionists assumed that Jews were one national body, similar to other European peoples. The only solution to the "Jewish Question," in their view, was emigration and statehood. Only this would put an end to the centuries of injustice and persecution. Only when in possession of their own country, would the Jewish people finally be able to rise to parity with other European nations.

In view of this development, in 1886, Rabbi Joseph Bloch from Floridsdorf, called into being the Österreichisch-Israelitische Union [Austrian-Israelite Union],[27] which was intended to provide a positive image of the Jewish community. It positioned itself in between Jewish nationalism and assimilation. Its founders viewed the Jews neither as an indivisible nation, nor did they believe in mass emigration. The first

26 Bruce Pauley: *From Prejudice to Persecution*. Chapel Hill, NC: University of North Carolina Press 1992, p. 8.

27 Rozenblit, p. 155.

task of the Union was an organised defence against anti-Semitism. The Union professed Austrian patriotism in that loyalty to the State and to the Habsburg monarchy were central tenets of their program. They were equally concerned with the achievement of a Jewish identity, with rights equal to those of the other peoples of the empire, within the framework of the Habsburg state. They appealed particularly to the Jewish middle class.[28]

In spite of their different approaches, such associations had one goal in common with Zionism. They wanted to unite all Jews in a general organization against anti-Semitism. Every German-speaking Jew must somehow take a stand against this new, racial anti-Semitism, regardless of how Jewish he felt himself to be. Complicating this considerable challenge were the divisions between the Zionists and the Austrian-Israelite Union, as well as between these two and the primarily religious "Israelitische Kultusgemeinde" (Israelite Cultural Association). This, in turn, was divided into liberal and orthodox factions. In light of this wide variety of opinions, one can appreciate that the question of Jewish identity in Vienna around 1900 was a complex issue indeed.

There was also a small number of Austrian Jews, however, who did not want to have anything at all to do with these larger groups. These were the painters, composers, philosophers, and writers who had each left their recognisable mark on German culture. The tremendous intellectual and artistic flourishing of the early 20th century, in which Vienna was a nexus of artistic modernity, has never been reached again. At the center of this creative blossoming were the assimilated, middle-class Jews.

Why was it the Jews? One answer could be that there is a strong tradition of learning, and respect for the learned, in Jewish communities. Freud attributed his adamant defence of psychoanalysis against widespread initial resistance to his Jewish background and the associated status of being an outsider in society. As a Jew, he noted, one is free from intellectual prejudice, and ready to enter into opposition against a united majority.[29] This mental attitude also rings true for one other prominent Jewish figure of public life: Arthur Schnitzler.

---

28 Wistrich, pp. 192–95, 311.

29 Shulamit Volkov: *Antisemitismus als kultureller Code*. München: C.H. Beck 2000, p. 151.

THE EARLY YEARS 1862–1894

The Schnitzler Family

Arthur Schnitzler was born on May 15, 1862, in the Praterstrasse of the Leopoldstadt. In those days, it was still called the Jägerzeile. This area in the present-day second district was already the Jewish quarter in the Middle Ages. It continues to be so up to the present. The life path of Schnitzler's father is an example of the successful ascent of provincial Jews into the Viennese upper classes, after the Emancipation that occurred in Austria in 1867, with the creation of the dual state of Austria-Hungary.

His father, Johann Schnitzler (1835–93), came from Groß-Kanizsa in Hungary, where his father Josef had had a cabinetmaker's workshop. According to one source, Josef was supposed to have been illiterate. Nevertheless, he succeeded in marrying Rosalie Klein from the family of Baron Gutmann de Gelse, who generously supported him financially, and enabled her grandson Johann to attend not only Gymnasium, but also to study medicine at the Universities of Budapest and Vienna. Until the required second doctoral dissertation in Laryngology was completed, he tutored to supplement his income. In 1861, shortly after completing his studies, he married Louise Markbreiter, the daughter of a respected Viennese doctor. On her mother's side, she came from the venerable Hungarian-Jewish family Schey.

In Vienna, where he opened his practice, Dr. Johann Schnitzler became the preferred laryngologist for the actors of the Burgtheater and the singers at the city and state operas. This professional success went hand-in-hand with assimilation, so that, according to his son Arthur's autobiographical notes, only his maternal grandmother still observed the rituals on Jewish holidays. In his family, quite tellingly, the matzo was used mainly as a coffee biscuit.

The father's unquestioning adoption of middle-class values and conventions exerted some pressure on the three Schnitzler children. Arthur's younger brother Julius was born three years after him (1865–1939), and two years after Julius came their sister Gisela (1867–1953). Julius Schnitzler would follow in his father's footsteps and become a renowned surgeon. His sister was later to marry the laryngologist Markus Hajek, who would operate on Freud's tumour in his last years – and, coincidentally, also on Kafka's laryngeal tuberculosis. In moments of self-doubt and marital crisis, Arthur would ask his siblings' advice time and time again, especially that of Gisela.

With Arthur, the father was later to have serious words, as the son, after receiving his medical degree in 1885, turned increasingly to literature. His literary inclinations were already apparent by the time he was eighteen. A year after graduating from the Akademisches Gymnasium, which was also attended by Peter Altenberg, Richard Beer Hofmann and Hugo von Hofmannsthal, in May 1880, Schnitzler recorded in his diary 23 completed dramas and 13 plays in progress.[30] After all, his father's patients and evening guests had brought him into contact with the glamour of the stage already at an early age. Johann, however, as a representative of the upper middle classes of the "Ringstraße Era," had a different view of the stage.

The Haute Bourgeoisie of Vienna

In 1857, the Emperor Franz Joseph I ordered the demolition of the old city walls. In their stead were laid out broad, tree-lined boulevards which were, over time, bordered by such exemplary public buildings as the Parliament, the University, the City Hall, the State Opera, the Burgtheater and the cultural and natural history museums, as well as the most exclusive hotels of the city. The Ringstrasse, which lent its name to an entire epoch, belonged to the upper classes of Vienna. Here, they manifested themselves in all their pomp and circumstance, building apartment buildings with lavish, neo-baroque facades that burgeoned with ornament – of which one Adolf Loos decidedly disapproved.

The Ringstrasse incarnated the self-confidence of the newly created "kaiserliche und königliche Monarchie," brought into being by the new

30 JiW, p. 101.

constitution of 1867. It also exemplified the political domination of the Liberals, who controlled the Austrian parliament. The Liberal ministers limited the clerical lobby's influence, and reformed suffrage. Under Liberal protection, the assimilated Jews, who since the Ausgleich were free to enter the professions of medicine, law, higher education and journalism, experienced a period of safety and prosperity. Dr. Johann Schnitzler embodied this new self-confidence, but also faith in the state and in middle-class values, which he imparted to his family. For the well-off bourgeoisie, the artistic callings, in particular that of the writer, smacked of general negligence and instability.

As an expression of this newly found Austro-Hungarian self-confidence, and of the Monarchy's pride in its technical and industrial achievements, Vienna hosted the world exhibition of 1873. Nevertheless, only six years later, the Liberal Party lost its majority in Parliament. Over the last two decades of the 19th century, the Social Democratic and the conservative, clerically-minded Christian Social parties gained more and more influence with the masses.

It is clear from *Jugend in Wien* (1968), that Schnitzler was fully cognizant of the atmosphere of tolerance and security during the Liberal government. In his diary as well as in his works, he always held up the tolerance of this era as a standard against which to measure the increasingly vocal anti-Semitism that, during Lueger's mayorship, became an officially recognised political means to achieve Christian Social goals.

As already mentioned, in 1875, the respected surgeon Theodor Billroth, who would supervise Schnitzler's doctoral research ten years later, publicly voiced his concern that the large numbers of Jewish students from the East would lower the academic standards of the University of Vienna.[31] According to their degree of nationalism, student fraternities, particularly the politically oriented "Burschenschaften" would no longer accept Jewish members. As late as the 1880's, both Schnitzler's later friend, Hermann Bahr, as well as Theodor Herzl, belonged to Burschenschaften. However, Herzl left in 1883 because of anti-Semitic comments directed at him, as did Bahr one year later for the same reason.

---

31 Rozenblit, p. 32.

Schnitzler himself remained distant from such associations throughout his life. But his first real encounter with anti-Semitism at the university level took place in these years. In his autobiography, he relates an episode reminiscent of the third act of *Professor Bernhardi.* He was on the committee of an association for the support of needy Jewish medical students. Christian and nationalist student groups demanded that forthwith, the association should support only "German, no Hungarian and Slav," and thus no Jewish students.[32] A likely predecessor of Dr. Schreimann from *Professor Bernhardi* was in this group, in that a converted Jew supported the German side, claiming objectivity because of his own Jewish background. Intrigues led to Schnitzler and his more liberal-minded colleagues being voted out of office and replaced by a soundly anti-Semitic committee. Similarly, Schnitzler declared that his opponent from this period of confrontation served as the model for a further Bernhardi character, the student Hochroitzpointner.[33] Later on, after Schnitzler was no longer involved, confrontations between the Jewish and non-Jewish members of this charitable society escalated to the point of violence, which was even reported in the Vienna dailies.[34]

University and Military Service

From October 1882 until October 1883, Schnitzler served one year as a medical orderly. In the army, the mocking term "Moses Dragoon" applied to the not particularly well-regarded medics, who were not considered "real" soldiers. Schnitzler notes that "some of them left much to be desired with respect to their military bearing and appearance, especially among the Hungarian and Polish Jews."[35] There is a report of a hardly pro-Semitic superior proposing several weeks of confinement to quarters for Schnitzler and several Jewish comrades, but the charges were subsequently dropped. Apart from this, Schnitzler does not mention any further anti-Semitic incidents during his military service. Rather, Schnitzler exploits

32 JiW, p. 157. [see FN 20]

33 JiW, p. 157–58.

34 Ibid.

35 Ibid., p. 141.

the glamour of the uniform to embark on various romantic adventures.[36]

In the year that Schnitzler receives his medical degree, 1885, Georg von Schönerer's nationalist party adds another point to their program: as a precondition for their reforms, the "removal of Jewish influence in public life is essential." This so-called "Aryan Paragraph" is then presented in parliament.[37] Two years later, Schönerer proposes an "Anti-Semitic Law," which places the immigration and residence of foreign Jews under strict regulations. Although it is rejected, German nationalist and clerical deputies vote for it, including the later mayor Karl Lueger.[38]

Schönerer loses his status as a deputy for five years, after breaking into the editorial offices of a liberal paper that was founded and run by the Jewish journalist Moriz Szeps. During this time, the predecessor party of the Christian Socials, which still calls itself "The Anti-Semites," is growing and increasingly attracting nationalistic as well as anti-Semitic elements.[39]

Schnitzler is Casanova's worthy successor, in that he knows many women and knows them intimately. He cannot live without these casual affairs, and he conducts them well passed his thirties. In his diaries are found countless women's names, which are sometimes only referred to by an initial. He compiles statistics of his sexual experiences, which add up to the following numbers: in 1887, 208 times; 1888, 400 times; 1889, 593 times; 1890, 181 times; 1891, 321 times; and 1892, over 400 times.[40] After his 30th year, he stops keeping record.

It was for good reason that, in *Ein Weites Land* (1911), he has Friedrich Hofreiter declare to Adele Natter, with whom he has had an affair: "If one has time and is in the mood, one builds factories, conquers countries, writes

---

36 Ibid., p. 143–44.

37 Robert Hein: *Studentischer Antisemitismus in Österreich.* Wien: Öst. Verein für Studentengeschichte, 1984, p. 31.

38 Adolf Gaisbauer: *Der historische Hintergrund von Arthur Schnitzlers "Professor Bernhardi."* In: Bulletin des Leo Baeck Instituts 13/50 (1974), pp. 113–63, p. 117.

39 *Niederösterreich im 20. Jahrhundert.* ed. by Stefan Eminger. Wien: Böhlau 2008, p. 400.

40 Arthur Schnitzler: *Tagebuch 1879–1892.* ed. by Peter Braunwarth et. al. Vienna: Verlag der Öst. Akademie der Wissenschaften, 1981–2000. The statistics stem from the respective entries for December 31 for the years 1887–91, and August 31 in 1892. The diaries are abbreviated TB.

symphonies, becomes a millionaire ... but believe me, all that is secondary. The important thing is you [women]! You! You!"[41]

This quotation, however, refers to more than merely superficial relationships with women. One year after a certain Betty betrays her husband with him, Schnitzler makes the acquaintance of Olga Waissnix in Meran, where he is treating a patient for a possible infection of the lymphatic system.[42] Olga is the first woman whose intellect and character have such a profound effect on him that a platonic relationship of several years' duration ensues. Schnitzler is 23. Her husband is the owner of the Hotel Thalhof in Reichenau, barely two hours away from Vienna. The relationship remains platonic, because Olga fears the consequences of adultery in a small town: social disgrace, according to the conventions of the time. Not to mention her own moral qualms. Their correspondence, conducted until her death in 1897, was first published in 1970. It testifies to Schnitzler's incomplete self-image as an author in these early years, and to the conflict between fulfiling his father's desire that he pursue a medical career against his powerful urge to write. Olga is the first woman to acknowledge him as a writer, and to encourage him continually in this regard.[43]

Olga Waissnix – First Literary Attempts

He first meets Olga in April, and already, on May 9, 1886, he records in his diary: "It was a tremendous blunder of mine to become a doctor, and, unfortunately, one that can no longer be remedied. Apart from a certain sharpness in observation and a clear understanding of certain issues, which I have my medical studies to thank for, I wish it could all be taken from me again – oh, I want to be free, quite simply: I want to be wealthy and an artist."[44]

---

41 Arthur Schnitzler: *Gesammelte Werke in vier Bänden*. Frankfurt/Main: S. Fischer 1961–62. Die dramatischen Werke Vol. 2, p. 250. Abbreviated as DW I or II.

42 TB 1879–92, 12.4.1886.

43 See Arthur Schnitzler – Olga Waissnix. *Liebe, die starb vor der Zeit. Ein Briefwechsel*. ed. by Therese Nickl and Heinrich Schnitzler. Wien: Molden 1970.

44 TB 1879–92, 9.5.1886.

From the literary point of view, Schnitzler is first published in 1880, when the *Liebeslied der Ballerine* and the essay *Über den Patriotismus* appear in the Munich journal *Der freie Landesbote*. Then, in 1885, the magazine *An der Schönen blauen Donau*, for which his later "Jung-Wien" (Young Vienna) colleague Paul Goldmann works, prints a poem of his. Also, several aphorisms as well as the prose sketch, *Er wartet auf den vazierenden Gott*, appear in the *Deutsche Wochenschrift*.

Around this time – between 1885 and 1887 – Schnitzler also writes *Erbschaft*, which is only first published in his collected works in 1932. In only a few pages, the mood swings from enjoyment of life to the opposite extreme. It is entirely possible that Schnitzler was speculating about what would happen if Olga's husband discovered his letters to her. But the constellation of husband-wife-lover was not all that unusual in Vienna at the time – and certainly not in Schnitzler's stories.

Four months after completing his medical studies, in September 1885, Schnitzler begins to assist in the Allgemeines Krankenhaus and in his father's polyclinic. Sometimes, he also helps out in his father's private practice. In November, he moves up in the medical hierarchy as assistant to Theodor Meynert, the head doctor in psychiatry. After April, 1887, he changes to the department for syphilis and skin diseases. He had already taken over, on January 1, the position of editor of the *Internationale Klinische Rundschau*, founded by his father. By 1893, over two dozen contributions by him have appeared in this journal. These are primarily book reviews. Nor is he otherwise motivated to do medical work. In January, 1888, he joins the surgical department of Dr. Joseph Weinlechner, but neglects his patient rounds, and tries to avoid the operating room as much as possible. Instead, he uses this time to turn his experience with Olga Waissnix into a short story, *Gabrielens Reue*. It gets to the point that his father, who observes this neglect of his medical duties with concern, wants to send him on an educational medical journey to Berlin and London.

Something already occurred in September of the previous year that could have come out of the world of the early plays, *Das Märchen* (1893) and *Liebelei* (1895). Schnitzler is strolling along the Ringstraße boulevard with a friend when they noticed an attractive, elegantly dressed young woman. Schnitzler follows her and speaks to her, which she does not seem to mind. It is not long before they succumb to their passion.[45] This girl, Jeanette Heeger, becomes Schnitzler's first long-term relationship. She is from the poorer outskirts, the "Vorstadt," and lives with her three sisters and a brother. She sews on commission for various shops to support her family.[46] Schnitzler was true to her for two years, which gave him ample time to study the petit-bourgeois milieu, the setting where Christine of the *Liebelei* is at home.

In the course of Schnitzler's relationship with Jeanette, a play is published that he wrote in 1886, *Abenteuer seines Lebens*. For the first time, Anatol and Max appear, along with an impulsive Vorstadt-girl, Cora. There is also Gabriele, who is torn between fidelity and passion, but in the end remains a loyal wife. The parallel between Gabriele, who also appears in *Weihnachtseinkäufe* (1893), and Olga Waissnix, is obvious. Indeed, Schnitzler, in May 1889, refers to Olga as the "adventure of his life."[47] Schnitzler opens a practice of his own, but since he hardly has any patients, he continues to write stories. *Der Andere* (1889) is one of his works from this time. It is a story written as a diary entry in the style of an interior monologue. In it, a lover, at the grave of his just-deceased beloved, sees another completely unknown man mourning. He tortures himself with the desecration of his love, as well as with the riddle of his beloved, whom he apparently never really knew.

Reichtum (1891) also dates from this time. A poor man awakens in the morning, still in tails, remembering that he won a fortune at a club the night before. However, he drank to excess and cannot remember where he buried the winnings. He continues his life in poverty, abandoning himself to alcohol. It is not until his dying hour that he remembers the hiding place. He calls his son to him, a painter, who follows his fathers' instructions and discovers the treasure. Thus elevated, he feels capable of painting a great painting. But to do so, he must experience the thrill of the card table, where he loses everything and then descends into madness. Schnitzler takes up the theme of this type of inherited misfortune again in his later work,

45 Ibid., 19.10.1887.

46 Renate Wagner: *Frauen um Arthur Schnitzler*. Wien: Jugend und Volk, 1980, p. 62.

47 TB 1879–92, 31.5.1889.

intrigued as he is with mysterious curses and behaviour patterns that recur over the generations.

Another work from these years is *Der Fürst ist im Hause* (first published posthumously). It is one of the few pieces in which Schnitzler focuses on a shy and introverted individual, a flute player in a large orchestra. Like Roland in *Ehrentag* (1897*)*, he is one of the many whose absence would scarcely be noticed, except that during a concert he suddenly falls ill and dies. Because the local prince is present, the director becomes frantic. At all costs, the misfortune must be covered up and no attention aroused. Here, the young Schnitzler parodies the overriding middle-class concern for propriety, and the need to have important occasions run flawlessly. The director assures the prince that all is well. There is no reason for concern. And the prince smiles on the proceedings benevolently.

Travels and Enemies — *Anatol*

Aside from the completion of these minor prose works, Schnitzler pursues his carefree existence. He goes to balls and to the derby, losing considerable sums there as well as at billiards in Vienna's coffee houses. His father strongly disapproves of this bohemian lifestyle, and insists, in April of 1888, that Arthur travel to Berlin to further his medical education. There he visits the Charité and the Friedrichshauser Krankenhaus. He takes one or another course, but the literature-obsessed son cannot feel genuine enthusiasm for medicine. One month later, he travels to London, where his uncle lives. There, too, he is more often at the theater or a concert than in the lecture hall. He embarks on one affair or another, with, for example, Claire, the manager of his boarding-house.[48] He also starts to write *Anatol's Hochzeitsmorgen* (1890).

In Ostende, a stop on the return journey, he indulges in a brief interlude with the married Adele Spitzer. She considers herself very attractive to men and wants to enjoy the sensual advantages of this appreciation without committing herself. For Schnitzler, she is as much a psychological study

48 JiW, pp. 303–304.

as a lover, and in his literary work we repeatedly encounter characters reminiscent of her type. In August, he is back in Vienna, where he calls off this affair for Jeanette's sake.[49]

Schnitzler launches into literary production. He finishes *Hochzeitsmorgen*, writes *Episode* as well as *Erinnerungen*, and sends these one-act plays, together with *Abenteuer seines Lebens*, to Samuel Fischer, who will only publish them if the author covers the costs himself. His verdict is: "We do not expect sales from 'dramatic conversations.'"[50]

The year 1889 brings increasing pressure on Schnitzler to revive his medical career. In January, his sister Gisela marries Markus Hajek, also of Jewish origin, who is by now a successful laryngologist. This is why Dr. Johann Schnitzler no longer objects to the match. The "Hungarian Jewish boy," as he called Hajek, has also achieved career success – and in medicine – while hailing from a similarly modest background. Nevertheless, Johann Schnitzler has so internalised bourgeois principles that he would rather have seen a suitor from a higher position in society.[51]

Schnitzler's brother Julius proves to be considerably more dedicated to his medical studies than Arthur himself ever could be. Julius intends to specialise in surgery. In this year, Schnitzler's first and last medical work appears: *Über funktionelle Aphonie und deren Behandlung durch Hypnose.* He is fascinated by hypnosis and reads Charcot, whose texts Freud is also working with. In the one-act play *Frage an das Schicksal* (1890), hypnosis is used to test a lover's loyalty.

It is worth noting an incident at the polyclinic in March. Schnitzler had declared himself ready to organize a ball. Not only is the event announced in the liberal papers, unusually, it is also mentioned in the Christian Social *Deutsches Volksblatt*. This is done on the initiative of an anti-Semitic assistant doctor who wants to make a demonstrative political statement, although it has been agreed not to advertise in the Christian Social papers. At the next committee meeting, Schnitzler states his disapproval. He calls for a vote of no confidence against the culprit, which passes successfully. At a

49 TB 1879–92, 25.8.1888.
50 Cambridge University Library (CUL), Briefe S. Fischer an Schnitzler. Folder B 121g, 27.11.1888.
51 JiW, p. 312.

meeting after the ball, however, his opponent accuses Schnitzler of the same degree of arbitrariness: Schnitzler had asked the conductor to play a waltz instead of the quadrille listed in the musical programme – a truly Viennese conundrum. The anti-Semitic doctor demands a public apology, which Schnitzler, of course, refuses. The tone of the discussion becomes more and more aggressive. A vote of no confidence against Schnitzler is averted by a single vote. He is then challenged to a duel, and his friend Louis Mandl urges him to accept. But, in his work, Schnitzler will frequently criticize the institution of the duel. And the son of the director does not respond to the provocation.

New Affairs, New Works

Schnitzler's affair with Jeanette is drawing to a close. Her successor is the 16-year-old Marie Glümer. Schnitzler meets her in July 1889, and she soon allows him to call her, tenderly, Mizi. She is an actress, and Schnitzler is her third lover. Judging by the standards of the time, she is a "fallen woman." Schnitzler addresses this particular problem of social convention and the situation with Mizi in *Märchen*, which he works on from November 1890 until March 1891.[52] He describes the inner conflict of Fedor Denner with a considerable dose of self-criticism. Although Fedor declares himself a defender of fallen women in his circle of friends, and speaks out against the double standard, he cannot forget the previous affairs of his lover, Fanny Theren (who is also an actress). The fairy tale of the fallen woman prevails, not lastly because of male vanity, to which Schnitzler observes himself falling victim time and time again. Just as with Fanny and Fedor, Mizi leaves Schnitzler, who is very much in love with her, in September 1890. She leaves for financial reasons as well, to accept a promising role in Salzburg.

Schnitzler's family is seriously dissatisfied with him. His uncle wants to marry his 28-year-old nephew to Helene Herz, a young woman from a well-to-do family. Even though Schnitzler finds her appealing, he foils his

52 JiW, pp. 312–13.

uncle's plans for the sake of Mizi Glümer.[53] Neither is Johann Schnitzler by any means happy about the publication of the one-act play *Episode,* which is inspired by the relationship with Jeanette, and features Anatol. Nor is he any more accepting of Schnitzler's two short stories *Mein Freund Ypsilon* and *Amerika* (both 1889) published in the magazine *An der schönen blauen Donau.* Poems of Schnitzler's also appear in print under the tell-tale nom de plume, Anatol. This does not exactly help him to distance himself from criticism of the protagonist of his one-act play cycle, with the inevitable allegations of autobiography by implication.

Amerika is a prose sketch, in which the narrator has just landed in the New World. He thinks back to a game he used to play with his love, in which they discovered their own America. The meaning varies from happy memories to sexual fulfilment. Schnitzler plays quite skilfully with the symbolism of the word "America" and its connotations of discovery. The narrator has actually crossed the Atlantic but longs for the other America left behind in Europe.

Mein Freund Ypsilon deals with a poet, the narrator, who has fallen in love with his own creation, the Prinzessin Türkisa. For her sake, he rejects a real-life woman. His health declines increasingly, the closer he comes to describing her inevitable death. In the end, he flings himself over the banister of a top story. Even though the plot is overstretched, Schnitzler's talent for structure is revealed here. He begins with Ypsilon's death and develops the narrative until the final moment of revelation.

"Jung Wien" and Bahr's *Antisemitismus — ein Internationales Interview*

Schnitzler's father is convinced that a doctor who writes novellas is not taken seriously, and makes this clear to his son in unmistakable terms. He also accuses Arthur of "a lack of scientific seriousness."[54] Nevertheless, Schnitzler turns increasingly to literature. Neither does his new circle of friends incur his father's approval. Since April 1890, he belongs to a loose

53 Ibid.
54 TB 1879–1892, 1.5.1886.

literary group called Young Vienna, which meets in the Café Griensteidl. Paul Goldmann, who helped him achieve his first publications, already belongs to the group, but only later in the year do Richard Beer-Hofmann, Felix Salten, Hugo von Hofmannsthal, Gustav Schwarzkopf, Hermann Bahr, and Karl Kraus join as well. Schnitzler will remain in friendly contact with most of these men throughout his life, even if, in many cases, the friendship slackens over the years. Kraus, the acid-tongued editor of the satirical paper, *Fackel*, from 1892 on, admires Schnitzler greatly at first, but then moves into the circle of naturalist writers in the Café Central. From there, he repeatedly launches biting attacks on him. Paul Goldmann also changes, in the course of the years, into a convinced Schnitzler critic. Felix Salten and Hermann Bahr belong to the minority in this circle which actually has to earn its daily bread with journalistic work. Most of the members of Young Vienna are from the Jewish upper middle class, and thus have both the leisure and financial security to dedicate themselves seriously to literature.

Today, from Salten's works, perhaps only his animal stories are remembered. One of them served as the model for Walt Disney's *Bambi.* Bahr's career is interesting in light of the "Jewish Question" of the period. As a student, he joined the nationalist fraternity "Albia," as Theodor Herzl, by the way, did also. Bahr was personally acquainted with the leader of the German Nationalist Party, Georg von Schönerer, and even became involved in the Pan-German movement. In 1884, he left his fraternity because of its increasing anti-Semitism. Instead, he openly acknowledged his Jewish background.[55]

In this context, it is worth noting the foundation of the "Verein zur Abwehr des Antisemitismus" [League for Defence against Anti-Semitism] in 1891. Its founding proves that the Jewish community of Vienna did not feel sufficiently protected by the Austrian Israelite Union, or at least felt the need to call another defensive association into being against increasing anti-Semitic sentiment. However, this defensive association was supported by Christians as well as Jews, and did not consider itself a religious association.

55 Pauley, p. 53.

Rather, it was an organization of the liberal middle class. The Union had much closer ties with the orthodox community.

The Association was active both in Germany, where it was supported by Mommsen and later by Heinrich Mann, as well as in Austria, where it was represented by the famous pacifist Bertha von Suttner. Its work was publicity rather than politics. With its mouthpiece, *Mittheilungen aus dem Verein zur Abwehr des Antisemitismus*, which was renamed *Abwehrblätter* in 1925, it sought to counter anti-Semitic propaganda from nationalist, clerical, and Christian Social journals.[56]

With respect to literary developments, Bahr always felt the pulse of his time. In 1891, he wrote the programmatic essay, *Die Überwindung des Naturalismus,* which distinguished the aestheticists of the Café Griensteidl from the naturalists of the Café Central. By this time, Bahr had left his Pan-German phase behind him, and had come to the conclusion that what was best in German culture was being preserved by Jewish artists. Following this conviction, he conducted interviews, as a journalist, with a number of intellectuals from various European countries on anti-Semitism. He published the collection of interviews as *Der Antisemitismus – ein internationales Interview* (1893). In the foreword, he writes:

> Whoever is anti-Semitic is so out of a craving for the intoxication of passion. He seizes the arguments that are at hand. When one disproves them, he will look for others. If he does not find them, that will not convert him. He doesn't want to do without the intoxication. The only thing that could heal him would be a nobler excess, if the masses were again given an ideal, a moral emotion.[57]

Bahr's book is a highly interesting historical document and important material for anyone concerned with the history of anti-Semitism. He talks to novelists who are anti-Semites because they loathe capitalism and the bourgeoisie. He also seeks out critics who, out of fear of socialism

56 Ibid., p. 52–53.

57 Hermann Bahr: *Der Antisemitismus – ein internationales Interview (1893).* ed. by Claus Pias. Weimar: VDG 2005, pp. 10–11.

and revolution, come to the same conviction. Notable are the intellectual acrobatics with which some of these theorists deny that they could be taken for anti-Semites, because they feel that they are promoting or combating much bigger ideas than "mere" Jewishness. But, ultimately, Bahr comes to the conclusion: "Anti-Semitism is the morphine addiction of the little people" – the shopkeeper, whose competitor is more successful, or the indebted husband, who, after speculating, cannot afford the interest on his loan any longer. Bahr writes further:

> My suspicion was confirmed, the [anti-Semitism] comes from a certain disposition of the nerves, a hysterical desire. Many people desire to be seized by passion, storm, and intoxication of the soul. Because they cannot find any great love in this forlorn age, they create narcoses of hate. One should find some kind of ideal for them.[58]

First Performances, Work on New Plays

The year 1891 sees the first performance of a Schnitzler play, *Abenteuer seines Lebens*, at the Rudolfsheimer Theater in the Mariahilferstraße. The public laughs, it would seem, at the wrong places, while the subtleties escape them. But on May 13, the play is repeated, to an enthusiastic reception, at the Josefstadt Theater. Even Schnitzler's father, who seemed indifferent to his son's work until then, is happy about his success. Schnitzler himself, however, is dissatisfied with the play, in which Anatol is torn between two women, inspired by Jeanette and Olga. It will not be staged again, and is not even included in the printed version of the *Anatol* cycle.

Die Braut is a short prose work that Schnitzler completes this year. Although it is only a few pages long, it underlines, with its unabashed portrayal of female sexuality, the modernity of its author. Because of its controversial content, Schnitzler avoided publishing it during his lifetime. It is most certainly drawn from his experiences with numerous poorer

58 Ibid., p. 141.

girls, "die Vorstadtmädel." Not only, but also because of this, Schnitzler's dramas caused scandals time and time again. *Die Braut* depicts human, but especial female sexuality as a primeval urge that cannot always be kept in check and that affects human behaviour consciously or unconsciously. In seizing on this notion, which clashed with the social conventions of his time, Schnitzler not only acknowledged Freud's revolutionary theories, but also one of the strongest themes of his contemporary artists.

Das Märchen, which treats the complications of being in love with an actress, is rejected for its indecency not only by the Burgtheater, but also by theater directors in Berlin and Prague. Nevertheless, encouraged by his literary colleagues, Schnitzler has the manuscript of this play printed at his own expense.

With the one-act *Anatol* plays, for the same reason, he sees no alternative to covering the publishing costs himself. The 1893 edition includes the plays *Episode* (1898), *Frage an das Schicksal* (1896), *Anatols Hochzeitsmorgen* (1901), *Agonie* (never performed), *Denksteine* (1916), *Weihachtseinkäufe* (1898) and *Abschiedssouper* (1893). Schnitzler leaves out *Anatols Grössenwahn* (1932), *Abenteuer seines Lebens* and *Süsses Mädel* (a fragment which, strictly speaking, is not part of the cycle). The entire cycle would be performed at the same time, on December 3, 1910, at Berlin's Lessing Theater and at the Viennese Volkstheater, with the exception of *Agonie* and *Denksteine*.

The *Anatol* Cycle

Anatol is a melancholy Don Juan who indulges in the pleasures of life, but later falls into melancholy reflections. He lives for his memories as much as for his love affairs. His close companion is the ironic, epigram-spouting Max, who knows how to take his friend's moods. These are the most light-hearted and humorous of Schnitzler's plays. The cycle already contains very well-observed female character studies. In *Frage an das Schicksal,* Anatol is desperate to know whether the flirtatious "Vorstadtmädel" Cora is true to him, and he hypnotizes her. Ultimately, he cannot bring himself to ask the fateful question. He orders Cora to wake up and kiss him. Anatol prefers love and ignorance to what could be a destructive truth. The closing line is left to Max: "One thing is clear: that women even lie under hypnosis..."[59]

Weihnachtseinkäufe presents us with a very different woman, the upper middle-class housewife Gabriele, who has always been shielded from the more unpleasant side of society. She is reserved at first, but eventually decides to help Anatol choose a Christmas gift for his girl from the Vorstadt. They cannot find anything in the shop window, and Gabriele gives him her own flowers for her, with the words: "These flowers, my sweet girl, are given to you by a woman who can perhaps love as much as you, but who did not have the courage to..."[60]

In *Episode* (1898) Max and Anatol go through Anatol's romantic souvenirs. Bianca has a rendezvous with Max. But Anatol, who thinks he knows that Bianca once really loved him, insists, because it is to be a purely friendly appointment, on remaining in Max's apartment. When Anatol again stands vis-à-vis Bianca, she does not recognize him. He leaves the apartment in a fit of anger.

In *Denksteine* (1910), Anatol cannot accept that a "fallen woman," Emilie, keeps a ruby in her drawer as a souvenir of her first lover. He insists (or pretends) that he cannot tolerate a lie from her, but the truth makes him even unhappier. After he has destroyed all letters and souvenirs of his earlier love affairs for her sake – or so he maintains – he demands that she, in turn, throw away this ruby. Then he discovers another jewel, a black diamond, assumes the worst and throws it in the fire. With a cry, she begins to search in the embers with a tong.

The cheerful actress Annie, who speaks her mind, is introduced in *Abschiedsouper* (1893). Anatol has invited her to a chambre separée to put an end to their relationship. Max is there for moral support. However, before Anatol can lay his cards on the table, she pre-empts him because she is in love with someone else. Max is greatly amused, while Anatol, not to lose face, tells her shameless lies about his alleged infidelities. Fuming, Annie storms out of the room, taking a pack of cigarettes from the table. "Not for me!" she declares, "They're for him!"

In *Agonie,* it is a question of a situation rather than a specific character.

59 DW I, S. 41.
60 Ibid., p. 49.

The issue is what men and women inflict on each other to obtain a proof of unconditional love – especially when the woman is already married. Anatol torments himself while he waits for Else, until Max suggests to him:

> Max: Naturally! You'd rather hide it from yourselves with a thousand tricks that you no longer feel the same way about each other, than to make a quick decision to separate. But why?
> Anatol: Because we don't believe it ourselves. Because in the middle of the endless desolation of these death throes, there are those rare, deceptive moments in which everything is more beautiful than ever before... !

Although Anatol basically knows that the affair with Else is over, he still torments her as she declares her love for him and maintains never to have felt anything for her husband. He wants to flee the country with her, until she brings him to his senses in that she reminds him that they can see each other as often as they want in Vienna. At the end, Anatol says, "'Now, with this kiss, I have made her into what she deserves to be... into yet another one!' He shivers. 'Stupid, stupid... !'"

Ilona, of *Anatols Hochzeitsmorgen,* is temperamental and the exact opposite of a "süßes Mädel." After a period of absence, Anatol met her again the night before. She finally grasps that Anatol is marrying the same day, and tries everything, impulsively, to hold him back. It takes all of Max's diplomatic skill to calm her down, so that Anatol can get ready and leave for the church. Soon afterward, she storms out of the house, vowing to return.

In *Anatols Grössenwahn* (1932), the older romancer looks back on his many affairs. Annette, who is in a group of guests at his house, flirts with him intensely, lets him hold her hand, and even throws herself on her knees in front of him. After she cannot persuade him to join the rest of the group, another former lover, Berta, appears on the scene. The humorous high points of the one-act play occur in the following dialogue, e.g., in this scene:

> Anatol: But we did adore each other so!
> Berta: Maybe so ... but you don't have to lose your head just because of that... !

Anatol is offended that Berta lied to him years earlier. She calls out, "I think I'm meeting up with an old friend, and he becomes as abusive as a lover." Anatol's pride is hurt, and he finally gets her to go back to the others. The last lines of the play are spoken by Annette to her new lover, who is jealous because she keeps looking over at Anatol and Max. She consoles him, "But, my sweet angel ... at such an old man!!"

What's interesting is the light in which Anatol's frivolous love affairs appear. The plays are basically written, not for him, but for his women. The women, with their diverse personalities, set the tone for the one-act plays. And none of them ends with Anatol as the winner, no matter how superior he feels. He values each meeting with a beautiful woman, even if it is only a conversation in front of a shop window, as with Gabriele in *Weihnachtseinkäufe.* In reality, it is the feminine characters who have power over him, and Anatol, who is in love with women in general, willingly submits to them.

These plays are all too often portrayed as light-hearted romantic adventures – as the literary equivalent of the frivolous, champagne-sprinkled world of *Die Fledermaus* (1874), in which one flirts, makes love, and parts the next day without regrets or sadness. But they do, in fact, contain the critical framework for condemning young Lotharios, which, in *Liebelei* and *Märchen,* comes into full realization. Schnitzler's life-long empathy for female characters, which only increases in the course of the years, is already evident in the Anatol cycle. Even though these one-act plays are not highly acclaimed works, Schnitzler succeeds in clearly portraying the weaknesses and vanities of the male lover in contrast to the qualities of the female characters. Here, he already delineates the financial and social dependence of the woman from the lower, but also from the middle classes, in keeping with the conventions of the time.

Breakthrough as an Author

Schnitzler continues to mature not only as a playwright, but also as a prose author. In 1892, he publishes *Der Sohn*, which contains the central idea for his second and last novel *Therese* (1928). A man who, between his debts and crimes, led a degenerate life, tries to kill his mother with an axe. Throughout his life, she indulged him in every whim, and continually met his financial demands as they became more and more outrageous. On her deathbed, she explains that all her sacrifices to her son could not atone for her original sin. The night after he was born, when his father had already left her, she had tried to smother the child. The next morning, however, he was still alive and breathing. She never forgave herself that sin. In spite of all her feelings of guilt, she was not able to avert her son's decline nor her own death.

From February until July, Schnitzler works on the novella *Naher Tod*, which concentrates on a feature that recurs throughout his work: the close proximity of love and death, of Eros and Thanatos. With clinical precision, he describes the psychological consequences of consumption on young Felix, who only has a few more weeks to live. At the outset, his lover, Marie, is willing to die with him. The closer death looms, however, the more desperately he clings to life, as embodied in Marie. Felix's increasing obsessiveness makes Marie more and more frightened of him. When, in the final stages, he tries to kill her, she leaves him for good, fleeing from proximity to death into the world of the living.

In 1894, Schnitzler sends the manuscript, now entitled *Sterben*, to Samuel Fischer. The publisher is concerned that the story may be too macabre, but at the same time, he is also convinced of its literary value. He draws up a three-year contract with the young author, which will be continually renewed throughout Schnitzler's life. In December, the story is published in the house's magazine *Neue deutsche Rundschau*. In the following year, it appears not only in book form, but also already in French translation as *Mourir*. The story is so successful that, in March, Fischer asks Schnitzler for more prose, in order to make the most of the public's enthusiasm.[61]

Nevertheless, 1893 is no easy year for Schnitzler. He still loves Mizi Glümer very much, and learns from her letters that she is no longer true to him. Although they have not even lived in the same city for years, Schnitzler's letters to her swing back and forth between agony and fury. He

61 Samuel Fischer und Hedwig Fischer: *Briefwechsel mit Autoren*. ed. by Dierk Rodewald and Corinna Fiedler. Frankfurt / Main: S. Fischer 1989, p. 53.

is well aware that the two "sweet young things," Minni and Fifi, with whom he is possibly just flirting, cannot replace Mizi.

Schnitzler's amorous entanglements are reflected in the prose of these years. In *Kleine Komödie* (1895), Schnitzler discards the usual first- or third-person narrative in favour of a fictional exchange of letters. Using this technique, a love affair unfolds before the reader's eyes both from the male and the female perspective. Alfred, from a wealthy family, and the actress Josephine, pretend to a life of bare subsistence. After they spend a brief holiday together, and their relationship becomes more serious, they decide to tell each other the truth. Josephine is delighted and hopes to consolidate their relationship. Whereas Alfred has no intention of supporting an actress used to a life of luxury. We have only a glance at their last letters before their next holiday together, in which Alfred has resolved to separate from the unsuspecting Josephine.

Death of the Father — the First Theater Scandal

The most serious event of this year – Schnitzler's father's death – occurs on May 2. In spite of their differences, Schnitzler suffers greatly from the loss of his father. He has always admired his intelligence and benevolence. It is impossible not to think of the character of the father in Thomas Mann's *Tonio Kroger* (1903), a literary exemplification of middle-class propriety who induces his son, after his death, to find the profession of novelist "a little careless" in contrast to an orderly, business-like, conventional existence that he now finds "very appropriate."

On May 1, 1893, Schnitzler notes in his diary: "Papa is extremely ill. I, hoarse, prescribe and make visits. [...] I feel nothing but boundless bitterness." One day later, he writes: "At 1:30 in the afternoon, my father died. – When I came home early, Julius already told me: Blood poisoning. – I held his pulse the last hour. – A terrible afternoon with all the triviality, horror, excitement, apathy and incomprehension. [...] The pain is lessened by the thought that he did not suffer after all."

On the next day, the following entry: "Impossible, the whole day, to come to a genuine sensation of pain. – Suddenly, in the evening, it came over me appallingly – how we were all sitting around the table for the evening meal – and – he was not there!"[62]

During Dr. Johann Schnitzler's last years as director of the polyclinic, anti-Semitic tendencies undermined his authority. His son would draw on these intrigues for *Professor Bernhardi*. Schnitzler now has the freedom to end his employment, both in the clinic and for the "Internationale Klinische Rundschau." He cannot yet live from writing alone, however, so he opens another practice in the Frankgasse and takes an apartment with his mother in the same building.

On July 14, he performs in the premiere of *Abschiedsouper* with the actor Josef Jarno in Bad Ischl. Because of censorship issues, in the same month he travels to Bezirkshauptmann von Aichelburg, who gives him a foretaste of future technical difficulties with stage performances. Jarno, with whom the author, as Max, stands on the stage, will later become the Director of the Josefstadt Theater. There, he will exert himself on Schnitzler's behalf. The critics call Schnitzler a "Naturalist," a grouping to which the socially themed *Märchen* will bring him closer.

This play premieres on December 1 in the Volkstheater. It experiences not only noticeably more attention from the press and the public than *Abschiedssouper*, it also develops into Schnitzler's first scandal. This, although the drama in three acts was approved by the censor.

Adele Sandrock, one of the most popular of the Viennese actresses, reads the drama, possibly through Hermann Bahr's mediation. She insists on playing the lead role, and all of a sudden the play and its author are the talk of the town. It is not a positive light in which the Viennese theater-going public views Schnitzler, in spite of Sandrock's involvement. The middle class sees its moral principles under attack – in particular, the role of the woman and the corollary right to cast out those who follow their hearts, and not parental directives. During the third act of the performance, the hissing of the public is unmistakable. This soon induces the director, von Bukovics, to drop the play after only one further performance.

The female lead, however, does not hold this against Schnitzler. The day of the premiere, she invites him to visit her and seduces him. Schnitzler, still

62 TB 1893–1902, 1.–3.5.1893.

smarting from Mizi's disloyalty, sees no reason to refuse.

It is worth noting here a letter that reaches the disappointed playwright in May 1894. Georg Brandes, the Danish literary critic, congratulates him on reaching new heights of creativity in *Märchen*. Both the dramatic construction and the female characters are successes, accomplished with a surer hand than in the *Anatol* cycle. This is the beginning of an amicable correspondence that continues until Brandes' death in 1927, and from which Schnitzler will draw valuable literary advice and support.

He finds another kindred spirit in Lou Andreas-Salomé, the only woman that Nietzsche ever loved, and who was later a close friend of Sigmund Freud's. She is introduced to Schnitzler by Beer-Hofmann. During her stay in Vienna, they make extended tours of the city's coffee-houses.

New Works in Prose — Increasing Anti-Semitism

In 1894, *Die drei Elixiere* and *Blumen* are published. In the first story, the narrator is obsessed with the question of whom his girlfriend loved before him. He travels to the Far East to procure a truth serum. He uses it in several amorous adventures and comes to find unbearable the thought that other men before him should have possessed his respective current love. He buys one more elixir, one that ensures total amnesia. The women he loves now think that he is their first lover, and he experiences new heights of passion. And yet he is still tortured by the certainty that he will not be their last lover. The only solution is to find another mixture, and this he gives to a beautiful girl he loves like no other before. "And the sweet child could love none other than him," the story concludes, "because she was dead!"[63] Fairy-tale like in its narrative, *Die drei Elixiere* deals with human vanity and insatiability. Schnitzler's diaries testify that he was obsessed with these issues in his own relationships.

Blumen is set right after the death of a young woman whose lover is

63 Arthur Schnitzler: Gesammelte Werke in vier Bänden. Frankfurt/Main: S. Fischer 1961–1962. Die erzählenden Schriften Vol. 1, p. 83. Abbreviated as ES I or II.

in mourning for her. Flowers arrive daily by post, because she fell ill so suddenly that he had no time to cancel the pre-ordered deliveries. The flowers confine the man into a state of fixation on death. He is only restored to normal life when a young, carefree girl from the theater, whom he invites to visit him, throws the wilted and mouldering flowers out of the window. With the symbolic power accorded to the flowers, this also reads like a modern fairy tale. Once more, Schnitzler deals with grief, mourning, and the effect of death on a young love.

Another story written in 1894 is *Der Witwer.* This first appears, however, in 1932. After his young wife's death, Richard finds his best friend Hugo's love-letters to her. But death has a reconciling effect: "He is incapable of hating. He sees too clearly." Hugo appears and suggests travelling with him to the North Sea to distract him. When Richard finds out that Hugo has been engaged to someone else since last winter, he throws the letters in his face.

To turn to Schnitzler's support for Herzl's literary ambitions, I would like to cast a light briefly on the development of pre-war anti-Semitism in Central Europe. In this context, it is worth mentioning the founding of the "Centralverein deutscher Staatsbürger jüdischen Glaubens" (Central Association for German citizens of Jewish Faith), the German equivalent of the Österreichisch-Israelitische Union, that was called into existence seven years earlier. Like the Union, the Centralverein saw itself as representing all Jewish citizens of the country. In doing so, it emphasized its support of the state and its patriotic views. This aspect is reflected in the name and consciously puts "German citizens" before "Jewish faith." The Centralverein was not primarily a religious organization, but rather wanted, first and foremost, to counteract with positive information the ever-increasing anti-Semitism in the population. A reconciliation between the German and Jewish cultures, whose fundamental estrangement nationalist-oriented groups loudly insisted on, was, in the opinion of the Centralverein, entirely possible. The organization worked toward this goal until its prohibition in 1938.

The mere fact that this sort of protective organization had to be called into being is an indication of the decidedly hostile tendencies in the population and press in the waning 19th century. This necessity, and the steady increase in anti-Semitism before 1933, is also reflected in the number of members. The first organization numbered 1,420, but grew to over 60,000 members by 1926. In 1923, there were 13 regional associations with 174 local groups.[64]

Before Theodor Herzl became the "Father of Zionism," and outlined his ideas in *Der Judenstaat* (1896), he wanted to become a playwright. In 1894, he turns to Schnitzler for advice. If Jacob Wassermann's *Die Juden von Zirndorf*, is a "Jewish" novel, it is Herzl's intention, with *Das Ghetto,* to create a similar work for the stage. This play is rejected by several German theaters, and in March 1895, by the Viennese Raimund Theater as well. The last paragraph of the rejection letter written by director Adam Müller-Guttenbrunn reveals how difficult it is at this time to present on stage, and thus to the public, a play defending the Jewish community against anti-Semitism.

> And, in spite of all of this – would *you* present it? And do you think that there is a large theater anywhere in Germany that would put on "Ghetto"? I don't think so! You can, nevertheless, leave the play here with me for several more days. I want to let others, completely impartial people whose opinion I value, read it. *If* the play is ever performed in Vienna, it can only happen in the R.-Th. We will get no thanks for it, neither from the Jews nor from the anti-Semites! (26.3.1895).[65]

This attitude anticipates the difficulties that Schnitzler himself will land in nearly twenty years later, when, with *Professor Bernhardi* in hand, he approaches various theaters in Germany and Austria. Before this last rejection, which Herzl takes as the final one, the friendship between Herzl and Schnitzler has developed to the extent that the latter accommodates as far as possible Herzl's complicated requirements with regard to the process of finding an appropriate stage. Herzl is asking that it should happen anonymously and with the use of a second address. He has, apparently,

64 *Politisches Handwörterbuch*. ed. by Kurt Jagow and Paul Herre. Leipzig: K. F. Koehler 1923, p. 1011.

65 CUL: Briefe Schnitzler an Herzl. Folders B 75.

serious reservations about being identified as the author of the play, which ends with the martyrdom of the protagonist. Nor does Herzl, in any way, hold back on adamant Jewish nationalism in this play, so that he has to resort to a pseudonym. For further security, Schnitzler is to assume the role of middle-man for him with the respective theaters. The stage play should be sent in different packets to the Deutsches Theater in Vienna (today the Volkstheater), because Herzl fears that the complete version could end up in the wrong hands.

That Schnitzler fulfils these tasks without grumbling speaks well for his friendship with Herzl in the mid-1890's. His advice to the future Zionist leader reveals his own opinion on German-speaking Jews:

> Thus, I am most opposed to the concluding sentence of this play, the actual final sentence that the dying Jacob Samuel says. Let him rather die wordlessly. This death says more, and something better, I believe, something completely different than the dying man's words. The dying man says: "Jews, brothers, one will only let you live again when you know how to die." – His death says, on the other hand: "This poor devil and noble fellow must let himself be shot down by this miserable good-for-nothing – because he is born as a Jew!" – – There was a time when Jews by the thousands were burned at the stake. They knew how to die. But they were not allowed to live in peace – because of it. [...]

Further on Schnitzler suggests:

> You can still put in the play what would be an effective opposite number: a Jewish fraternity member, who, after 30 duels is driven from the fraternity because he is a Jew. [...] And here I see it again: the figure of a <u>powerful Jew</u> is what I am downright missing in your play. It is, in fact, not true that in the Ghetto that you are talking about, all Jews go around depressed or in a pitiable state of mind. There <u>are</u> others – and it is exactly those who will be most deeply hated by the anti-Semites. Something along these lines must also be said in the play. Your play is daring

> – I would also like to have it defiant. (17.11.1894)[66]

In his reply, Herzl expressed himself openly:

> That's why it is enough to be daring, and I don't want to be defiant. Otherwise, they won't hear me until the end. I am addressing a population of anti-Semites! (27.11.1894)

Schnitzler put this sentence practically word-for-word in the mouth of Dr. Pflugfelder in *Professor Bernhardi.* A few weeks later Herzl explained:

> Above all, I do not want to engage in the defence of J[ews] or their "salvation." I only want, with everything in my power, to put the question to discussion. The critics and the public should then defend or attack. If only I can get on the stage, my purpose is achieved. I couldn't care less what happens after that. [...] I do not want to be a likable writer. I want to express myself – from the heart. If this play is out there in the world, I will have a lighter heart. (17.12.1894)[67]

However, Schnitzler's mediation was not successful. In 1897, the play appeared under the title *Das neue Ghetto,* in the Zionist periodical "Die Welt." It only achieved performance one year later, in Vienna's Karlstheater.[68]

---

66 Ibid.

67 CUL: Briefe Herzl an Schnitzler. Folders B 39.

68 Bettina Riedmann: "… die Legenden, deren Entstehung man miterlebt": Arthur Schnitzler und Theodor Herzl. In: *Arthur Schnitzler und das 20. Jahrhundert.* ed. by Konstanze Fliedl. Vienna: Picus 2003, pp. 192–210, p. 200.

FIRST SUCCESS 1895-1900

Liebelei

For a long time, it was assumed that Schnitzler's first idea for *Das Arme Mädel* came to him in 1891. The latest research shows, however, that the earliest inspiration is to be found already in his student days, from the sketch of *Das Fräulein am Brunnen* from 1881.[69] Ever since his affair with Jeannette Heeger, he is very familiar with the petit- bourgeois milieu in which the play is set.

From September to October 1894, Schnitzler develops the play further and renames it *Liebelei*. His Young-Vienna friends, to whom he soon reads the play, are convinced of his talent. Why shouldn't it be performed in the Burgtheater? It is very convenient that the director of this theater, Max Burckhard, lives one floor above Schnitzler. Countless aspiring playwrights have to send their manuscripts by mail, whereas Schnitzler can give it to him on the street. Burckhard takes it on, and even though a year will pass before the play is premiered on October 9, 1895, Schnitzler has made it onto the greatest stage in Austria-Hungary. Not only Adele Sandrock, but another of the public's favorites, Adolf Sonnenthal, will star in it. Sonnenthal had, by the way, refused with rather pointed criticism to act in earlier Schnitzler plays.

The public is even more enthusiastic than the critics. The night of the premiere, the author receives repeated curtain calls. At the next performance, the theater is entirely sold out. *Liebelei* becomes one of Schnitzler's most frequently performed pieces, and remains on the programme of the Burgtheater until 1910.

There are only four characters in the play: Fritz, Theodor, Christine, and Mizi. The first act takes place at Fritz's, where the four friends have gathered for a pleasant evening. After supper, just as everyone is thoroughly enjoying

69 Vivien Friedrich: Schnitzlers Filmskript zu *Elskovsleg* im Kontext der Textgeschichte von *Liebelei*. In: *Arthur Schnitzler und der Film*. ed. by Achim Aurnhammer. Würzburg: Ergon 2010, pp. 45–44, pp. 48–49.

themselves, the doorbell rings. Outside stands the husband of the woman with whom Fritz is having an affair, who promptly challenges him to a duel. Once the man leaves, they conclude the evening as light-heartedly as they can, leaving the young ladies in the dark. Theodor and Mizi make up one couple and Fritz and Christine the other.

It is clear that Christine is far more attached to Fritz than vice versa. She is overjoyed when he comes to visit her the next day, if slightly ashamed of the humble rooms she shares with her father, a violinist. In the third act, Fritz has been shot, and Mizi and Theodor call to bring the news. Christine's character offers an actress the chance to range an entire spectrum of emotions. She is driven to desperation by fully grasping all aspects of the tragedy: Not only has the man she truly loved been killed, he has been killed for another woman whom she never knew about. In addition to this, she has not even been asked to the funeral to pay her last respects. Whereas for all the other characters, this was merely an affair, for Christine it was true love. Resolved to risk all, she runs to the cemetery, leaving her father to speak the final words of the play: "She will not come back – she will not come back!"[70]

Otto Brahm, Director of the Deutsches Theater in Berlin, has asked, after Burckhard has taken on the play, for permission to perform *Liebelei* in the German capital. Of course, Schnitzler consents. Brahm is one who stages, promotes, and fights for modern theater. He was one of the first to present Gerhard Hauptmann, and he also introduced the German public to Ibsen. He shows the same initiative with regard to Schnitzler in Wilhelminian Germany, and they soon develop a true friendship.

Schnitzler first meets Brahm in person, along with his publisher Samuel Fischer, at the Berlin premiere of *Liebelei*, on February 4, 1896. The same year sees successful performances of the play in Frankfurt, Munich, Cologne, and Graz, where, ironically, Mizi Glümer plays the character Mizi on the stage. The play continues its tour onto the stages of Bratislava, Prague, Verona, Milan, Athens, and Sofia. *Liebelei* lays the basis for Schnitzler's success in Russia, where he would remain the most frequently performed German-speaking author well into the 1920's. In 1897, *Liebelei* makes the

70 DW I, p. 263.

leap over the Atlantic, where it is staged in German in New York, with the English titles *Flirtation* (1905) and *The Reckoning* (1907). To Schnitzler's success as a prose author, is added his breakthrough as a playwright. His reputation is now established.

The Type of the "Süßes Mädel"

With his invention of the "süsse Mädel" (the affectionate, but street-wise young woman: the sweet young thing), Schnitzler breathed new life into the image of women in the late 19th century. At the time, the standard literary female types included the naive, happy bride; the obedient, virtuous housewife; the stern or laughable old maid, and the beautiful seductress. These occur, above all, in the novels of popular authors of the time, but to some extent also in Gottfried Keller, Charles Dickens and Honoré de Balzac. It was only around 1900 that psychologically-oriented novelists began to break up these types and bestow upon them individual characteristics.

Schnitzler plays with the standard literary female types of the fin de siècle. But he submits neither to the symbolistic cult of the "femme fatale," which celebrates her deadly erotic aura, or to that of the pale, child-like and sexless "femme fragile" who is hardly capable of surviving without assistance.[71] In contrast to these typecast females images in the art of his time, which are reflected in the pictures of Franz von Stuck, in Schnitzler's characters, the human individual is always recognizable. This is a function of his highly developed interest in the female psyche.

A great deal has been written about the "süsse Mädel" – nearly every standard cliché was invoked in connection with it. Contemporary critics labelled, at least once, almost every female character of Schnitzler's a "süßes Mädel." In a letter, Felix Salten even slots the more mature Frau Berta Garlan into this category.[72] However, one can already outline the

---

71 For a detailed analysis of female types of the Fin-de-Siècle, see: *Frauen – Körper – Kunst – Literarische Inszenierungen weiblicher Sexualität*. ed. by Karin Tebben. Göttingen: Vandenhoeck & Ruprecht 2000; as well as Emil Brix und Lisa Fischer: *Die Frauen der Wiener Moderne*. Munich: R. Oldenbourg, 1997.

72 CUL: Briefe Felix Salten an Schnitzler. Folder B 89, 7.11.1903.

type fairly exactly: of decisive importance are her social origins, because the "süßes Mädel" comes from of the poorer Vorstadt. Jeanette Heeger is her real inspiration. And it was with these poorer daughters of the petite bourgeoisie that Schnitzler primarily consorted in the last years of the 19th century.

She is naturally attractive and babbles cheerfully away in the dialect that one speaks on the other side of the Ring, in Hernals or Ottakring. She is not subject to middle-class morality, but instead distracts herself with her love affairs from the daily handwork that she, still living with her parents, has taken on to support her siblings. Naturally, she is still burdened with social disapprobation. Should she, in the language of the outskirts, be in a family way, there is no longer any prospect for her of social recognition. She will become one of the ostracised, the "fallen women," according to the double standard that Schnitzler so ruthlessly exposed in *Märchen*.

Not to say that the "süßes Mädel" is in any way naive, as one might assume. In the *Reigen*, she knows exactly what she must say to men – above all to the well-off husbands – to keep them happy. She keeps secret the love affairs in her own social milieu, which almost certainly mean more to her. In stories like *Die Braut*, one sees that this young woman is invested with a very active sense of her own sexuality in an era in which the middle-class ethos tabooed every indication of a female sexual drive. She could pass for a sweet young thing, but as one with a shady side. She is, in fact, not so much a victim as is Christine, but rather someone who inflicts pain herself. In doing so, she has abandoned herself to her "fundamental human drives," and thereby is closer to the "femme fatale" than to the cheerful, flirtatious girl from the Vorstadt. The actress Annie, from the Anatol-play *Abschiedssouper*, is another example of a strong-minded, clever young woman who knows how to get what she wants. In amorous matters, she is definitely in a position to go her own way.

Whereas the "süßes Mädel" in *Reigen* is a general type, in *Liebelei*, she becomes psychologically more detailed, and is depicted as an independent figure. Fritz calls Christine a "süßes Mädel" several times. She is in love to the point of self-sacrifice – as opposed to Annie, who, on the evening that Anatol wants to end the relationship, pre-empts him by leaving him first. Christine becomes – as have the female characters in the other early dramas *Das Märchen*, *Das Vermächtnis* and *Freiwild* – a trusting victim of the cavalier young men of the upper middle class, cornered by the unwritten laws of a society that gives women markedly less freedom than men. And mostly with tragic consequences. As a realistically drawn character, the "süßes Mädel," holds potential for effective social criticism.

Mizi II und *Freiwild*

Back to reality – there are a few changes in Schnitzler's private life. His relationship with Adele Sandrock, affectionately called "Dilly" in his diary, is on quite a superficial level, because they have no real intellectual interests in common. She had helped to increase the impact of his plays on the Viennese stage, and the young author was enchanted that the popular actress had chosen him as a lover. But by March, 1985, the affair is over, and the next girl is already at hand – and this time, no one from the outskirts. Marie Reinhard is the daughter of a soundly middle-class family, who comes to Schnitzler's practice for treatment of problems with her voice. In his diary, he nicknames his new lover "Mizi II," so as not to confuse her with Marie Glümer ("Mizi"). This only happens, however, after he has broken up with "Dilly."

Marie Reinhard expects to be courted and married, which is why she has guarded her virtue. This is extraordinarily tempting for Schnitzler, and he quickly falls in love with her. Unfortunately for Marie, Schnitzler is not in the least interested in marriage. For a girl of her social background, she is exposing herself to considerable risk.

The correspondence with her exists owing to the documentation of Schnitzler's Scandinavian trip in August 1896. In the course of this trip he visited, among others, Georg Brandes and Ibsen. The letters to Marie are noticeably cooler than those to Mizi Glümer. On the other hand, in Marie Reinhard, he has found a young lady with whom he can discuss contemporary literature on an equal footing. These themes are completely lacking in the letters to her similarly named predecessor.

Schnitzler has already met Clara Loeb in January of the same year on her 21st birthday, and he finds her charming. In his diary, he records:

> I know you. She: "Certainly, because I always smile at you when we meet in the street." [...] Pleasant sensation – satisfied vanity. The little girl enchants me, she promised to send me her own writings, became very confiding.

Decades later she will, as Clara Pollaczek, enter his life again and participate with Schnitzler in one of the more serious relationships of his later years.

In 1896, Schnitzler is working on another play, *Freiwild* (1898). This addresses his problematic situation with Mizi Glümer – as in *Märchen* – as well as the question of the duel that he was fairly recently confronted with. Whereas *Liebelei* concentrates on the fate of Christine, the female protagonist, *Freiwild* deals with society and its institutions. This, Schnitzler's first criticism of the military, comes through clearly: the officers who, with their mindless dash exalted by the effect of their uniforms, elevate themselves to the level of masters of a provincial town. As the title suggests, they regard the girls of the theater as their personal harem.

As favourably inclined as is Max Burckhard to Schnitzler, he cannot perform the play at the Burgtheater. Not only does it call into question one of society's ironclad institutions, the duel, but it portrays officers in a disrespectful manner. "Can't you make a postman out of him instead?" Burckhard asks the author – but in vain. The premiere, in fact, takes place at Brahm's Deutsches Theater in Berlin on November 3. The reviews are largely favourable, but the piece is soon taken off the programme, because the house is nearly empty. In his diary, Schnitzler calls the anti-Semitic criticism "raving."[73]

The one-act play, *Die Überspannte Person,* written in 1894, is published in the same year. It recalls the *Anatol* scenes in their light-hearted humour, but does have its serious moments.

---

73 TB 1893–1902, 1.12.1898.

A Meeting with Ibsen — Questions of Style

From July until August, Schnitzler travels to Norway, in order to flee not only his sense of being torn between Mizi I and II, but also to escape the Viennese reviewers. In Christiania, (today Oslo), he meets Henrik Ibsen. They converse about the symbolist movement in Berlin, Vienna, and Paris, about which Ibsen maintains he knows nothing. In discussing novelists who rank form over all else in literature, the Norwegian writer complains, "How can a word be at all beautiful if it has no content?"

Ibsen wants to recommend *Liebelei* – which he congratulates Schnitzler on – to the director of the city's theater. Ibsen's aversion to Strindberg becomes apparent as they talk. But the two playwrights part on very good terms, and Ibsen asks Schnitzler to greet Otto Brahm from him: "He is for me a very beloved old friend."[74]

Schnitzler does not consider himself to be the naturalist his contemporary critics have come to make him out to be. He does not write novels against social injustice as does Zola. But there is an unmistakable note of criticism in his plays, especially with respect to the strict conventions of the middle classes. It was Ibsen, whom Schnitzler admired, who showed him the way, not only on the issue of social criticism, but also with regard to modern dramatic technique, with such plays as *A Doll's House* (1879), *Enemy of the People* (1882), and *Hedda Gabler* (1890). In this context, the parallels between *Enemy of the People* and *Professor Bernhardi* are astounding. On the return journey, Schnitzler stops in Copenhagen to visit Georg Brandes, with whom he had been corresponding since the staging of *Märchen.*

Schnitzler's affections still swing back and forth between the two Mizis. In the letters to Mizi Glümer, Schnitzler mentions a rushing in his ears that will not go away. In autumn, he is diagnosed with otosclerosis, the ossification of the inner ear, which will worsen in the course of his life. It will later deprive Schnitzler, who had always loved music, of the pleasure of concert-going. Certainly, this unceasing twittering and rustling in his ear also reinforces his hypochondriac tendencies.

It is worth mentioning that Karl Kraus leaves the "Griensteidl" group

74 TB 1893–1902, 25.–26.7.1896.

toward the end of 1896. From now on, his milieu will be the naturalist circle around Polgar and Altenberg in the Café Central. Aside from a slap in the face that Felix Salten gives Kraus because of a cheeky review in the *Wiener Rundschau*, the differences between the two groups will be debated in their respective journals. In Kraus' *Demolirte Litteratur* of the same year, his former companions are lampooned in scathing satires.

Reigen and both Mizis

From December until January 1897, Schnitzler composes the *Reigen* (1920). *Liebesreigen,* whose title he soon shortens, is probably Schnitzler's best-known play, a dance through fin-de-siècle society. These ten scenes, each of which ends with the act of love, show the emptiness behind the facade of late-century bourgeois respectability, as well as the futility of the search for fulfilment. The absurdity of the ceremony surrounding the sexual act as well as the interchangeability of the partners is made clear to the public. The series begins with a prostitute and a soldier and continues up the social scale to a maid and her young master, an actress, a poet, a married couple, and, finally, a count, who closes the circle again with the prostitute.

Reigen does not feature individual characters, whose psyche Schnitzler normally likes to explore, but social types, which lends the play its satirical poignancy. Samuel Fischer recognises the literary potential of the work, but realises, at the same time, that it is impossible to publish for fear of censorship and scandal. Schnitzler then has 200 copies printed at his own expense, which he distributes among his friends. Even though, in the dedication of the book, he asks for discretion, *Reigen* soon becomes known beyond the borders of Austria. Schnitzler considers official publication once more, but once more he is confronted with Fischer's resistance. The author turns to the Viennese publishing house Freund. The first edition is printed in 1903, and the first run soon reaches 40,000 copies. In 1914, Schnitzler switches to the larger publisher Benjamin Harz, who manages to sell 75,000 copies by the year's end. Although, even before the First World War, Schnitzler is criticised by numerous anti-Semitic reviewers for "Jewish indecency," the real scandal does not occur until 1920. It is not until Schnitzler's death that the Fischer publishing house buys the rights to *Reigen*.[75]

In January 1897, it is clear that there will be a major change in Schnitzler's private life: Marie Reinhard is pregnant. Their relationship is by no means harmonious, because Schnitzler still corresponds regularly and intimately with Mizi Glümer. He has no intention of marrying, even though he seriously compromises Marie with his decision. According to the moral values of society at the time, she will become one of the "fallen."

There are dramatic incidents with both girls because of Schnitzler's Jewish background. He accuses Marie Reinhard of moving in "brainless anti-Semitic circles," and learns that she is made to suffer for her interactions with Jews. In June 1898, he learns through Felix Salten that the industrialist Carl Armbruster, although in love with her, refuses to court her officially for precisely that reason.[76]

Mizi Glümer is latently anti-Semitic, which Schnitzler attributes to her simple upbringing in the poorer part of town. He resolves not to take it to heart. At one point, however, when she mentions that a friend of Schnitzler's "jüdelt," he can no longer control himself. He calls her a "Vorstadt-harlot" and seizes her by the throat, threatening to slap her in the face and throw her down the stairs if she says one more word against his friend. She, pale as death, gets up and wants to get dressed. Both of them burst into tears. Schnitzler feels he has gone too far, and begs her forgiveness. At first, it was as if an "irremediable rift" had opened up between them. Even after reconciliation, they were both horrified that it could even come to such scenes.[77]

Schnitzler begins to come to terms with his situation in the play *Das Kind*, which he later renames *Das Vermächtnis* (1898). At the same time, the earliest version of his first novel, *Der Weg ins Freie* (1908), is taking shape in his mind. At this stage, however, it is still conceived as a drama entitled *Die Entrüsteten.* Here, too, he draws on the experience of extra-marital pregnancy, which will form the main plot line. In contrast to *Das*

---

75 Giuseppe Farese: *Arthur Schnitzler – ein Leben in Wien 1862–1931*. München: C.H. Beck 1999, pp. 77–78.
76 TB 1893–1902, 11.6.1898.
77 TB 1879–1892, 7.5.1891.

Kind, however, the idea behind this is a satirical comedy.

Dark and sober thoughts, on the other hand, dominate the prose works published this year: *Die Frau des Weisen*, *Der Ehrentag*, *Halbzwei* und *Die Toten schweigen*. The first two stories take up the theme of marital infidelity. *Die Frau des Weisen* partially employs the technique of the interior monologue. After seven years of separation, a young man meets a woman who was once dear to him. Even though she is now married and has a child, they become close once more. It was she who had sent him away all those years ago. Her husband had seen them in an intimate embrace and feared the worst. Now it becomes clear that Frederike, unlike her lover, never knew that her husband had seen them, and that the husband had obviously kept quiet about the incident himself. The young man leaves, never to see her again.

In *Die Toten schweigen,* Emma and her lover are going for a ride in the Prater park. Just after they kiss, an accident occurs that costs the young man's life. Torn as she is, Emma cannot wait for the doctor's arrival, to whom she would have to give her name and address. She leaves the young man's body lying in the street, and returns home. On seeing her child sleeping peacefully, she promises herself to tell her husband everything.

Ehrentag shifts to the notion of human meddling with fate. A group of friends decide to honor the actor Roland, who is only ever allowed to play minor roles, with thundering applause at the theater that evening. Schnitzler describes Roland's mind-set in the next scene. He has so often been humiliated and made fun of that he takes the audience's response to be new heights of ridicule. In the end, he is found hanged in his dressing room.

In May, when Marie's condition can no longer be hidden, she travels to Switzerland to be with her mother. Schnitzler goes to Bad Ischl in the summer, where he launches into an affair with the married woman and mother Rosa Freudenthal. Even though the affair does not last long, he feels the passion for her that has faded out of the relationship for Marie Reinhard. He briefly returns to Vienna to find an apartment for Marie, where she can have the child, and finds one in the suburb Mauer. Marie's parents, needless to say, are unhappy, and insist on marriage. But Schnitzler, on the contrary, decides, as he travels back to Rosa, that the child must be adopted.

On November 4, Olga Waissnix dies after a long illness. Schnitzler loses a good friend who understood him and supported him with regard to his literary efforts.

A Tragic Occurrence during Lueger's Time in Office

It is in this year that Dr. Karl Lueger, after four ballots and decided resistance from the Kaiser, is elected mayor of Vienna.[78] Although Lueger is himself not a racial anti-Semite, he uses anti-Semitic language opportunistically in order to win favour for his ambitious communal projects. His notorious exclamation, "I determine who is a Jew!" makes clear that he is entirely open to financial support from wealthy Jewish donors. In Lueger's own words: "You know, anti-Semitism is a very good means for agitation, and for climbing up in the political ranks; but once you're on top, you no longer have any use for it. It is the sport of the rabble!"[79]

Lueger stays in office until his death in 1910, and under his aegis, anti-Semitism becomes socially acceptable. The young Hitler is in Vienna at this time, and calls Lueger "the greatest German mayor of all time."[80] It is thanks to Lueger's leadership that the atmosphere for the city's Jewish intellectuals noticeably deteriorates. Thus, it is no coincidence that the only two "Jewish" works of Schnitzler's entire career are both produced in this first decade of the 20th century. In *Der Weg ins Freie,* for instance, Schnitzler will contrast the anti-Semitism that his parents' generation was confronted with, which could still be effectively silenced by conversion, with the racial anti-Semitism of the present.

The month of September brings a tragic event that hits Schnitzler even

78 Alan Palmer: *Twilight of the Habsburgs. The Life and Times of Emperor Francis Joseph.* London: Phoenix 2001, pp. 273–75.

79 Alexander Spitzmüller: *Und hat auch Ursach, es zu leben.* Vienna: Frick 1955, p. 74.

80 Adolf Hitler: *Mein Kampf.* München: Franz Eher Nachf. 1943, pp. 54–65.

harder than the loss of his parents. On September 24, after a long and painful labour, Marie Reinhard gives birth to a stillborn child. In *Der Weg ins Freie,* the protagonist Georg von Wergenthin echoes Schnitzler's own feelings of those days:

> I was not only far removed from the unborn child, but also from its mother in a way so uncanny that I cannot hope to describe it to you, and that I can hardly imagine it today. And there are moments when I cannot help thinking that there must have been some connection between my distance from them and the death of my child. Do you think that is entirely impossible?[81]

Das Vermächtnis

The year 1898 is the year of *Das Vermächtnis,* a drama in three acts. In the middle of a pleasant chat between Anna and Franziska about Hugo, Franziska's brother – for whom Anna harbours affection – and Franziska's fiancé, Hugo is suddenly carried into the room, fatally injured after a fall from his horse. In *Liebelei,* death brings the play to a conclusion, and in the *Anatol* cycle it is missing entirely. Here, it breaks brutally into the first act.

This play is highly critical of the callous laws of society. Again, the women suffer most from these cast-iron rules, whose staunchest supporters are men. The fate of Toni, the female lead, is not as central for *Das Vermächtnis* as is Christine's for *Liebelei,* but the parallels are evident. As in *Freiwild,* and to a lesser degree in *Märchen,* society is the real issue here, whose strict rules Schnitzler attacks in a manner very much reminiscent of Ibsen.

Max Burckhard, the friend of modernism and Schnitzler's supporter at the Burgtheatet, wants to see *Das Vermächtnis* performed. But a work of his own, *Die Bürgermeisterwahl,* is too close to reality for both the audience and his superiors at the Ministry. The play costs Burckhard his directorship. In January, 1898, Paul Schlenther is appointed his successor, and working with him will by no means be as easy as it was with Burckhard. Schlenther

81 ES I, p. 956.

postpones Schnitzler's latest play to the beginning of the next year, in part because of anti-Semitic criticism, in part, because, in his eyes, the play glorifies free love. In fact, the play is staged at the Burgtheater earlier than that, on November 30. But, thanks to Brahm, its premiere has already taken place in Berlin on October 8.

Three Successful One-Act Plays

In the months between the negotiations with Schlenther and the premiere of *Das Vermächtnis,* Schnitzler finishes three one-act plays: *Paracelsus, Der grüne Kakadu* and *Die Gefährtin.* These three works premiere at the Burgtheater on the same evening on March 1, 1899.

Paracelsus is a historical work, in which the famous doctor throws a marriage into confusion by hypnosis. Set in Basel in the early 16th century, Paracelsus makes Justina, the wife of a well-established smith, believe through hypnosis that she was unfaithful to him with a young aristocrat, Anselm. She is wracked by guilt, and her husband insists that Paracelsus reverse the hypnosis. But the doctor refuses, for he was once in love with Justina and unable to marry her because he was poor. Thus Justina was obliged to spend her life with a crude individual who is by no means her intellectual equal. When Anselm, to everyone's surprise, makes his own claims on Justina, the situation becomes ever more confused. Paracelsus releases her, again through hypnosis, from her false memories, in order to find out what has really happened between her and Anselm. In the end, it turns out that Justina was true to her husband. All appears to be well, but there is a moment of tension as Paracelsus is offered a permanent position in Basel. He refuses it, however, to carry on his life of travel. In his own words:

> It was a play! What else should it be?
> Which of the things we perform on earth is not a play,
> As tremendous and profound as it seemed to be! [...]
> I toy with the souls of men. A meaning
> Is only found by him who seeks one.

Dreaming, waking, all flow into one,
Truth is a lie. Safety is nowhere to be found.
We know nothing of the other, nothing of ourselves;
We're always acting, who knows this is wise.[82]

This is not only reminiscent of Shakespeare's famous line, "All the world's a stage," but also of Schiller's aphorism from his essay *Über die äesthetische Erziehung des Menschen* (1795): "A human being is acting only when he is being human in the fullest sense of the word, and he is only fully human when he is acting." The last sentences of Paracelsus can be taken as an expression of Schnitzler's interest in the fluid boundaries between reality and imagination, between conscious and subconscious. That we know "nothing of ourselves" reflects the deep-seated insecurity of modern man in the era of Freud. With the discovery of the subconscious, Freud declared the rational man to be no longer "master in his own house."[83]

In Berlin, the censors banned *Der grüne Kakadu*, whereas in Vienna, the one-act-play, in spite of its allegedly revolutionary tendencies, is allowed on the stage. It is important to mention, however, that the Burgtheater director Schlenther, under pressure from the Prince of Lichtenstein and the artistic director Plappart, removes the play from the schedule in the fall in spite of all contractual agreements. Only in October of 1905 will it again be performed in Vienna, at the Deutsches Volkstheater, and then with great success.[84]

Development of Narrative Style and a Loss

Apart from *Freiwild* and *Paracelsus*, S. Fischer publishes a collection of short stories, *Die Frau des Weisen*, in which are included, in addition to the

82 DW I, p. 498.

83 Cf. Sigmund Freud: Eine Schwierigkeit der Psychoanalyse. In: Imago: *Zeitschrift für Anwendung der Psychoanalyse auf die Geisteswissenschaften* 5 (1917). pp. 1–7.

84 The correspondence between Schnitzler and director Schlenther can be found in: Otto P. Schinnerer: The Suppression of Schnitzlers *Der grüne Kakadu* by the Burgtheater. Unpublished Correspondence. In: *The Germanic Review* 6/2 (1931), pp. 183–92.

story by the same name, *Ein Abschied, Der Ehrentag, Blumen,* und *Die Toten schweigen.*

Ein Abschied, a short novella in this collection, is a minute psychological depiction of a young man impatiently waiting for the married woman he loves. Schnitzler traces every worry, every association, every fear with which Albert tries to explain her absence. Ultimately, it turns out that she is mortally ill. He sees her body on the deathbed after she has passed away, and feels ridiculous, in spite of his acute worries, when comparing his own to her husband's tremendous grief. He leaves with the feeling that "his dead lover had chased him away because he had renounced her."[85]

On a train journey to Berlin in October of the same year, Schnitzler reads Édouard Dujardins *Les lauriers sont coupés,* the first novella written entirely using the technique of the interior monologue.[86] Much later, this will have considerable influence on *Ulysses* (1922), but it also inspires Schnitzler's *Lieutenant Gustl,* which appears in 1901.

The spring of 1899 brings yet another painful loss for Schnitzler. Only a few days after strolling through the Prater together, Marie Reinhard gets appendicitis. Her condition worsens so rapidly that two specialists, one of whom is Schnitzler's brother Julius, cannot help her. On March 18, before she dies, she is conscious until the end. He records her tender last words in his diary: "I know that you are there. That is why I cannot go."

At this point he stops making his otherwise daily entries in his diary until the beginning of April. Schnitzler explains, "Impossible to write here as though she were still alive. Above all, not that horrible day. She died on 18th March and I saw her die." On April 2, he writes: "Monstrous sorrow." And on April 29: "Monstrous desolation."[87] For years afterward, he remembers the anniversary of her death in his diary.

In the fairy tale-like novella *Um Eine Stunde,* which appeared that year, he describes a desolate young man at the deathbed of the woman he adores. The Angel of Death appears, and he begs the angel for one more hour of life for her. He can only fulfil the wish, the Angel says, if they find another human being willing to yield an hour of his life. In their search,

---

85 ES I, p. 254.

86 TB 1893–1902, 2.10.1898.

87 TB 1893–1902, 18.3., 1.4., 29.4.1899.

they encounter a philosopher and a murderer condemned to death, among others. But none of them wants to give up their final hour. The young man then offers his own life for her, and the Angel vanishes. Soon, however, the girl dies. The young man cries out that he has been deceived, but the Angel replies, "Do you believe that it is given to you to see through all your love and pain into the depths of your soul, where your true desires are hidden? You will meet me once more, and then I will ask you whether I have deceived you or whether you have deceived yourself."[88]

If we take this to represent Schnitzler's own state of mind after Marie Reinhard's death, it reflects an almost ruthless honesty with himself. At the same time, the notion that one cannot see into the "depths of one's soul," i.e., into one's subconscious, reflects the decidedly modern concepts of Freud.

Another story inspired by Marie Reinhard's death is *Die Nächste.* Gustav grieves for his young wife, Therese. While walking aimlessly in the streets, he suddenly thinks he recognizes her from her walk. He follows this girl, and even though her voice is different, physically, she is the very image of his wife and she even has the same name. They become lovers, but at the same time, Gustav feels suffocated by her presence. The only way to free himself is to kill her. She has cast the same spell over him that the flowers did in the story *Blumen*. Whereas in that tale, someone else throws the mouldy flowers out of the window to free him, here, the protagonist has to take his liberation into his own hands, even if this may well mean a term in prison.

On March 22, 1900, Schnitzler writes to Hugo von Hofmannsthal that he:

> ...suffers from loneliness without equal. – I always have to think about how I tried to describe people who lose what they love most – that is eternity, that is infinity: – solitude, which one cannot help, becoming lonely by one's own actions, becoming isolated.[89]

---

88 ES I, p. 318.a

89 Deutsches Literaturarchiv Marbach (DLA): Manuscripts Collection. Briefe Schnitzler an Hofmannsthal 1891-1928. Folders 377–81, 22.3.1900.

In the next letter, dated one day later, he mentions:

> I am working on nothing but the long novella, which will probably become, judging by the material, an offshoot of the *Femme de trente ans*, a *Veuve de 30 ans* – maybe I will finish it on the cruise along the Dalmatian coast."[90]

Frau Berta Garlan and Reality

Schnitzler manages to distract himself from his sense of emptiness by meeting his childhood sweetheart, Fännchen. She has been a widow for several years now and asks him in a letter if they can meet again in Vienna. In Schnitzler's diary entry from May 24, he notes: "At first, I found her annoying. But then, the triumph of the urge!"[91]

This event forms the core for the later story *Frau Berta Garlan* (1901). Here, a widow is also lured by her former lover from a provincial town to Vienna, and the high hopes that she places in him are bitterly disappointed. Compared to Schnitzler's other short prose, there are long-drawn out, perhaps unnecessary, sections. But this is a precise and realistic study of a female character, for whose psychological aspects he could draw on his own observations.

As so often in Schnitzler's work, the plot begins with a death and is used to explore the survivors' reactions. Berta seems to have 'stumbled into' her marriage as an inexperienced young girl. Rather than love, she felt gratitude towards her husband because of his devotion, and because he provided her with security after the death of her parents. Because she is from a well-to-do family, and lacks any work qualifications, she is afraid of having to earn her own living. But already in the first days of her marriage, she is aware that she does not love him.[92]

Her husband dies young, and after a period of mourning, which she

---

90 Ibid.
91 TB 1893–1902, 24.5.1899.
92 ES I, p. 394.

follows according to the custom, she is once more quite carefree and content. She is concerned that, at 30, she is considered old for a woman, by the standards of the time, and enjoys the attentions of her handsome nephew. She longs increasingly to see her childhood sweetheart again, Emil Lindbach, who is a successful musician in Vienna, and with whom she is corresponding. She agrees to a meeting in Vienna, and they spend the night together. For him, this is merely a distraction, whereas Berta expects more from him in the future. After she has left Vienna, she writes a long letter to him confessing her love. His reply is merely the suggestion that she should come to Vienna every four to six weeks, his engagements permitting, to spend a day and a night with him.

Her disillusionment finds a parallel in developments in the neighboring couple's relationship. Berta's friend Anna Rupius sees through many of the illusions that Berta still believes in. She cannot help telling her one day: "But you are really very naive." Anna herself travels to Vienna regularly to see a man. Just before Lindbach's reply arrives, Anna commits suicide. "'But why, Berta reflects, if she loved only her husband?' [...] Berta could not understand." She is aware of Anna's affair in Vienna, but her view of human relations is simplistic. Herr Rupert grieves for his wife, and says that her death was wholly unnecessary for – "I would have raised it, raised it like my own child."

Berta is greatly shocked by this. She cries and is disgusted with herself because "she was not one of those people who had the gift of an easy conscience, who are allowed to drink the joys of life without hesitation." She thinks of Lindbach, for whom she had to "die" just like Anna Rupius, and who "wanders the streets of the big city unpunished and probably without any trace of regret, who could live on, like any other... no, like the thousands and thousands of others who had touched her dress in passing and stared at her with desire."

In Schnitzler's era, a woman risked everything by living out her sexuality. One mishap could cost her social, financial, and professional standing. A repulsive individual like Herr Klingemann runs free in this provincial town, seducing cooks and housemaids, whereas Anna Rupius has to pay with her life for the affair with which she betrayed her invalid husband. Who the lover was or what Rupius himself suffered from is secondary. This novella is a condemnation of middle-class morality around 1900, because it describes in detail the strict punishment of a woman who is not ready to submit to its rules. Lindbach is granted his pleasure "for a day and a night," but Berta is, according to the standards of the time, considered a "fallen woman." Berta is honest, trusting, and capable of self-sacrificing love – not one with an "easy conscience." Yet the mores of the period do not prevent her from being exploited.

This weakness of a woman's position is further underlined by Anna's death. She hid her affair from her husband as well as her abortion. After the dramatic turning point, it finally dawns on Berta at the end:

> And she began to realize the great injustice in the world, that the longing for pleasure is given to the woman just as much as to the man; and that it becomes sin and demands punishment for the woman, if the longing for pleasure is not, as the same time, longing for a child.

Meeting with Olga Gussman — The Murder in Polná

This year, incidentally, Schnitzler's work is officially honored for the first time. He is awarded the Bauernfeld Prize, one of the highest literary distinctions in Austria. In later years, other recipients of the prize include Hermann Hesse and Joseph Roth.

Also in 1899, Schnitzler first meets his later wife, Olga Gussmann. She is twenty years younger than he and reveres his plays. By letter, she asks him for an autographed picture that she comes to collect in July. As he asks her who she is, she replies with the following, still under the pseudonym "Dina Marius:"

> Quite simply: a girl of 17 years, who wants to have her own life and be herself completely. There were a couple of pathetic shadows that live in a swamp that wanted to prevent me doing

> so, but I chased them away and reached out joyfully toward the sun. [...] I'm glowing. - I can't do otherwise.[93]

But it is not until October one year later that the formal "Sie" becomes "Du," and the end of his letters change from "Your devoted Arthur Schnitzler" to "I kiss your eyes."

This previously unpublished correspondence extends over the next thirty years. It is extraordinarily rich not only as a body of personal documentation, but it is also of scholarly interest, since Schnitzler discusses his literary work with Olga in greater detail than with some of his fellow writers. It is difficult to say if, even in his diary, one can come closer to Schnitzler than in these letters, which so faithfully reflect the roller coaster ride of his later marriage, and with it the inner life of a sensitive, emotional personality. Excerpts from this correspondence are to be found in the appendix.

With regard to the political background of these years, a murder case in the Bohemian town of Polná is shockingly relevant. On April 1, the body of a Catholic seamstress was found in a little village near Iglau (today Jihlava), with no sign of a possible culprit. A few statements by the village inhabitants were sufficient for the police to arrest the Jewish shoemaker's assistant Leopold Hilsner on suspicion. With the throat of the victim having been cut and Easter not far away, Hilsner was accused of having committed ritual murder to acquire Christian blood for Pessach. On the evening of April 10, 300 Polná villagers looted Jewish shops and shouted anti-Semitic abuse. As the case becomes known all over Europe, songs and postcards on the subject begin to make the rounds. Based on the testimony of further "witnesses," Hilsner was condemned to death, which called forth protest from Tomas Masaryk, a Czech patriot and professor at Prague. In a series of open letters, the future President of Czechoslovakia insisted on Hilsner's innocence. Even though the highest Court of Cassation revoked the death sentence the next spring, in the new trial, Hilsner is once more sentenced to death by hanging. At this point, Emperor Francis Joseph finally gave in to the strong international protest and pardoned Hilsner.

---

93 DLA, Briefe Olga an Arthur Schnitzler. Folder 1220, 23.6.1899.

But only with the end of the Habsburg Monarchy is the young man finally released from prison.[94] The disturbing thing about this case is not only the persistence of the medieval legend of Jewish ritual murder through to the end of the rational and progressive 19th century, but the authorities' willingness to make an example of the innocent Hilsner.

On September 29, Schnitzler writes from Wiesbaden to Gustav Schwarzkopf: "Polna makes me furious even at this distance. In Germany, you always feel that Austria is the stupidest country in the world."[95]

Schnitzler as a Historical Playwright

In the last years of the 19th century, Schnitzler's relations with Paul Schlenther, the director of the Burgtheater, reach a low point. From spring of 1898 until September of 1899, Schnitzler is working on the Renaissance drama *Der Schleier der Beatrice* (1900). It stands out among his other plays, which are all, with the exception of *Paracelsus* and *Der grüne Kakadu,* set in contemporary Vienna. *Der Schleier der Beatrice* is a concession to Historicism, which was most visible in the architecture of the period, above all in the monumental neo-baroque, neo-classical, and neo-gothic buildings of the Ringstrasse. Adolph von Menzel's paintings of the Prussian court under Frederick II also reflect this popular style of the period.

Der Schleier der Beatrice is not one of Schnitzler's strongest plays. The main reason for this is that it is in verse throughout, which prevents the characters from revealing the psychological motives for their thoughts and actions as persuasively as in dramas with conventional speech. The verse simply does not cut as close to the reader as is usual with Schnitzler. In the late work, *Der Gang zum Weiher* (1931), Schnitzler again forces himself to use verse, and his diary entries attest to his intense frustration with this technique.

Der Schleier der Beatrice is set in Bologna in the 16th century, as the city is

94 Georg R. Schroubek: Der 'Ritualmord' von Polná. Traditioneller und moderner Wahnglaube. In: *Antisemitismus und jüdische Geschichte*. ed. By Rainer Erb and Michael Schmidt. Berlin: Wiss. Autorenverlag 1987, pp. 149–71.

95 Briefe 1875–1912, p. 379.

under threat from the troops of Cesare Borgia. One modern element of the play is the importance of the dream, in which Beatrice imagines she is the duchess, with all the duties that a duchess owes her duke. Because of this fantasy, which her lover Filippo already considers an act of unfaithfulness, he rejects her. This theme recurs a quarter of a century later in *Traumnovelle*. On the way to church with her bridegroom, Vittorino, she offers herself to the Duke of Bologna, who duly marries her. Beatrice is in this regard a modern woman, because she chooses her sexual partner herself. But when Vittorino commits suicide, Beatrice's spontaneous decision brings her brothers and her sister Rosina against her.

Beatrice is presented as a contemporary woman, who is aware of her own sexuality. However, the manner in which she switches from Filippo to Vittorino, then on her wedding day to the Duke, and at the wedding ceremony, back to Filippo, is unconvincing. The precision with which Schnitzler normally describes a character's rational or irrational motives for adultery is entirely absent here, mainly, as noted above, because of the use of verse that he has imposed on himself. There is no apparent reason why Filippo, in addition to Vittorino, should suddenly swallow poison. Although he is a poet, Filippo is portrayed as melancholy rather than impulsive. We are not told of any personal crisis that might have driven him to desperation. The impending military threat from Borgia's troops, which could have contributed to the suspense, does not do so, because there is no mention of it in the entire third act, which focuses on the various amorous entanglements.

There is another play from this period, *Lady Windemere's Fan* (1892), by Oscar Wilde, which deals with the delicate complications of a lady's accessory being left behind. Whereas in Wilde's piece, the plot centers on the fan, its meaning for several characters and its timely retrieval before a catastrophe, in *Der Schleier der Beatrice*, it is merely a sidelight. There is a strong chance that, after his first major success with *Liebelei*, Schnitzler wanted to create a truly great and lasting work in the tradition of Grillparzer's historical dramas. We can also point to the strong-willed female protagonists in Schiller's *Maria Stuart* and *Die Jungfrau von Orleans* – all plays written in verse, true to the classical tradition.

Brahm is not interested in Schnitzler's new play, since he prefers

Schnitzler's contemporary dramas to the historical ones. The author himself has the feeling that the play can only be properly performed at "his" Burgtheater. Schlenther promises to stage the play in February 1900, but does nothing further about it. Schnitzler waits for weeks and weeks and keeps inquiring about the beginning of rehearsals. In June, he is given a vague but implied rejection. Early in September, he insists on a yes-or-no answer, and the play is turned down.[96]

Schnitzler is angry and disappointed, because Schlenther had already used this delaying tactic with *Vermächtnis,* which was soon taken off the programme, and with *Der Grüne Kakadu*, which never even premiered. Together with Bahr and other intellectuals, he draws up a public letter of protest against Schlenther. It is directed against the arbitrariness in general of theater directors with regard to playwrights.[97] The public is, however, not on the playwrights' side. The anti-Semitic press is in an uproar against the supposed Jewish dominance of the theater and the press, and Karl Kraus openly takes sides with Schlenther.

This dispute has another painful consequence: Schnitzler is told that *Der Schleier der Beatrice* had originally been nominated for the Grillparzer Prize, but was then withdrawn so as not to offend Schlenther. In December, the play is finally performed at the Lobe-Theater in Breslau. Schnitzler is dissatisfied with the actors' performance, and so are the reviewers.

96 Renate Wagner and Brigitte Vacha: *Wiener Schnitzler-Aufführungen 1891–1970*. Munich: Prestel 1971, pp. 34–36.
97 Ibid.

ASCENT TO FAME:

Leutnant Gustl and *Der Einsame Weg* 1900–1907

The new century began with a gruesome occurrence in light of the ever-increasing anti-Semitism in German-speaking countries. On March 13, 1900, the torso of an 18-year-old high-school student, Ernst Winter, was found on a frozen lake near Konitz (Chojnice) in what was then West Prussia. Because of the way the limbs were cleanly severed, suspicion fell on the Christian butcher Hoffman, as well as the Jewish butcher Lewy. Hoffman blamed Lewy, and soon the anti-Semitic press as well as the rumours simmering in the population declared it to be a case of Jewish ritual murder. Even today, neither party has been proven guilty beyond a doubt. The criminal expert Johann Braun, sent from Berlin, came to the conclusion that Hoffman had caught the boy being intimate with his daughter and committed murder in the heat of the moment.

It is remarkable that several thousand citizens in the town, workers as well as the prosperous classes, took Lewy's guilt to be self-evident, and vociferously demonstrated against him and his family. The anti-Semitic fury of the people was discharged in the destruction of shop windows and the plundering of Jewish shops. The military had to be sent to Konitz twice, because the local authorities were completely overwhelmed by the hysteria of the population. On the second occasion, it was only with the deployment of 500 soldiers, who were stationed on public squares and before Jewish apartment buildings, that order was restored to this small West Prussian town. The synagogue of Konitz, unfortunately, could not be saved, as it had already been put to the torch.[98]

98 A detailed account of this murder case can be found in Johannes T. Groß: *Ritualmordbeschuldigungen gegen Juden im Deutschen Kaiserreich 1871–1914*. Berlin: Metropol 2002; and also in Christoph Nonn: *Eine Stadt sucht einen Mörder. Gerücht, Gewalt und Antisemitismus im Kaiserreich*. Göttingen: Vandenhoeck & Ruprecht 2002.

The *Gustl* Affair

For Schnitzler, the main event of the century's turn, at which time Freud's *Traumdeutung* also first appears, is the scandal that develops around *Leutnant Gustl*. He finishes the novella in only one week in July, during a stay in Reichenau. In his diary, he records after completion his "feeling that it is a masterpiece." Olga, who has stood by him during the controversy around *Der Schleier der Beatrice*, has travelled with him.

"*Leutnant Gustl*" is the first work in German literature to use the interior monologue, and it secures Schnitzler his place in literary history. Even though other novellas of his from this period use the interior monologue selectively, Schnitzler will only use it one other time as comprehensively, that is, in *Fräulein Else* (1924). There, he uses it to trace, with astounding realism, every thought and association of the female mind.

Fräulein Else is a story imbued with social criticism, which attacks the restraints placed upon a young woman in spite of the new freedom in society after the First World War. *Lieutenant Gustl*, on the other hand, criticizes the officers' caste. This novella has been analysed so thoroughly in previous scholarship[99] that a brief overview should suffice.

Gustl is a rather crude individual who feels somewhat out of place at a concert. His thoughts reflect the superficial anti-Semitic stereotypes held by an army officer. Speaking about the husband of his flirt, Steffi, he muses:

> Must be a Jew as well! Of course, he's in a bank, and the black moustache ... He's even supposed to be an officer of the reserve! Well, he better not come to my regiment for training! That they still appoint so many Jews as officers – anti-Semitism doesn't mean a thing! [...] The Mannheimers themselves are said to be Jews, baptised of course ... you don't even notice their origins – especially the wife ... so blond, a beautiful figure... Was rather

99 To list only two of the more recent examples: Ursula Renner: Dokumentation eines Skandals: Arthur Schnitzlers 'Leutnant Gustl'. In: *Hofmannsthal-Jahrbuch* 15 (2007), pp. 33–40; and Jörg Pottbeckers: Hatte Leutnant Gustl Hunger? Einige späte Bemerkungen zur Entstehung des inneren Monologs bei Arthur Schnitzler und Knut Hamsun. In: *Studia austriaca* 20 (2012), pp. 85–106.

> amusing on the whole. Great food, excellent cigars ... Well, who has the money?[100]

Once the concert is over, and Gustl goes to the cloakroom, he cannot help but notice: "It's amazing, half the audience is Jewish... you can't even enjoy an Oratorio in peace and quiet."

On the way to the exit, he gets into a scuffle with a baker, who grabs his sword. A mere civilian has grasped his weapon! The remainder of the story depicts Gustl's dilemma. According to the army's strict code of behaviour, he has no way to restore his honor other than suicide. The situation is reminiscent of Officer Karinski's compulsion for duelling in *Das Märchen*, in itself a satire on the army's code of honor. The entire night, Gustl aimlessly walks the streets of Vienna and then the Prater. Early in the morning, while eating his last breakfast, the waiter casually drops into conversation that the baker died of a stroke in the night. Gustl is overjoyed. "What mad luck that I went into the coffee house," he thinks, "Otherwise, I would have shot myself for no reason at all. He is hardly able to contain his delight. Noticing a passer-by looking at him in the street, he mutters: "Wait, my friend, just you wait! I'm in a good mood... I'll beat you into steak tartare!"[101] [strictly speaking: Krenfleisch, M.H.]

These last paragraphs prove the hollowness of the officer's code of honor, which appears to be an external construct first and foremost, rather than a question of self-worth. At the same time, they show that Gustl has not learned a thing from the whole affair, and may well find himself in exactly the same situation before long.

Schnitzler probably takes the outraged reaction of the army as unavoidable, but he is primarily concerned with depicting one of the underpinning principles of the duel, the military's cast-iron definition of honor, as hollow and ludicrous. He has repeatedly attacked the duel, rather than the military, in his work, starting with the short-story *Erbschaft* and continuing to a later play about journalists, *Fink and Fliederbusch* (1917). Schnitzler puts the spotlight on duelling's anachronistic sense of honor. However, anyone who attacks the institution of the duel also attacks the

---

100 ES I, pp. 338–39.

101 Ibid., pp. 365–66.

military caste, for whom honor is one of the sovereign principles. Small wonder, then, that Gustav Davis, the editor-in-chief of the conservative journal *Reichswehr*, which is favourable to the army, tears Schnitzler's latest work to pieces. Other papers speculate whether or not Schnitzler will challenge the editor to a duel. But nothing can have been further from his mind.[102]

He is soon commanded, by the "k. k. Landwehrergänzungsbezirks-kommando Nr. 1," to appear before an advisory committee on issues of honor. Schnitzler counters, however, citing several paragraphs of military law, and he ignores all further demands to appear in person. Thus, in June, he reads in the newspapers that the honor committee has deprived him of his rank of officer for having offended military honor. He has not only damaged "the honor and prestige" of [the] imperial and royal army," but also, very notably, "has not responded in any way to the attacks of the journal *Reichswehr*."[103] During this scandal – Mayor Lueger has already been in office for four years – the anti-Semitic papers outdo each other in their polemics. In July, the satirical journal *Kikeriki* prints a spiteful caricature of "Aaron Schnitzler," as well as other offensive articles.[104]

Schnitzler's Processing of the *Gustl* Scandal

In the same year, Schnitzler works on a prose sketch entitled *Die grüne Krawatte.* Here Schnitzler depicts, immediately after his experience with the *Gustl* affair, the fickleness of critics and the public. This includes, of course, anti-Semitic reviewers, for whom the green tie could possibly be a symbol of Schnitzler's "immorality," and those wearing it, "decadent Jews." The sketch is about a man who decides to wear a green tie for two days in a row, a blue one the next day, and a violet one the day after that. The people

102 Otto P. Schinnerer: Schnitzler and the Military Censorship. Unpublished Correspondence. In: *The Germanic Review*, 5/3 (1930), pp. 238–46. Vgl. ebenfalls von Theodor Sosnosky: Unveröffentlichte Schnitzler-Briefe über die "Leutnant-Gustl-Affäre." In: Neues Wiener Journal, 26.10.1931; see also Heinrich Schnitzler: Die Wahrheit über "Leutnant Gustl." Eine Dokumentation. In: *Die Presse*, 25.12.1959.

103 Schinnerer, p. 243.

104 Ibid., p. 245.

admire the green tie at first and imitate him, but when he puts it on again the next day, they already begin to complain about his lack of imagination. But, then, when he does change his tie, they become furious. This arbitrariness continues to the point that the crowd starts yelling that people who wear green ties are thieves and murderers. The parable is symbolic of Schnitzler's life-long fight against reviewers who misinterpret his work, and, in doing so, reinforce stereotypes and misunderstandings.

The fragment, *Der Boxeraufstand*, written in 1900, is not published until 1957. The play is worth mentioning because it illustrates Schnitzler's interest in the nature of fate, which can swerve off from an apparently unavoidable course at the last minute. In this case, however, human intervention is responsible for the change. Immediately after the suppression of the Boxer Rebellion in China, a Chinese prisoner, awaiting execution, is reading a novel. When a European officer expresses his surprise at the prisoner's apparent calm, he replies, "What will come to pass in the next hour is never certain."[105] Indeed, for reasons of sympathy he cannot explain, the officer sets him free, whereas the other prisoners are executed.

Although Schnitzler touches on the question of female honor comparatively often, he rarely addresses the honor of the disadvantaged. In *Wohltaten, still und rein gegeben*, a poor student, Franz, longs for nothing more than a bite to eat. A well-dressed stranger gives him a gold coin. Although realizing that he has given too much, the stranger lets Franz keep it anyway. Franz eats a good dinner and spends the night with a prostitute, after which he is left with hardly anything. The next morning, he is once more impoverished. After having briefly tasted the pleasures of life and being denied them for the future, Franz stews in his own frustration. The stranger appears once more, and Franz strikes him in the face. Franz is taken away by the police, but he has settled what he feels to have been his debt.

Ein Erfolg is one of Schnitzler's rarer humorous prose works. Like the previous stories, it deals with various aspects of honor. A girl provokes her boyfriend, the policeman Engelbert, to the point that he arrests her, and the man she succeeds in making him jealous with. The two of them, who did

105 Ibid., p. 546.

not know each other, become acquainted thanks to Engelbert. As neither takes him or his threat of arrest seriously, they go off together. From that day on, Engelbert, who was always too kind to seriously reprimand anyone for the minor offenses he saw, is a changed man. He is soon bringing more cases into court than his colleagues. The well-deserved promotion is not far off.

In May, Schnitzler suffers another personal tragedy. Olga, who is pregnant and close to term, is unable to give birth to the child. The ensuing operation entails complications, and the child does not survive this time. For Schnitzler, this is not the traumatic incident, however, as with Marie Reinhard.

Until September, he works on a series of one-act plays: *Literatur, Die Frau mit dem Dolche, Lebendige Stunden, Die letzten Masken* and *Der Puppenspieler. Lebendige Stunden* consists of an intense dialogue between Heinrich, the son of a woman who has just died, and her former lover, Hausdorfer, who is a retired official. Hausdorfer eventually shows her last letter to Heinrich. In it, she outlines her intent to end her own life, because she sees that Heinrich's deep concern for her is getting him into professional difficulties. Her disease would have given her two or three more years to live, and, for his sake, she would have carried on. Heinrich feels that Hausdorfer should not have shown him the letter, as his mother had requested that it be kept secret. This way, her sacrifice has been rendered void. Hausdorfer asks: "What is all your scribbling worth, and even if you are the greatest genius, what is it against one hour, one living hour, in which your mother sat here in the armchair and spoke to us [...]?" Heinrich counters that, with his writing, he can ensure that those hours last – and leaves.[106]

Die Frau mit dem Dolche is a curious melange of past and present, which begins in an art gallery in Vienna. Two elegant young people, Pauline and Leonhard, meet in front of a picture of a woman with a dagger. Leonhard remarks on the striking similarity between the woman in the picture and Pauline. She concurs and mentions, "Why not? My mother is from Florence." They play with the idea that they could have met each other

---

106 DW I, p. 702.

in an earlier century, and Pauline replies, "Perhaps – maybe we just don't remember?" In the course of their dialogue it becomes clear that Pauline's husband, an actor, was unfaithful to her. He even wrote a play about his affair, in which he starred. Pauline confesses that she is sexually attracted to Leonhard but cannot love him. "Haven't I already told you this once before?" she asks. The plot switches abruptly to the 16th century, with the same characters. Paola and Lionardo have spent the previous night together – which in the present had not been possible. Lionardo wants to deepen their relationship, whereas Paola makes it clear that she will stay with her husband. When the husband, the painter Remigio, arrives, Paola and Lionardo confess to their adultery. Lionardo insists that Remigio kill him, or he will kill Remigio. But before Lionardo can leave the house, Paola plunges her dagger into his heart. Back in the present, Pauline had planned to leave Vienna with her husband, but now the stage directions state: "*Her expression reflects her realization that there is a fate above her she cannot escape.*" She promises Leonhard to see him again in the evening.

Die letzten Masken is set in a hospital, in the room of an aged dying journalist named Rademacher. He asks a young actor to fetch his friend, Weihgast, a poet and playwright much more successful than himself. Rademacher has had to watch the decline of his own popularity against the background of Weihgast's rise to success. His envy has turned to hatred. Before he dies, he wants to let Weihgast know that he had an affair with his wife for two years. She was completely bored with Weihgast and begged Rademacher to take her away with him, but he was too poor to support her. Before Weihgast arrives, Rademacher rehearses this confrontational scene with his actor friend, Florian, not without a certain cruel pleasure. Weihgast, however, proves himself to be a genuine friend in his concern for his afflicted colleague. And he relates how his only support against all the adversities of life has been his wife, his two children and grandchildren. In the end, Rademacher keeps his secret to himself. In a final twist, we learn that Florian, who displays all the confidence and exuberance of youth, and expects to leave the hospital soon, does not have long to live, either.

Literatur provides a rather ironic perspective on a wife very much drawn to literature, and her husband, who is quite the opposite. Her former lover, a real "Kaffehausliterat," visits her. They realize that they have used the same love scenes in their respective poems and prose, which would give away their relationship to the public. Catastrophe is averted when the volumes of poetry that are already in print are destroyed. Then the husband, all unknowing, throws the only remaining copy into the fire.

New Plays — Familiar Tensions

Brahm, with his aversion for historic pieces, is not favourably inclined towards *Die Frau mit dem Dolche.* But Schnitzler leaves *Der Puppenspieler* out of the collection rather than give up any of the other one-act plays. The other plays are grouped together in the cycle *Lebendige Stunden,* which is published in the same year. Later, *Frau Berta Garlan* and *Sylvesternacht* appear in print separately. *Sylvesternacht* is a dramatic dialogue between a young man and a married woman. She tells him of a female friend who used the liberties of New Year's Eve for an excursion into the Prater with her lover, only to return to her guests an hour later. He imagines she is talking about herself, but she replies:

> AGATHE: You are most certainly mistaken. And anyway, it doesn't matter at all whether it's one's own or someone else's past. It's long distant.
> EMIL: But it can happen again.
> AGATHE: What can you be thinking? Nothing recurs.[107]

Schnitzler here shows the interplay of reality, memory and the past, as it takes place in the magical atmosphere of New Year's Eve. In the cycle *Marionetten,* he is to develop this theme further. Ever since, as a child, Schnitzler saw an actor look up from the stage into his parents' box in greeting, he has been fascinated by the fluid boundaries between these various fields of perception, in which his profound interest in the human psyche plays a role. *Die Frau mit dem Dolche* is also an unusual tapestry of past and present, with hints of reincarnation, the repetitive nature of

107 Ibid., p. 687.

history, and the immortality of the human soul, as the plot jumps back and forth between the Renaissance Era and an of the present. This playing with different levels of reality reaches its high point in *Traumnovelle.*

The premiere of the four one-act plays of *Lebendige Stunden* takes place in the first days of January, 1902. The cycle finds strong resonance with the public, especially *Literatur.* Goldmann, however, finds it is again time for Schnitzler to write a humorous piece. His critical review contributes to a growing distance between them.

At the same time, in January, it is definite that Olga is pregnant again. Schnitzler looks for a villa for her and finds one, after some time, in Hinterbühl, on the slopes of the Vienna Woods. On August 9, their son Heinrich will be born there. Olga pressures Schnitzler to marry, but he will not be moved. He wants to maintain his independence, but is also seriously worried about whether he can support his family financially. In fact, he has always harboured a fear of poverty, and is required to conduct lengthy discussions by mail with publishers and theater directors about royalties and the pirated editions of his works throughout his life.

The differences with Olga worsen and are aggravated by his otosclerosis. On December 4, he notes in his diary: "Sometimes it seems to me that the darkening of my existence dates from autumn '96, from the time the rustling in my ears began. Since then, it has not left me for one second."[108]

One of the fundamental problems in his relationship with Olga is her conviction that she is an artist, and her insistence on an artistic career. When Schnitzler first met her, she wanted to become an actress. Now, she intends to become a professional singer, which for the father of her child, in view of the fact that she is twenty years younger than he is, awakens the old anxieties from the Mizi Glümer era. When they argue, she threatens to put her career before the family. On December 15, 1902, he records in his diary:

> Her career. I spoke of the inconveniences of being engaged permanently in certain towns, and she read into this a hostility to all her ambition, an attempt to talk her out of her career. The frightening thing about these discussions is that they swirl

---

108 TB 1893–1902, 4.12.1902.

> up the depths in which hate rests, – as it exists between every couple that loves each other. – There are always reconciliations, and we console each other that it is only love... what remains is fatigue, and the grim but recurring conclusion: We should not have found one another.[109]

As it develops, even if Olga has some success with her public recitals, it eventually becomes obvious that she does not have the talent for a career as a professional singer. In the coming year, the clearer this becomes to her – although she tries to deny it – the more serious the tension between herself and her husband.

One hour after his son is born, Schnitzler sets pen to paper for the work that will become his first novel, *Der Weg ins Freie*. In the course of this year, he also writes *Die Fremde* (not renamed until 1907), originally called *Dämmerseele.* Each of these stories addresses some sort of betrayal and estrangement. The first one is told from the perspective of a young man whose wife has just left him, a mysterious woman whom he never really knew. She continued to lead a life of her own, with tragic consequences. In *Die Griechische Tänzerin,* a husband commits adultery under his wife's nose, leading the narrator to suspect that her death was not natural, as presumed, but suicide. *Exzentrik* is a humorous variant on these Schnitzlerean themes. In a coffee house at 3 a.m., an unusual guest, possibly a parody of Peter Altenberg, discovers that his actress girlfriend has been unfaithful to him three times with performers from a visiting circus: once with a dwarf, once with a giant, and once with the leader of a group of acrobats. *Andreas Thameyers letzter Brief* describes a husband's despair that his wife has given birth to a black child. *Die Weissagung* addresses another theme with which Schnitzler is preoccupied: predetermination, and the extent to which an individual can control his own fate. The protagonist sees his own death scene in a dream, and tries to flee until, in the end, he finds himself in precisely that same situation in reality and can no longer escape the inevitable.

---

109 Ibid., 15.12.1902.

One-Act Plays and a Competitor

Schnitzler finishes the one-act play, *Der tapfere Cassian*, which he includes in the Marionetten-cycle. He also continues to work on the drama *Die Egoisten*, which he had begun already in 1900 as the novella, *Der Junggeselle. Der tapfere Cassian* is set in a small German provincial town in the late 17th century. Schnitzler has learned from his experience with *Der Schleier der Beatrice* and uses contemporary vernacular rather than verse. The whole play is a dynamic dialogue, with unexpected turns which end with a complete reversal of the original situation. Surprising plot turns are typical for Schnitzler, but here they are condensed into a single act. The author enjoys playing with the reader's expectations, just as he is fascinated by the shifting perceptual levels of reality and fiction, both from the character's and the audience's perspective.

Why does he call this a "puppet play," in spite of the realistic characters? In comparison with the other plays in the *Marionetten* cycle, it looks as though here, Schnitzler intended his characters to be in a state of predetermined fate beyond their control. This is especially clear in *Der Puppenspieler. Zum grossen Wurstel* is the only play in the cycle that actually uses puppets, in the framework of a puppet theater on the stage, including its own audience, adding these levels of narrative to the real stage and real audience.

In October, Schnitzler visits Gerhart Hauptmann, on Otto Brahm's recommendation and by the playwright's own friendly invitation. Hauptmann is the other major name at Brahm's Deutsches Theater. The naturalist has, with his plays *Vor Sonnenaufgang* (1889) and *Die Weber* (1894), shaken the Berlin public out of its complacency, especially with his unabashed presentation of the working population and its tribulations. Although Schnitzler corresponds with a number of literary personalities, such as the brothers Thomas and Heinrich Mann, he only meets with them when they are coincidentally in Vienna. Ibsen is the only one that he travels to seek out, in Norway. Although Schnitzler and Hauptmann get along well, Schnitzler's diary shows deprecatory comments on Hauptmann's mainly positive reviews. It is possible that Schnitzler felt that his dramatic and literary talents were under-appreciated compared to Hauptmann's.

In March of 1903, Schnitzler is awarded the Bauernfeld Prize once more for the cycle *Lebendige Stunden*. Brahm decides to stage *Der Schleier der Beatrice* at his Deutsches Theater, in spite of its lack of success at the Breslau performance. Alfred Kerr praises the play as the "strongest of Schnitzler's work so far." But Goldmann, his longtime companion from Jung Wien, damns the play in the *Neue Freie Presse*. It is generally known that Schnitzler and Goldmann are friends, so that this negative review is taken as well-intended honesty, which in no way benefits Schnitzler. Although the play is not a success, it continues to be performed.

Der einsame Weg and Marriage

Back in February, he discussed *Der einsame Weg* (as the play *Die Egoisten* is now called), with Olga and Gustav Schwarzkopf. He realizes that there are two separate dramatic strands here, which can easily rupture the framework of a single play. He divides them into "the bachelor play" and "the doctor play." Starting with the seminal idea of a priest who is not allowed by a doctor into the room of a dying patient, out of the latter develops, by 1912, *Professor Bernhardi*. In the words of Renate Wagner, *Der einsame Weg* marks "the transition from [Schnitzler's] early period into his phase of maturity." It focuses on the two "egoists," Julian Fichtner and Stephan von Sala, who, throughout their lives, have always taken from people, depending on what they needed at the time, without ever giving anything back. Now, in their old age, they are alone and realize that they themselves are at fault. In Salas' words:

> Did we ever sacrifice anything without advantage to our sensuality or our vanity? Did we ever hesitate to cheat and lie to honest people, if only to get one more hour of happiness or pleasure from it? ... Did we ever risk either our peace of mind or our lives – not on a whim nor out of folly... no, only to enhance the well-being of an individual who had given everything to us? […] And do you believe that we have the right to ask back from one human being – man or woman – anything we have given them?

The plot is set in the Wegrat's family house, with the stage direction so familiar for Schnitzler's plays: "Vienna – Present." Frau Wegrat is ill and passes away in the second act, leaving her husband and two children, Felix and Johanna. Johanna is a mysterious, intriguing character, with her head full of unusual, poetic thoughts. Felix is currently serving his year in the army.

The actress Irene Herms visits her old friend Julian Fichtner, a friend of the Wegrats, who has returned from his travels and is back in Vienna. It turns out that Fichtner left her many years ago over a brief affair of hers. Fichtner was, however, Irene's one love, and she tells him: "That silly story during my engagement abroad, dear God, you really could have forgiven me that." Fichtner was, however, too proud. She wishes that the two of them could have settled down to a fulfiled life with their child. Now it is too late, and she is a spinster, just as he is an old bachelor.

It is eventually revealed that Felix is, in fact, Fichtner's son, the result of a love affair with Gabriele, Wegrat's wife. Fichtner's attempts to win Felix over are unsuccessful. Felix rejects his true father, who left him all these years for the sake of his own escapades, and remains with Wegrat, who adopted him, and for whom he feels a filial affection.

This development runs parallel to the tragedy of Johanna's and Sala's love. When Sala asks Johanna to be his wife, and to come on an expedition to the Far East with him, she is deeply touched. But at the same time, she is aware that Sala – unknown to him – is in the clutches of a fatal disease and does not have long to live. Overwhelmed by the impossibility of her happiness in the face of his death, she drowns herself in Sala's pond.

When one reflects that this was the year Schnitzler married, *Der einsame Weg* seems somewhat downhearted. It smacks of age and resignation, although Schnitzler was only 41 years old when he wrote the play. Nevertheless, the atmosphere is melancholy, sustained by the reminiscences of their irretrievable youth on the part of the two protagonists, Fichtner and Sala. The density of the plot and the well-constructed dialogue make *Der Einsame Weg* one of Schnitzler's most successful dramas.

His decision to divide the two plays enables Schnitzler to complete the drama in July 1903. As if this had resolved some inner conflict – but also to provide his son with an intact and legitimate home – he finally gives up his resistance to marriage. Thus, he confesses to Olga already in April, before a trip to Linz:

> My beloved, before I leave, I want [...] to say to you that I have never left you with such a feeling of the complete, indissoluble, everlasting, sense of belonging together as I have this time, and that [I] love you terribly, even unto death, in all happiness and all desperation, (the one without the other is certainly impossible)[110]

On 26th August, he weds Olga Gussmann in the synagogue of the Schopenhauergasse.

Zwischenspiel and Herzl's Death

Aside from the fact that Schnitzler is convinced of the literary qualities of *Reigen,* Schnitzler knows the piquant play will sell. The censors pass it without amendment, as in April, 1903, it appears in the Wiener Verlag. It soon reaches a print run of 40,000. His friends jokingly call him the "pornographer," and his brother Julius tells him of mutual acquaintances who are outraged. Schnitzler has an almost physical reluctance to open the morning newspaper. In June, the Munich Dramatic Association stages Scenes 4 to 6 and immediately calls down sanctions from the Bavarian government.[111] When Bahr wants to do a public reading of excerpts and submits it to the responsible authorities for approval, the expected ban follows. In 1904, *Reigen* is confiscated in Germany. In 1912, in Budapest, however, the provocative series of scenes is staged without the knowledge of the authorities, as is done likewise in Moscow and St. Petersburg in the year of the revolution, 1917. The major scandals, however, do not occur until the stagings in Vienna and Berlin.

With *Der Einsame Weg,* nevertheless, Schnitzler wins his audience back. In February, 1904, at the premiere in the Deutsches Theater, Berlin, its reception is lukewarm. But the next evening, the house is sold out. The play

110 DLA, Briefe Arthur an Olga Schnitzler. Folder 518, 8.4.1903.

111 Harmut Scheible: *Arthur Schnitzler*. Reinbek bei Hamburg: Rowohlt 1976, p. 140.

becomes one of Schnitzler's most enduring successes.

Before the first night, he has his publisher send a copy to the Burgtheater. Schnitzler is not surprised at Schlenther's refusal. The Volkstheater in Vienna is another option, but remembering his bad experiences with *Lebendige Stunden,* Schnitzler decides to rely entirely on his friend Brahm.

In July 1904, Theodor Herzl dies. Schnitzler attends the funeral service on August 1. Although he maintained opposition to Zionism throughout his life, looking back, he concedes his admiration for Herzl.

In these years, there is a change in the world of German theater: Brahm goes to the Lessingtheater in Berlin, and Max Reinhardt takes over the Deutsches Theater. Reinhardt wants to begin the season with the one-act plays *Der tapfere Cassian, Der grüne Kakadu* and *Das Haus Delorme.* But out of solidarity with Adele Sandrock, the actors refuse to rehearse for the latter, because Sandrock's family is easily recognizable as the model for the characters. When the play is banned by the censors, Schnitzler is actually relieved, because this saves him trouble with the actors. *Cassian* is a failure with the Berlin public at the Kleines Theater. *Der grüne Kakadu*, on the other hand, is a resounding success in the German capital. Schnitzler has no intention of fighting for *Das Haus Delorme*, and the play first premieres only in 1979.

From July 1904 until August 1905, Schnitzler is working on a "comedy" in three acts, *Intermezzo (Zwischenspiel,* originally *Neue Ehe).* It is a dialogue between the composer Amadeus and the singer Cäcilie. This is the first time that Schnitzler depicts a serious long-term relationship between a man and a woman. Amadeus and Cäcilie must acknowledge that they are no longer in love. They agree to turn their relationship into a close friendship. At first, this solution succeeds. They both continue to see their young child, and they also carry on their productive professional cooperation. They both have relationships with others, and Cäcilie soon becomes a protégée of Graf Sigismund. At the end of act two, however, Amadeus is enthralled by the new woman she has become, and they spend the night together. But this means that Amadeus lays claim to her, and in order to dispose of his competitor, he wants to challenge the Count to a duel. Before it comes to this, however, the Count visits him. They agree that Amadeus has the legitimate claim to Cäcilie. The dilemma seems to be resolved, but Cäcilie feels compelled to tell him that she cannot return to him. "We meant so much to each other, Amadeus, that we must keep the memory of it pure."[112] They part, and before the curtain drops, Cäcilie bends her head over the piano and weeps.

Schnitzler even manages to win over Schlenther for the performance, so that with this play, Schnitzler returns to "his" Burgtheater. There are "bravo" cries and joy at Schnitzler's homecoming, but the final act of the premiere on October 12 ends with sharp whistles of disapproval. The staging of the *Kakadu* at the Volkstheater, on the other hand, is received with great enthusiasm. At one performance, Schnitzler is called to the stage eight times.[113]

Komtesse Mizzi and *Das Wort*

Komtesse Mizzi is a one-acter in which Schnitzler reclaims his mastery of dramatic dialogue. It is published in 1908 and premieres the year after. After the publication of his novel, on the other hand, Schnitzler can turn all his creative energy to his master works: *Der junge Medardus* (1910), *Das weite Land* (1911) and *Professor Bernhardi* (1912).

A new short story is published in 1905, *Das Neue Lied.* A young woman, a singer, is blinded in an accident, which alienates Karl, with whom she is in love. Her latest song, about the joys of youth, only worsens her depression. In the end, her lifeless corpse is found in the middle of a courtyard. It is unusual for Schnitzler to depict the rejected and abandoned in society, but he does it here with his usual psychological precision. *Das neue Lied* is reminiscent of *Ehrentag*, in which the unlucky Roland is driven to suicide by exposure to what he perceives to be public ridicule.

Schnitzler puts the finishing touches on *Komtesse Mizzi* between June and July 1906. The play demonstrates all the suspense and turns of plot of a typical Schnitzlerean drama. The action takes place at the country estate of a count, elevating the usual middle-class setting to an aristocratic social sphere. A prince visits his friend, the count, to announce the impending

112 DW I, p. 959.
113 TB 1903–8, 14.10.1905.

visit of his son. Mizzi, the count's daughter, is 37 years old and unmarried, "but still very good-looking." When the count excuses himself, we learn that the prince's son is also Mizzi's child. She tells the prince that she would have come with him and left everything behind her, had it not been for his "cowardice." This was a strong word at the time, and if it had been uttered between men, the natural response would be a challenge to a duel. But the prince lets it pass, reminding her that he proposed to her twice. Mizzi declined both times, because he "never really knew her at all."[114]

When the 17-year-old son arrives, he grasps that Mizzi is his real mother. After she has left, he tells his father so. In the end, the whole group leaves for a summer holiday in Ostende. It remains open whether this trip will bring general reconciliation.

At the same time, Schnitzler is working on a play about Peter Altenberg, a coffee-house writer par excellence from the circle of Alfred Polgar and Karl Kraus. The work, which will soon be called *Das Wort* (1969),[115] is a satire on that competing literary group, which also includes Adolf and Lina Loos. Schnitzler uses two real events for the play. In August, 1904, he notes in his diary that Lina advises Altenberg, an alcoholic who is perennially without funds, to commit suicide rather than accept the donations collected for him by his friends, because she finds this solution more poetic.[116] In January, Altenberg himself tells a young painter, who is in love with Lina and was rejected by her, to kill himself – which the young man actually does. The plot of *The Word* builds up to this point, with which the play in the final act finds its climax.

Anastasius Treuenhof, the fictional equivalent of Altenberg, utters the line: "I call self-sacrificing people, those who work for others, Christians, and people who work for themselves, Jews. There are many Christians who are Jews and many Jews who are Christians." His colleague Rapp retorts: "Which brings the entire racial question to a satisfactory conclusion."[117]

The two characters who cause damage with the words they use are Lisa

114 DW I, p. 1045.

115 An excellent performance by the Theater in der Josefstadt from 1969 is available as a DVD ("Edition Josefstadt"), with Klaus Maria Brandauer, Hans Holt and Vilma Degischer.

116 TB 1903–8, 7.8.1904.

117 DLA, Das Wort – Manuskripte, Dramatisches. Folders 69–70.

van Zack and Treuenhof himself. Lisa lies shamelessly both to her husband and to her young lover, Willi. Willi takes her promises, which are just a game to her, very seriously. In the final act, Willi realizes that Lisa lied to him for weeks and will stay true to her husband. He is desperate. Treuenhof, however, claims that the concepts of truth and lie are only words, invented by men. Women aren't familiar with these ideas, he says, although they "parrot mindlessly what men tell them." He continues in disbelief, tapping his head: "Truth and lie – in the realm of the erotic!" Treuenhof heaps rather harsh criticism on Willi, going so far as to suggest that he should kill himself.

Treuenhof, when asked for advice, seems to do no more than utter hollow epigrams. When van Zack admits that he suffers badly from Lisa's possible infidelity, Treuenhof tells him that if he really loves her, he must step aside and let her go away with Willi. For those who admire Treuenhof, namely women, he is seen as authoritative because of his knowledge of the world and his former accomplishments as a poet. They believe in him, but Treuenhof, as he states, no longer believes in himself. It appears, looking at the advice he gives, that he is usually wrong and trying to produce some kind of original effect, rather than to actually help the people who turn to him. This insincerity becomes especially clear when Willi's family begins to expect the worst, and they ask Treuenhof what he said to him. Treuenhof answers, "Words! Only words! What are words after all?" Willi's father replies: "Words! Are they only there to play with? We have nothing but our words!"

This conflict is related to another Schnitzlerean theme: the difference between people who take things "lightly" and those for whom words – and promises – carry more weight. Willi's father obviously takes the words he hears from people as the truth. But Lisa tells her friend Neumann, who disapproves of her two-faced conduct, not to take it to heart. "Don't take it so seriously." Treuenhof uses exactly the same expression after he has told Willi that he has lost all faith in him, that he deserved no better than to lose Lisa, and that he was "born only half a man." The consequences are disastrous. The same dualism occurs, by the way, in *Das Weite Land,* in that Genia Hofreiter makes every attempt to adapt to the easy-going ways of her husband, but in the end fails in the attempt.

Although Schnitzler records, in May of the following year, that he does not believe in the play,[118] *Das Wort* is perhaps the most Viennese of his dramas. It is not only an accurate study of a social milieu, it is also the study of a particular institution and its clientele. And this institution – the coffee house – exists in this special form only in Vienna. Schnitzler never completed the play, and it was subsequently never performed in his lifetime. But in 1969, the Josefstadt Theater dared to stage *Das Wort*. With its excellent cast, it was a great success, and conjured up Schnitzler's Vienna most authentically.

The *Marionetten*-Cycle

The lack of success of *Ruf des Lebens* is balanced to some degree, by the success of a puppet play, *Zum grossen Wurstel* (1906). Schnitzler can, in his three "puppet plays," which he had combined in the cycle *Marionetten*, effectively play with the shifting boundaries between the stage and reality, which he enjoys confusing the audience by violating. As a child, he once observed actors in costume greeting up from the stage to his parents' box.[119] Ever since then, Schnitzler had been fascinated by the flowing boundaries between acting and real life.

Der Puppenspieler is a puppet play to the same extent that *Der tapfere Cassian* is, which is to say, not at all. This brief one-act play explores the concept of fate and predetermination on several levels. Two old friends, the musician Eduard and the poet Georg, meet by chance in the street after not having seen each other for years. At one point, Georg confesses to having been the puppet master behind Eduard's marriage with his wife, Anna, who is present. He had felt sorry for Eduard, who was shy and prone to melancholy, and told Anna to pretend as if she were in love with him. Anna obliged Georg, for the somewhat perverse reason that she was in love with him and wanted to make him jealous. This is news to Georg, who learns that he could have been in Eduard's place today, in a secure married life, if he had only come back to her. Instead, he travelled the world restlessly and

118 TB 17.5.1907.

119 JiW, p. 27.

gave up his promising career as a writer. Just before he leaves, he informs his friends that he, too, was married once, and had a son. Georg claims that he died, but given that Anna starts at his words, and then avoids her husband's eye, it is left open whether her child, who is also named Georg, is, in fact, Eduard's son.

The one-act play, *Zum grossen Wurstel,* named after the puppet theater in the Prater, seems like a summary of Schnitzler's experiences with the theater. Apart from the acting characters, there is a "Poet," who functions as a playwright, and a "Producer." These two squabble over which parts of the play to leave out, and which are the most effective. Different members of the audience appear on the stage, such as the "Benevolent Man," the "Naive Man," and the "Vicious Man." Schnitzler treats the characters with irony, parodying his own invention, the "Süßes Mädel," and the "Demonic Duchess" (a catch-word of the time). The "Protagonist" is rendered an anti-hero. In this respect, although he is not a real character, this puppet hero resembles the heroes of Schnitzler's greater dramas. Both Medardus as well as Professor Bernhardi are by no means typical heroes, and fail in their cause, if they even have one. Here, the Protagonist says: "People call me a hero/I don't really have to be one." And later: "I am the hero of the play, nothing else./ Once I have done my duty,/ I will remain, hopefully, undamaged,/ Packed into a green box/With the greatest care."[120]

When the plot between the Hero, Liesl, the Duke and the Duchess gets too spicy, a "Bourgeois" in the audience wants to take his daughters away. But they insist that they do not understand what is happening. There is even a "Man in the Theaterboxes," who sits in the real audience, complaining loudly. He is repeatedly taken to be real. In the final scene, the puppet strings are cut, and the poet muses: "Am I a god?... a fool?... am I just like you? Am I myself – or just a symbol?"In the same year, the cycle appears in book form with S. Fischer, which also includes *Der tapfere Cassian* and *Der Puppenspieler*.

Der tote Gabriel is published in 1907. This story also includes an Anastasius Treuenhof, but only as a marginal figure. Gabriel is dead, and Ferdinand and Irene, who was very fond of him, discuss his relationship

---

120 DW I, pp. 875, 878.

with the actress Wilhelmine. Ferdinand is now Wilhelmine's lover as well, and when they visit her, she proves to be totally indifferent to the fact that a man committed suicide because she was unfaithful to him. Here, the loss of a beloved being, a recurrent theme in Schnitzler's work, is examined from the female perspective.

In the same year, Schnitzler writes the story *Tod eines Junggesellen,* which appears in print the next year. A writer's last will requests his friends to gather at his bedside to hear the reading of a posthumous letter. The letter states: "I have had all of your women. Every one."[121] Two of the women in question have already died, and as for the others, the husbands resolve not to confront them about it. In the end, therefore, nothing changes. The situation brings to mind a line from *Der Einsame Weg:* "A lie which has proven strong enough to carry the peace of a family is just as worthy of admiration as a truth, which could do no more than destroy the image of the past, sully the feelings of the present, and confuse the view of the future."[122]

121 ES I, p. 968.
122 DW I, p. 775.

DER WEG INS FREIE —

Schnitzler's Cautious Sounding of the "Jewish Question"

Schnitzler had conceived his first novel, in the period between 1894 and 1900, as a comedy entitled *Die Entrüsteten.* It was intended to address the issue of seduction, set in the petit bourgeois milieu, apparently inspired by his experience with Marie Reinhard. The novel is a comprehensive bourgeois social panorama of Vienna in 1900, including the intellectual currents of the time: socialism, anti-Semitism and Zionism.

As a novel that addresses certain "Jewish Questions" of the era, *Der Weg ins Freie* by no means stands alone. Aside from Jakob Wassermann's *Juden von Zirndorf* (1897), which Wassermann considerably diluted for the 1906 edition,[123] in this context, Georg Hermann's thoroughly successful book *Jettchen Gebert* (1906) must be mentioned. It deals with the destiny of a daughter from a bourgeois Jewish house who must bow to family conventions – with tragic consequences. Auguste Hauschner, who wrote a very insightful review of *Weg ins Freie*, also stepped forward with her own published works, which are set among the Jewish middle class of Prague and Berlin: first *Die Familie Lowositz (*1908), and two years later, the sequel *Rudolf und Camilla*. Both novels touch on questions of Jewish identity.

The great success of Schnitzler's novel finally brings him financial security. He considers it, as he wrote to Brandes, the best work that he has done so far. In fact, it will become one of the most profitable books of the Fischer Verlag and undergoes, by 1929, 136 print runs.[124]

But in spite of the high sales figures of his novel, Schnitzler is not completely satisfied. Certain critical articles, particularly if they are written by friends, affect him deeply and can preoccupy him for days. In the end, Schnitzler decides that his book was generally misunderstood, and adds: "In the place that produced it, the novel will come into its own only in the purer atmosphere of later years."[125]

---

123 Jakob Wassermann: Die Juden von Zirndorf. Cadolzburg: ars vivendi 1995, p. 277.

124 Farese, p. 130.

125 TB 1909–1912, 1.1.1909.

His otosclerosis has now progressed to the point that it disturbs him as he is working, aggravates his hypochondria, and deprives him of the full pleasure of the concerts that he, as a music-lover, regularly visits. Thus, he notes in 1911, on the occasion of a memorial concert for the recently deceased Gustav Mahler, that he does not hear the "pianissimi" at all anymore, but that the "forti" can fortunately penetrate the incessant rushing noise in his ears.[126]

Originally, when Schnitzler had conceived the work as a drama and called it *Die Entrüsteten,* it dealt with the seduction of a girl from the lower walks of society, as well as her brother's revenge. Schnitzler worked on this theme between 1894 and 1900. He finished the novel in October 1907. In May 1908, Schnitzler was already sketching the first act of *Professor Bernhardi.* Although the work on the novel merged into that on the drama, and, for a period, he worked on both at the same time, a further four years lay ahead before he could finish the dramatic work.

In *Der Weg ins Freie* (1908), Schnitzler unfolds a social panorama of the Jewish haute bourgeoisie of his home city, including several different perspectives on anti-Semitism. There is, for example, the position of Salmon Ehrenberg, who has Zionistic tendencies, and finds pleasure in irritating his assimilation-oriented family by speaking Yiddish. His son Oskar, on the other hand, irritates his father with his pronounced sympathy for Catholicism and the aristocracy.

The plot of the novel is relatively straightforward. The young nobleman and composer Georg von Wergenthin loves Anna Rosner, who comes from the petit-bourgeois milieu. The only hope for a girl in Anna's position to find social recognition is in marriage. Georg, however, cannot bring himself to marry her. Their relationship reaches a tragic climax with a stillbirth that leads to the parents' alienation from each other. At the end, Georg leaves Anna, and also Vienna, to take the position of court choir director in Detmold.

Georg's friend Heinrich Bermann embodies a moderate stance on the so-called "Jewish Question." Bermann, who is older than Georg, ultimately loses an election to a German nationalist deputy of dubious reputation. Bermann's political career illustrates the decline of Austrian liberalism. He

126 Ibid., p. 2.12.1911.

passionately discusses philosophical themes and, as a character, presents a counterweight to Leo Golowski's Zionism.

Another character worth mentioning is Jakob Rosner, Anna's brother. In the first chapter, his parents are disappointed by his lack of ambition and continual demands for money. He, nevertheless, soon finds work with a Christian Social paper and willingly assumes the appropriate political views. Jacob is the only character in the whole novel who sets a clear goal in life and succeeds in reaching it.

Der Weg ins Freie appears in the *Neue Rundschau* of the Fischer Verlag from January to June 1908. It is first published in book form in June.[127] After the first critical reviews, Schnitzler is outraged by the fact that he is now apparently generally perceived as a Jewish author. However, the publication of a work in which most of the characters are of Jewish origin was public acknowledgment thereof. On January 13, 1910, Schnitzler notes in his diary, that "'Der Weg ins Freie' [...] above all is not well enough understood."[128] In September of the same year, he expresses his disappointment over the fact that the literary value of his characters is not adequately appreciated, because the Jewish theme weighs too heavily: "Will I ever experience that the character of 'Heinrich Bermann' is grasped purely artistically, without prejudice?"[129] After the author had reread his work in March of 1912, he recorded: "After the 4th chapter, I had the decided feeling that this book is barely understood and appreciated. – "[130]

Schnitzler protested vigorously against his book being viewed as a Jewish "roman à clef." On January 8, 1907, he makes an entry in his diary: "At table a discussion of my novel [...] as a roman à clef; annoying doubts on my side as to whether one could (make a deliberate effort to) forget this sensationalizing of a work of art. – "Two days later he adds: "Worked badly at home; rather irritated by the roman à clef interpretation."[131]

Schnitzler was fully conscious of his Jewish background, but he saw himself first and foremost as an Austrian author. In a letter to the Jewish

127 ES II, p. 993.
128 TB 1909–1912, 13.1.1910.
129 Ibid., 24.9.1910.
130 Ibid., 30.3.1912.
131 TB 1903–1909, 8.1. & 10.1.1907.

National Fund, which had asked him for financial support for a Zionist project, he states:

> I see myself, in fact, in no way as a Jewish writer, but rather as a German writer as far as something like that can be proven, belonging to the Jewish race, whose blood, in any case, is predominantly Jewish and who also, in some of his qualities, finds much that may be considered characteristically Jewish.
> I write in the German language, live within a German cultural circle, certainly owe by far the most to the German culture among all the cultures, even if I also know exactly what I owe to the Hebraic, Greek, and Roman cultures, not to mention the Romanic culture. Neither the Jewish-Zionist resentment nor the silliness and shamelessness of the German nationalists will move me the slightest to disregard the fact that I am a German writer. Not even the suspicion that I want to ingratiate myself with the Germans, nor even with their most miserable representatives, will hinder me from feeling what I feel and knowing what I know [...][132]

But the critics had touched a nerve. Schnitzler described his novel, in a dispute with Hofmannsthal, as "one of the most personal of my creations."[133] This is not only because of the autobiographical parallels to his relationship with Marie Reinhard, but also because of questions of German-Jewish identity that preoccupy him. And in 1915, Schnitzler writes: "I [...] have, understandably, never been able to decide, in all my more than twenty years of writing activity, to counter with one word all the anti-Semitic distortions, aspersions, and calumny."[134] He intended his work – in spite of the theme of *Der Weg ins Freie* and *Professor Bernhardi* – to be understood not only from the Jewish perspective. That is also the main reason why Schnitzler so decisively opposed the play- or roman à clef approach.

---

132 CUL, MS Unabgesandte Briefe, Folder 124 B, Nr. 3.

133 Briefe 1875–1912, p. 632.

134 Briefe 1913–1931, p. 76.

Distanced Sympathy: Schnitzler's Approach to Zionism

As the letter to the Jewish National Foundation indicates, Schnitzler always maintained a critical distance to Zionism. In his opinion, it was a worthwhile, meaningful, philanthropical measure for the impoverished and persecuted Jews of the East. But he himself withheld support for the movement.

> One cannot overestimate what this movement has accomplished and will continue to accomplish, particularly for poor, persecuted, and tormented Jews. One can't deny the fact that hundreds of thousands of Jews, indeed, through persecution by their host countries, even more through the knavish behaviour of their respective governments, have been driven out of their native lands and desperately need a new home. It goes without saying that countless Jews [...] merely through disgust at the enmity that they were subjected to, leave their homelands in wounded pride and seek another, and that to them, the one that looks most fitting is the place where 2,000 years ago their ancestors lived.[135]

In 1902, Schnitzler declines the invitation to write something for the Zionest organ *Die Welt*. In the same way, he refuses to participate in 1907 in land purchases in Egypt; or to give speeches before Zionist organizations, such as before the Galician-Jewish Student Association Bar Kochba in 1909.[136] In April 1914, Schnitzler refuses to give a speech on the tenth anniversary of Theodor Herzl's death. His rationale was the following, "that in my innermost heart, I never felt so allied with Herzl that I deserved on such an occasion to speak out publicly on his behalf."[137]

Schnitzler's acquaintance with Herzl had begun on the day in 1892

135 CUL, MS Unabgesandte Briefe, Folder B124, Nr. 7.

136 TB 1893-1902, 18.12.1902; TB 1902-1908, 9.1.1907; TB 1909-1912, 26.2., 30.10., 25.11.1909.

137 Briefe 1913–1931, p. 38.

that the latter had sent him a congratulatory telegram on the premiere of his drama *Das Märchen,* which Herzl greatly admired. In 1894 and 1895, Schnitzler works as an intermediary to enable the performance of Herzl's play, *Das Ghetto* (see section "New Works in Prose – Increasing Anti-Semitism").

In their correspondence, the two get along very well. But as they meet for the first time in 1895, after Herzl's return from Paris, all is not so harmonious. Schnitzler mistrusts Herzl's personal ambition. It is precisely Herzl's increasing political activity for Zionism that estranges Schnitzler. In 1895 and 1896, they repeatedly discuss the settlement of Palestine, and Schnitzler expresses his skepticism each time.[138]

Recognizing their differences, personal meetings and letters between the two become increasingly rare. In July, 1904, Schnitzler nevertheless notes in his journal that he was "badly shaken" when he heard of Herzl's death.[139] More than once, he notes his regret that he had not openly demonstrated to Herzl his admiration for him, and that he felt misunderstood by Herzl. On August 7, he finds words of praise for the famous Zionist leader. "[A man] very important to note, worldwide fame, wanting to found states, mourned by millions when he died – Jews in Odessa shut their stores as the news of his death arrived."[140] In September, 1906, Schnitzler notes: "I remember also Herzl, who couldn't stand me (in later years, who really behaved stupidly toward me – and never really found out how much I respected him, even admired him)."[141] Schnitzler describes these feelings in December again: "Much about Herzl (who couldn't stand me, as I know, and had no real idea who I was, while all along, I really admired him)."[142]

But all of his admiration for Herzl doesn't change Schnitzler's attitude toward Zionism. He acknowledges Herzl's efforts because he championed a cause with unwavering determination. But Schnitzler does not want to be harnessed to a political movement himself.

---

138 DLA, MS Charakteristiken aus den Tagebüchern – Theodor Herzl. Folder 187, Nr. 453.

139 TB 1903–1908, 4.6.1904.

140 Ibid., 7.8.1904.

141 Ibid., 24.9.1906.

142 Ibid., 7.12.1906.

> But that one could be a convinced convert or a convinced Zionist are both equally incomprehensible. That would mean that one could predict the future. One can only speculate or have an opinion about which solution could be more advantageous for oneself, for one's relatives, for a people, that one belongs to with or without love, with pride or with shame. It is not cowardice to be assimilated and it is not bravery to be Zionist. One can be an acknowledged Jew and nevertheless assimilated. [...] Also, without feeling solidarity, one can abhor the obvious injustice that the Jews experience.[143]

"To foresee the future," means here to know the solution of the Jewish Question in advance. At present, one could only speculate about the various proposed solutions. Here, Schnitzler's individualism comes to the fore. The last sentence in the above quotation refers to Schnitzler's stance on the "eastern Jewish" refugees. Even though he did not share their social or religious background, his sense of justice was offended by the persecution that they were increasingly subjected to during this period.

On the one hand, Schnitzler distances himself from Zionism on the basis of personal differences with Herzl; and on the other hand, because of his conviction that this is geared more to the impoverished Jewish refugee from the east than to the assimilated member of the middle class.

Besides that, Schnitzler feels very closely allied to Austria and the city of his birth. After all, he is one of the most successful authors of the German-speaking world and relies on a German public for his living.

Schnitzler's Jewish Identity

Schnitzler left his home city of Vienna only for occasional trips. In a short statement in 1904, he writes: "I don't love my fatherland because it's my fatherland, but because I find it beautiful. I have a strong sense of being at home in my native land [Heimatgefühl], but no patriotism."[144] Schnitzler

143 CUL, MS Aphorismen, Folder A 5.

144 Ibid.

thus distinguishes between attachment to his homeland as such and to the political construct of the state. He feels allegiance not to the dynastic entity, but to the nature and culture of the land. He expands on this allegiance in an interview with James L. Benvenisti for the *American Hebrew and Jewish Messenger* on February 29, 1924:

> I have my roots here in Vienna, where my home was in my youth and is now. I have grown up identifying myself with the unique Viennese culture. Should I leave this land, only because some rude and badly brought-up blockheads of anti-Semites tell me that I don't belong here?[145]

Even if Schnitzler's cultural identity in a larger sense takes in the entire German-speaking world, he identifies in particular with Austria. His dilemma arises from anti-Semites denying that anyone of Jewish origin could be a true Austrian. In an unpublished statement, he defends his position.

> They don't count us among their kind. I'm glad for this. They think that I'm no Austrian like them. Above all, nobody can deny that I'm myself, which is sufficient to begin with, and that I was born in Austria. If millions of cretins find that I don't belong here, I know better than they that I'm more at home here than all of them.[146]

Thus, Schnitzler's cultural identity is threefold: Austrian, German, and Jewish. In a letter to his sister-in-law, Lisl Steinrück, in the first months of World War I, he expresses this tripartite allegiance as follows:

> It's going for us Austrians – almost like – us Jews – ; by the way, in respect to foreign countries one could almost say: us Germans

---

145 James L. Benvenisti: Arthur Schnitzler foretells Jewish Renaissance. An exclusive interview with the eminent litterateur. In: The American Hebrew and Jewish Messenger, 29.2.1924, ZAS MF 320. The English original text is reproduced in Riedmann, pp. 396–98.
146 CUL, MS Aphorismen, Folder A 5.

> - like us Austrians - and us Jews. *We* are misjudged. Strange, that during these times, we must feel that we are all these things at once. I am Jew, Austrian, German. It must really be so – because I feel offended in the name of Jewishness, Austria and Germany, if one repeats something bad about any of one of the three.[147]

During the war, Schnitzler feels a certain antagonism between his Jewish origins on the one hand, and his strong adherence to both German-speaking culture and attachment to his native Austria on the other. This is made more acute by the nationalism of the war propaganda. In 1915, he writes:

> And now I experience as a German, as a member of the German people, with millions of other Germans, with hundreds of thousands that don't count me among them, [...] in spite of the belonging, that from enmity endured together is more strongly welded than from air breathed in common, [or] commonly loved works and people; now I experience it again, so that I ask myself, together with those who don't count me as one of them: Why don't you know us? Why don't you want to know us? And this question goes far out into the world, in all directions in which the nations [...] live, which also, with long-nourished civic resistance, turn against the greater Germany in which I, an offspring of the Jewish race, and an Austrian, felt the whole time that I belonged, with equal rights and equal responsibilities. And I now ask the Germans, who like me [...] send up this question to the truly neutral heavens [...]: Why don't they know us? Why don't they want to know us?[148]

In the later course of the war, Schnitzler's identification with the German and the Austrian cause decreases, as he becomes increasingly sceptical of the government's war aims, as well as the nationalist propaganda. His sense of

147 Briefe 1913–1931, pp. 68–69.

148 Arthur Schnitzler: *Aphorismen und Betrachtungen*. ed. by Robert O. Weiss. Frankfurt/Main: S. Fischer Verlag 1967, p. 198.

German, Austrian, and Jewish identity remains fairly consistent, however. In his own words: "I am an Austrian citizen of the Jewish race, professing to the German culture."[149] As such, and given his strong attachment to his native Vienna, he sees no reason to emigrate to Palestine.

"Avoidable Causes of Anti-Semitism" — Schnitzler against Religious Orthodoxy and the "Renegades"

In keeping with his assimilated background, Schnitzler was not raised to be religious. In *Jugend in Wien*, he describes, as mentioned previously, that his family used matzos to accompany coffee. This only underlines to what degree an orthodox ritual was transformed into a secularised, refined ceremony of the middle classes.[150] In October of 1912, Schnitzler inquires of his son's religion teacher, Salomon Zimmels, whether Heinrich could be released from the hours of instruction in the synagogue.[151]

Three years later, during the war, Schnitzler is asked for a donation to provide unleavened bread to Jewish prisoners of war for Passover. Instead of a donation, Schnitzler sends a letter to the Israelite Cultural Association in which he lays out why he considers this idea not only to be "outdated" but, rather, also dangerous. "Why? he asks, "is a committee formed on the issue of ritual diet etc., etc., in a time during which there are so many more important, timely, and, as I would like to emphasize, less controversial things to deliberate on and to do?"

Furthermore, according to Schnitzler, the Rabbis should, instead of spreading religious superstition, finally enlighten the Jews "for once and for all."

> Now or never, not only with the prisoners of war [...] would be the opportunity to point out the outdatedness, the superstition and the danger of all those ritual practices that don't have

149 TB 1917–1919, 1.11.1918.
150 JiW, p. 18.
151 Briefe 1875–1912, p. 702.

> the least thing to do with the essence of religion, with true reverence for God. One not only suspends the ritual dietary regulations that are no longer appropriate for our time and our climate, rather, what seems to me to be much more important, one finally gets around to transferring the Sabbath to Sunday. Even the most orthodox Jew will let himself be convinced by his rabbi without difficulty that God, who, after all, tolerated the development of Christianity, is completely indifferent as to whether one sanctifies the Sabbath or Sunday.[152]

Schnitzler could not state his disapproval of Jewish ritual more plainly. He is convinced that in wartime such a marked adherence to ritual only gives impetus to anti-Semitism.

> Perhaps I'm exactly the one to articulate it, who am, with regard to dogma, completely lacking in faith, but never denied my ethnic identity, [...] that such a rigid adherence to the externals of religion counted for me as one of the causes, and, in fact, the avoidable, the few avoidable causes, of anti-Semitism.
> And I fear the accusation from the Jews' side of being one of the assimilated as little as it ever irritated me if the German nationalists tried to deny me my Germanness. And I would personally have the feeling of engaging in dishonesty, indeed cowardice, if I committed myself to supporting a superstition, which, with goodwill [...] and with some degree of political insight, the Jews who are called to be religious leaders of their comrades in faith could have long ago gotten rid of.[153]

Schnitzler accents his individualism in that he protests equally vigorously against the accusations of religious Jews as well as against German nationalists. If he does not openly point out what he feels is one of the motives for anti-Semitism, he would consider himself a coward. His

152 CUL, MS An den Ausschuss zur rituellen Beköstigung der jüdischen Kriegsgefangenen und Zivilgefangenen an den Pessachfeiertagen, March 1915, Folder 60, Nr. 68–72.
153 Ibid.

own position was thus neither in "Jewish-Zionist resentment" or in the "shamelessness of German nationalists." One can justifiably ask the extent to which Schnitzler, who took a stance toward Jewry as critical as his stance toward Zionism, felt himself to be a Jew at all. His Jewish background was for him apparently rather a cultural than a religious or even ethnic heritage. To acknowledge his origins was for him a question of integrity. For the Jews who denied their background for opportunistic reasons, or who even converted to Catholicism, he had nothing but contempt. In *Der Geist im Wort und der Geist in der Tat* (1927) he writes:

> You may hold your new belief in as high esteem as you hold your former, you are in any case, a worse person than you were, because you are now a renegade. And if you pray just as devoutly to the new God as to the one you abandoned, the new God is no better for it than the old one was, but you have become a worse person.[154]

Jews like the ones depicted above went so far as to take up anti-Semitic positions themselves, to deny their own background. An example is Karl Kraus,[155] about whom Schnitzler wrote to Gustav Schwarzkopf in September, 1899:

> Little Kraus sits in the theater [...]; his attitude towards the anti-Semites is, in fact, the most disagreeable that I have ever experienced. If it were insight, or the intention to be fair; but in the end, it's nothing so much as cringing – something like that which I once experienced in a tramway, where a shabby Jewish kitchen helper made room for Lueger and said: "Please, doctor," and was thrilled not to get a kick from Lueger – in other words, the attitude of little Kraus toward the anti-Semites – is very Jewish.[156]

The attribute "Jewish" is used in its negative sense here to describe

154 Schnitzler, *Aphorismen und Betrachtungen*, p. 260.
155 For a thoroughly-researched, recent biography on Karl Kraus, see FN 7.
156 Briefe 1875–1912, p. 379.

complete subservience to the non-Jewish majority. One of Schnitzler's favourite expressions to label this type of "Jewish" comportment was "Esoi." It comes from an anecdote in *Der Weg ins Freie.* A Jew travels alone in the compartment of a train, his legs stretched out in front of him on the opposite seat. As one of the other passengers comes in, he takes his feet off the seat right away, until the new arrival addresses him with a Yiddish accent. "Ä soi," the first Jew says, a corruption of "Ach so," and stretches his legs out again on the opposite seat.

This lack of respect of the Jews among themselves, as well as their cringing in front of anti-Semites like Lueger, strikes Schnitzler negatively. Cringing was, naturally, but not exclusively, practised by renegades. In an aphorism that probably dates from 1914 or 1915, Schnitzler writes:

> Not to acknowledge your Jewishness is worse than cowardice, it is stupidity. It means to deny that one comes from father and mother, that these parents have had their own father and mother, it means to deny that one is a creature at all, a very particular being, an individual among others.[157]

Schnitzler uses here the expression "cowardice," which he also uses frequently in aphorisms on the mutability of political convictions. In Schnitzler's opinion, the turning away of a Jew from his own background presents a failure of character but also of morals.

> The renegade is always a human being who is vaguely aware of his inferiority and who undertakes the cowardly or malicious attempt to make his family, his nation, and his race responsible for his highly individual inadequacy.[158]

What about his own attitude toward his Jewish identity? Publication of *Der Weg ins Freie* appears to be a public acknowledgment of it. Schnitzler, however, always contested this. The reasons for that will be illuminated below.

---

157 CUL, MS Aphorismen, Folder A 5.

158 Arthur Schnitzler: *Ohne Maske – Aphorismen und Notate.* ed. by Manfred Diersch. Leipzig: Kiepenheuer & Witsch 1992, p. 205.

A Provocative Publication — Schnitzler's Public Acknowledgment of his Jewish Background

As early as May, 1900, Schnitzler wrote to his friend Georg Brandes:

> It will in fact hardly be possible to write something "wienerisch" about Vienna, in which the anti-Semitic question does not play a role – and my way of thinking with regard to it will please neither the Christians nor the Jews.[159]

It was not Schnitzler's style to water down his ideas merely in order to avoid a scandal. His wife Olga was completely captivated by the third chapter, of *Der Weg ins Freie* in which Leo Golowski and Heinrich Bermann conduct their discussion of the "Jewish Question," and she maintained that such passages "would strike like a bomb [!]"[160]

Schnitzler was very well aware of the dangers that he exposed himself to as he undertook, as an author of Jewish origin, to write a novel about Vienna. To the later director of the Burgtheater, Alfred von Berger, Schnitzler reports the following incident:

> The two gentlemen conversed about literature, and, as the conversation turned to me, they both claimed unanimously to be very offended by my attempts to get at the Viennese soul, the deeper understanding of which must naturally remain, to me, a Jew, unknowable. And after they had properly scolded me, one of them remarked: "And he's not even supposed to write his things himself; a poor Christian student does it for him." –
> This is not made up, revered Herr Baron. And to think that it is not even certain if these two gentlemen really represent the most narrow-minded examples of this pleasant species, so widespread in the Viennese atmosphere that it darkens the horizon.[161]

---

159 CUL, MS Briefe Schnitzler an Brandes. Folder B17b Nr. 2, 3.5.1900.

160 TB 1903–1908, 23.10.1907.

161 Briefe 1875–1912, p. 563.

In view of this, one can assume that Schnitzler was aware of the risks that he ran in publishing his novel – and that he was prepared to deal with the consequences. A further proof of his appreciation of the problem of an Austrian-Jewish author lies in his statement: "It was not possible, especially for a Jew in public life, to ignore the fact he was a Jew, because the others didn't do so: the Christians did not and the Jews even less."[162] From this it is clear that, although Schnitzler continually contested having written, with *Der Weg ins Freie*, a roman à clef, the work is nevertheless of decisive importance for understanding his own Austrian-Jewish identity. After all, in a literary career of over thirty years, Schnitzler only produced two works that deal mainly with Jewish themes. It was unavoidable that Schnitzler would be perceived first and foremost as a Jewish author, when he published a novel that was set in the higher social circles of the Viennese Jewish community. And that is exactly what happened.

If one considers Schnitzler's intellectual independence as well as his lifelong dislike of politics, it was impossible for him to accept Zionism or Jewish nationalism as an answer to the Jewish Question. Instead, Schnitzler felt that every Austrian Jew should solve this problem for himself. In this respect, the important thing was never to deny one's cultural background, but rather to stand by it, regardless of how high the anti-Semitic waves rose. Schnitzler was an enlightened, anti-political individualist. Enlightened, because he rejected Jewish orthodoxy and the "renegades" who converted to Catholicism. He confronted every form of politics with profound skepticism, and all his life cultivated an appropriate distance to political movements. Schnitzler was an individualist because, in spite of all opposition, he clung to his personal moral convictions. Even though *Professor Bernhardi* presents the key document with regard to Schnitzler's position as an Austrian Jew, it is worthwhile, at this point, to refer to a quote from an interview for the *American Hebrew and Jewish Messenger*: "Everything that I have to say on the subject of the Jewish question is to be found in my book, *Der Weg ins Freie*."[163]

162 JiW, p. 328.

163 Benvenisti, 'Arthur Schnitzler foretells Jewish Renaissance', ZAS MF 320.

The Strange Behaviour of Hugo von Hofmannsthal

Der Weg ins Freie was not one of Hofmannsthal's favorite works. On June 6, 1908, Schnitzler noted in his diary: "Drove to Hugo's with O. Rodaun. [...] Not a word about the novel, not even thanks. Only a joke about Stanzides. I had to laugh inwardly."[164]

Why did Hofmannsthal behave as though Schnitzler had never written *Der Weg ins Freie?* With regard to his own background, Hofmannsthal was an aristocrat of Jewish origin, whose grandfather had converted to Catholicism. In his circle of friends, Hofmannsthal was known for his anti-Semitic remarks. Nevertheless, he himself was not spared anti-Jewish caricature, for example, as it appeared in the magazine *Kikeriki.*[165] His *Ödipus* (1906) was even denigrated as being written in "Jewish German."[166] Hofmannsthal was well aware that this was because of his circle of Jewish literary colleagues. Even when it was a step too far to break with them for this reason, he still tried, with regard to literary as well as personal matters, to distance himself from them. He married into a well-off Jewish family, which displayed tendencies similar to his own. About Hofmannsthal's brother-in-law, Hans Schlesinger, Schnitzler puts on record: "Really believes in purgatory and everything else in the catechism. Is now happy and content. Will even possibly become a priest. A Jew should either be intelligent or not born at all."[167]

Because these attitudes were widespread in his wife's family, Hofmannsthal soon also behaved like a practicing Catholic. His belief found expression in such plays as *Der Schwierige* (premiered in 1921) and *Der Unbestechliche* (premiered in 1923), which both, after all sorts of complications and confusions, end with a harmonious marriage. To Hofmannsthal, marriage was holy. For him, the family was the fundamental

164 TB 1903–1908, 6.6.1908.

165 Bettina Riedmann: "Ich bin Jude, Österreicher, Deutscher." Judentum in Arthur Schnitzlers Tagebüchern und Briefen. Tübingen: Max Niemeyer 2002, p. 223.

166 Steven Beller: Vienna and the Jews 1867–1938. A Cultural History. Cambridge: Cambridge University Press 1989, p. 205.

167 TB 1909–1912, 10.1.1911.

symbol of social stability. What probably put Hofmannsthal off in *Der Weg ins Freie* was not only the Jewish component, but possibly also the extramarital relationship of Georg and Anna, with the tragic stillbirth as a consequence. In July, 1908, Hofmannsthal wrote to Schnitzler:

> I mean my not-at-all happy relation to your novel. Because, in fact, I like you very much, and naturally can't draw any distinction between you and your work, this seriously disturbed me for several weeks. It would have been just as agonizing for me to have to talk about it as it was awkward to remain silent.[168]

In his diary, Schnitzler notes that he feels touched and reflects: "In order not to be 'disturbed' by this novel, one must be more distant emotionally from its writer than one had had any idea of."[169]

At the end of October two years later, Hofmannsthal leaves the book in a train – half accidentally, half-deliberately, as he admits to Schnitzler.[170] Schnitzler takes great offense at this, as Hofmannsthal's indifference, if not aversion, to his novel becomes clear. He regards the incident as "completely incompatible with our artistic and personal relationship, as I've perceived them up to now."[171]

For Schnitzler, Hofmannsthal's behaviour was symptomatic of that which he characterizes as "snobbism." Hofmannsthal almost certainly had concerns because of his family's Jewish origins; also because he himself was branded as a Jewish author by the anti-Semitic press. His emphatic, well-displayed sympathy for Catholicism, his anti-Semitic statements and his contact with editors like Felix von Oppenheimer could, combined, be judged as efforts to gain distance on his Jewish background. In Schnitzler's journals one finds several examples of Hofmannthal's "snobbism." In November of 1914, Schnitzler speaks with Raoul Auernheimer about "Hugo, whose feudalism now appears to be developing again" (Article in the

---

168 CUL, Briefe Hofmannsthal an Schnitzler. Folder B 43,2, 24.7.1908.

169 TB 1903–1908, 25.7.1908.

170 CUL, Hofmannsthal an Schnitzler. Folder B 43, 29.10.1910.

171 CUL, Briefe Schnitzler an Hofmannsthal. Folder B 43a, 2.11.1910.

Oe[stereichischen] R[undschau]).[172] One month later he notes: "Hugo, as a politician, doesn't want to admit the evil effects of Catholicism."[173] After a lecture of Hofmannsthal's in April of 1917, Schnitzler again mentions his "snobbism,"[174] and at the end of the year he even writes: "This unusual mixture of Satanism, jealousy, insecurity, desire to dominate, ambition, cavalier attitude, haste – all on the basis of his snobbism."[175]

In that Hofmannsthal reduces *Der Weg ins Freie* to its Jewish aspects, he finds himself in the ranks of those critics again for whom the book was "too Jewish," a Jewish novel. This oversimplification on the part of a good friend and capable writer disappoints Schnitzler the most, as his tirade in the journal indicates. As late as April 1929, Schnitzler remembers how deeply Hofmannsthal's "snobbishly spiteful" rejection of his novel decades before affected him.[176] Only a few weeks afterwards Hofmannsthal writes to him:

> I've reread the novel as you recommended, from Chapter 5 to the end. But I now like this work even less, and I could also give reasons for it. The objections begin with the main character, who doesn't appear to me to be quite consistent [...].[177]

In spite of all of this, the friendship between Schnitzler and Hofmannsthal survives the crisis over *Der Weg ins Freie* and continues until Hofmannsthal's death.

---

172 TB 1913–1916, 13.11.1914. More on the friendship between Schnitzler and Hofmannsthal in the essays by Jacques Le Rider and Giuseppe Farese in the edited volume: *Arthur Schnitzler im 20. Jahrhundert*. ed. by Konstanze Fliedl. Vienna: Picus 2003.

173 TB 1913–1916, 18.12.1914.

174 TB 1917–1919, 26.4.1917.

175 Ibid., 22.12.1917.

176 TB 1927–1930, 1.4. & 13.4.1929.

177 cited in Giuseppe Farese: Arthur Schnitzler und Hugo von Hofmannsthal. In: *Fliedl*, pp. 290–304, p. 303.

Otto Stoessl's Review in the *Oesterreichische Rundschau*

A particularly nasty example of anti-Semitism in the press is found in Otto Stoessl's review of the novel in the *Oesterreichische Rundschau*, whose publisher was a friend of Hofmannsthal. Schnitzler's furious reaction to it – unusual in contrast to the composed silence that he normally bestowed on his critics – is reproduced below, because it has not before been mentioned in research.

The *Oesterreichische Rundschau* was a middle-class paper that was loyal to the Habsburger dynasty and, thus, maintained a neutral posture in questions of nationality, in accordance with the imperial principle of Austria. Although the paper's orientation was officially liberal, it was edited by Christian-minded aristocrats: Baron Felix von Oppenheimer, Leopold von Chlumecky and Alfred von Berger, who, from 1910 until 1912, also led the Burgtheater as director. Karl Glossy, who later joined the Censorship Advisory Board for *Professor Bernhardi,* also belonged to the editorial staff.[178]

Oppenheimer repeatedly asked Schnitzler to work on his paper. Because the author thought highly of the paper and of its publisher, he seriously took this under consideration.[179] The book review by Stoessl showed, nevertheless, that the neutral political posture of the editors was not always reflected in the journalistic contributions to their paper. Stoessl, a railway functionary with literary tendencies and himself a Jew, published plays as well as prose. The novel, *Das Haus Erath* (1929), which is set in an idealised, pre-modern Austria of the early 19th century, can be considered typical of his work.[180] He regarded modern literature with great skepticism, particularly the direction that was developed by the novelists of the Café Griensteidl circle. Stoessl labelled their regular haunt "Café Megalomania."[181]

---

178 Andrea Willi: *Arthur Schnitzlers Roman "Der Weg ins Freie." Eine Untersuchung zur Tageskritik und ihren zeitgenössischen Bezügen.* Heidelberg: Carl Winter 1989, p. 138.

179 Briefe 1875–1912, pp. 522-23.

180 Willi, pp. 135–36.

181 Ibid.

In the review, Stoessl accused Schnitzler that his book:

> [...] takes place in the very particular milieu of wealthy Viennese Jewry, that mistakes what is basically an eternal ghetto for the world and is [...] inclined to, because it has enough money to buy travel tickets [...] and with the purchase of a great deal of valuable real estate, also believes that it has acquired intrinsic spiritual values. Who, however, would seriously want to take this, in every sense, limited segment of a society for the world, if only for the Viennese world...[182]

Schnitzler responded to criticism only in very rare cases, even more rarely to those who fundamentally misunderstood his intentions. But that kind of vulgar yet successful anti-Semitic attack on him in a supposedly friendly newspaper now forced him to compose a wrathful statement entitled, *Gegen Kritik und Fälschung*, which he ended up not sending in the end.

> It is not stupidity, at least not stupidity alone, but, rather, conscious falsification if Herr Stoessl maintains that the novel *[Der Weg ins Freie]* takes place in the "very particular milieu of the rich Viennese Jewry, which takes its basically eternal ghetto for the world and is inclined to spend money," – because with this he suppresses the fact that more than half the characters do not at all belong to the rich Viennese Jewry and an equally large number are not Jews. It is not stupidity, but rather deliberate falsification if Herr Stoessl, who characterizes himself as distant from society, labels my characters not as true-to-life creatures, but, rather, only as successful stereotypes of the kind usually found in these circles. It is not stupidity, but rather deliberate falsification, if the dialogue of the novel is compared with the local studies from the Sunday and Monday papers [...].[183]

---

182 Otto Stoessl: Der Weg ins Freie. In: *Oesterreichische Rundschau*, Vol.18, Nr.1, 1 January 1909, pp. 79–78.

183 CUL, MS Gegen Kritik und Fälschung, Folder A 15.

What Schnitzler cannot grasp, in light of this false representation of his novel, which no longer qualifies as criticism, is why the editors nevertheless continually ask him to work for them.

> Then the question still remains unresolved, what induces the editor of a magazine that presents its readers with such a grotesque caricature of an author, to continually call upon that same author to work for him. [...] Leave whatever you want in your paper, the silliest and most deceptive things, but at least have the good taste not to repeatedly call on me to work with you.[184]

Ultimately, Schnitzler and Oppenheimer talk this over and find their way back to friendly, if formal, relations. In 1910, Schnitzler publishes excerpts from *Das weite Land* in the *Oesterreichische Rundschau.*[185] Oppenheimer himself comes from an old Jewish family on the Rhine. Thus, Oppenheimer as well as Hofmannsthal have Jewish forebears. After Oppenheimer's second inquiry about Schnitzler's working with him, in August, 1909, Schnitzler notes, "Oppenheimer's letter indicates a bad conscience and a not much better Hugo."[186]

It is worth mentioning the close relationship between the Baron and Hugo von Hofmannsthal.[187] Hofmannsthal's first loyalty, as one is forced to conclude, was to the Catholic aristocrats, and only after that to his friend and literary colleague Schnitzler. If Schnitzler, therefore, sometimes found his and Oppenheimer's postures objectionable, even so, it is debatable that he would have passed the same verdict on them as on Stoessl: "O.St.: Critic, Jew, who ingratiates himself with the anti-Semites, scoffs at the non-German, cringing."[188]

---

184 Ibid.

185 TB 1909–1912, 22.9.1910.

186 Briefe 1875–1912, p. 607.

187 Ibid., p. 900.

188 Arthur Schnitzler: *Entworfenes und Verworfenes*. ed. by Reinhard Urbach. Frankfurt/Main: S. Fischer Verlag 1977, p. 204.

Apolitical Liberalism — A Contradictory Concept?

Before the revolution of 1848, the Viennese Jews were critical of the Habsburg state, not the least because of Count Metternich's restrictive measures. From this, one concludes that no rightist, dynastic patriotism could find a foothold in the Jewish community. In their circles, one found, rather, liberal-democratic as well as "greater-German" tendencies, which oriented themselves toward certain currents in the German Union. When the revolution in Vienna broke out, it was the Jewish medical students who erected the first barricades. And it was a Jewish doctor from Budapest, Adolf Fischhof, who gave the revolution a concrete political programme in a spontaneous speech before the enthusiastic Viennese citizenry. It seemed almost natural that the Jews of the city supported such liberal measures as freedom of religion and the press.

In the era of liberal government in Austria, which roughly dates from 1860 to 1880, the Jewish citizens identified strongly with the state – the complete opposite situation, for example, of British liberalism. In Great Britain, liberal theory distanced itself gradually from the values of the Enlightenment and of political emancipation and tended toward increasing support for the free market economy. Just as in Bismarck's German Empire, the National Liberals and the members of the Jewish Centralverein became patriotic, loyal citizens, the Jewish Liberals in Austria developed an unconditional loyalty to government and dynasty which far outdid the loyalty of all the other nationalities of the Danube Monarchy. They appreciated that the Kaiser guaranteed their constitutional rights and insisted on the equality of his subjects regardless of their religious or ethnic differences. This went so far that, in June of 1917, the *Oesterreichische Wochenschrift* wrote, "In fact, the Jews are not only the most loyal supporters of the monarchy, over and above that, they are the only unconditional Austrians in our state."[189]

The atmosphere, not only in Schnitzler's parents' house, but in the whole liberal era of his childhood, was defined by a tolerance among the citizenry

---

189 Nichts gelernt und nichts vergessen. In: *Oesterreichische Wochenschrift*, Heft 24, 22 June 1917, p. 390.

that disappeared after the loss of power of the Liberal Party toward the end of 1870. In *Jugend in Wien*, Schnitzler remembers:

> Then, it was in the later bloom of Liberalism that anti-Semitism existed, it's true, as it has since, as an emotional impulse in many souls disposed that way, and as an idea with a high potential for expansion; but it played no significant role either as a political or a social factor. The word was not even coined, and it sufficed to label people who were particularly maliciously minded almost dismissively as "Judenfresser" [Jew-eaters].[190]

The *Neue Freie Presse* was, at this time, the only Austrian daily paper with an international circulation and reputation. The editorial staff and most employees were of Jewish origin, which is why the Editor-in-Chief Moriz Benedikt and his right hand, Eduard Bacher, were eternally vigilant against their newspaper being equated with purely Jewish interests. This brought them, however, the accusation of serving two masters. Josef Fränkel points out that Benedikt and Bacher, as German-speaking Jews from Bohemia, revealed those exaggerated Germanophile attitudes that were typical for men of their background.[191]

Their uncompromisingly neutral posture in Jewish affairs, to the extent of completely ignoring them, led Lueger to the statement that "the primary creator of Austrian anti-Semitism is the Jewish liberal press." It is remarkable that Karl Kraus put the blame for the First World War primarily on Moriz Benedikt, who "was guiltier of the outbreak and continuation of the war than some of the statesmen or generals who were directly involved."[192] This, as well as the background of the two editors-in-chief, indicates that the alignment of the paper corresponded to the patriotic, loyal, Austrian model citizen – very much the orientation of the Centralverein in the German Empire.

It is further indicative that Benedikt and Herzl, after Herzl became

---

190 JiW, p. 78.

191 Josef Fränkel: *The Jews of Austria: Essays on Their Life, History and Destruction.* London: Vallentine & Mitchell 1970, p. 88.

192 Ibid.

the editor of the literary section, quarrelled over Benedikt's public refusal to take the part of Vienna's Jews on particular issues of the day. Benedikt refrained from making any definitive statements on the "Jewish Question," whereas Herzl insisted on a comparatively militant Zionist position. This is only one example of a posture that Fränkel delineates as "the laughably Austrophile, ostrich-like inability of the editors to look reality in the face."

In this context it is not surprising that Raoul Auernheimer, in his review of *Der Weg ins Freie* in the *Neue Freie Presse* mentions not a word about the novel's Jewish characters. He breaks the novel down on the one hand into Georg's conflict between "the world of the artist and middle-class happiness," and, on the other hand, his decision between Anna Rosner and Else Ehrenberg. In December of 1910, Schnitzler writes to Auernheimer: "In fact, I forget that in the N. Fr. Pr. – as a rule, there is no Jewish question, so also no Jewish answer, therefore also no Jewish dialogue."[193] Because Auernheimer, in spite of all his goodwill toward his friend, does not address a single Jewish theme of the book, Schnitzler notes after reading the review only that: "Auernheimer's Feuilleton on the '*Weg*' in the N. Fr. Pr. very kind and superficial."[194]

Interestingly, Schnitzler had originally conceived of a haracter based on Auernheimer for *Der Weg ins Freie*. In an earlier draft of *Entrüsteten*, he introduces Jonas, a son of Ehrenberg, as an "ambitious, unprincipled, liberal journalist."[195]

For the younger generation in the novel, represented by Berthold Stauber and Heinrich Bermann, the faith in social and political progress, as it was held up by their fathers, is nevertheless shaken by this ever-stronger anti-Semitism. In the eyes of the youth, it is much more than a side issue, which is how the elders would gladly dismiss it. Anti-Semitism strikes at the core of their identity – even if they formerly were not so conscious of their Jewishness – in that their affiliation with their home country and their culture is denied them, and they are reduced to being second-class citizens. The second generation after the emancipation is much less sure of itself, not only when it is a question of their Austrian-Jewish identity, but also

193 Briefe 1875–1912, p. 640.
194 TB 1903–1908, 3.6.1908.
195 CUL, MS Die Entrüsteten, Folder A 132.

with regard to their moral convictions. If Schnitzler depicts Dr. Stauber's liberal generation with a certain nostalgic sympathy, the author is, in fact, too clear-sighted to deny that this era is over for good. Liberal values are no longer suitable for fin-de-siècle Vienna, Lueger's Vienna and that of his Christian Socials. Liberalism has no answer to offer to the increasingly outspoken anti-Semitism. Its pre-eminence lasted only two decades, and although it was a time of enlightened tolerance and culture, now those values belong to the past.

Heinrich Bermann as Schnitzler's Mouthpiece

In the aphoristic vignette *Vaterland*, dated 1904, Schnitzler writes:

> I love this land, whose woods and valleys are well known to me. I love the language that my father spoke. But how can I love a governmental structure that gradually expands through love of conquest [...], how can I love this master of whom I know nothing except that he [. . .] has power over me [. . .]
> - No! If you call that fatherland, I do not love it, nor does anyone.

In a draft of the novel, Schnitzler brings out a highly developed, pronounced individualism that culminates in the phrase, "he felt solidarity with no one." Bermann, a novelist and questioning spirit, postulates:

> We have our homeland (that is not what is lacking); we are only lacking fellow citizenry and therefore – which is all the same to me – a fatherland. [...] As little as I would feel myself to be the brother of a butcher's worker or of an idiot of a count if I were forced to go into battle with him, I feel myself to be equally unrelated to a Jewish kitchen worker or a show-off banker, because a street urchin or a government representative throws the same swear words at us. I choose my brothers myself, and

> they don't need to know anything about it.[196]

In an unpublished statement, also from 1904, Schnitzler writes:

> I don't feel solidarity with anyone because he coincidentally belongs to the same nation, the same rank, the same race, the same family. (I'm not proud of anyone, not even of myself.) It is exclusively my concern with whom I want to feel related. (I acknowledge no obligation on this issue.) I have fellow citizens in each nation, comrades in every rank, and brothers who have no idea of my existence.[197]

The phrasing in places is almost identical. According to the manuscript, Schnitzler worked from January to March of 1905 on the chapter that contains a thorough discussion of the "Jewish Question" between Bermann and Golowski. Schnitzler left out the above passage in the final version of the novel, possibly because in this scene he wanted to concentrate rather on Golowski's arguments for Zionism rather than on Bermann's personality. Bermann's inner conflict comes into focus, on the other hand, in the sixth chapter in his discussion with Georg. Why didn't Schnitzler therefore insert the passage here? In all likelihood, he found it too personal.

Not only does Bermann want to stay in his own country, he feels himself to be Austrian and wants to live among his countrymen, not "among a lot of Jews." Herein lies the root of his dilemma. He is not only connected to the nature, but also to the culture and people of his home country, even when they – or a part of them – reject him. On the one hand, Bermann loathes any form of anti-Semitism. On the other, he rejects Jewish "cringing" and efforts to ingratiate, just as decisively as he does Zionism. He knows that he belongs to Austria. Torn as he is between the two halves of his identity, he comes to the conclusion:

> For our time, there is no solution, that's clear. No all-encompassing one, anyway. Rather, there are a hundred

196 CUL, MS Aphorismen, Folder A5.
197 Ibid.

> thousand different solutions. Because, in fact, it's a situation that, until further developments, each one must come to terms with himself, as best he can. Each one must see for himself how he finds his way out of his aggravation, his desperation, or out of his disgust to somewhere where he can breathe freely again. Maybe there really are people who, to do that, have to stray all the way to Jerusalem [...]. The important thing is for each one to find his inner way. [...] Not to let himself be put off. Yes, that must be the daily prayer of every respectable human being: steadfastness![198]

This is Professor Bernhardi's programme in embryonic form: every German-speaking Jew must find his own position on the so-called Jewish Question, and steadfastly hold to it, without ever denying his Jewish identity. This concept is also mentioned on two earlier occasions: in the first chapter, Berthold Stauber speaks of "doing the right thing." Besides that, Heinrich Bermann insists, in conversation with Leo Golowski, that we are only able to attain "that which is given us within our being and our ability to perform." From this statement in *Der Weg ins Freie* one can draw a direct line to Bernhardi's assertion in the fifth act of having done "the right thing."

In conclusion, one should note a diary entry from July of 1914 that underlines Schnitzler's identification with Bermann: "Patriotic sensibilities. A sense of belonging. Leo contradicts. I call to his attention that 'we' have already had this conversation in 'Weg ins Freie.'"[199] Since the musician and mathematician Leo Van-Jung provided the real model for Leo Golowski, one can conclude from the pronoun "we," that Schnitzler saw his own views embodied in Heinrich Bermann.

Anticipating *Professor Bernhardi* – Anti-Politics

The statements of Stauber and Bermann are early manifestations of that which will later be formulated as Bernhardi's code of behaviour: the enlightened, anti-political individual, who stands against the politicised

198 Arthur Schnitzler: *Der Weg ins Freie*. Frankfurt/Main: S. Fischer 1992, p. 236.
199 TB 1913-1916 , 27.7.1914.

masses or officials. These observations prove that Schnitzler's aversion to politics was already very pronounced during the period that he was working on the novel. He will also develop this further in *Fink and Fliederbusch.*

In the previously mentioned interview with Benvenisti in 1924, Schnitzler clarifies this point:

> The solution of the Jewish problem has to be found by every individual for himself. There is no one single solution for everyone. Zionism appears to me to be anything but a solution. [...] This doesn't keep me from admiring Zionism. I admire people who can reach so high and dream so gloriously, but they will never be able to convince me.[200]

The similarity with Bermann's statement in the novel published 16 years earlier is astounding. Resemblances between the characters of Heinrich Bermann and Professor Bernhardi are not to be overlooked. One can even maintain that the former already carries within it the seeds of the latter. Schnitzler's interest was not in laying out sociocultural theories after the fashion of his friend and colleague Jakob Wassermann. Schnitzler found his position as an Austrian-Jewish author relatively early, because he did not come from a religiously observant home, and religion was therefore never a determining theme for him. The Jewish Question is for him purely a personal affair. Although Schnitzler only formulated this clearly in 1924, his position manifested itself indeed since his public stance as an author of Jewish background, which took place irreversibly with the publication of *Der Weg ins Freie*. In *Spiegelbild der Freundschaft*, Olga writes: "It was, in any case, a destiny, the difficulties of which he, in all manliness, was willing to take on, that he confronted without deviating, namely to be that which he had always acknowledged himself to be: a European Jew of German culture."[201]

200 Benvenisti, 'Arthur Schnitzler foretells Jewish Renaissance', ZAS MF 320.

201 Olga Schnitzler: Spiegelbild der Freundschaft. Salzburg: Residenz 1962, p. 96.

THE GREATEST TRIUMPHS ON THE STAGE 1909–1912

In January of 1909, *Komtesse Mizzi* is performed at the Volkstheater in Vienna. The play is well received by the public, even if the critics are protective of the nobility. A performance at the Burgtheater, the bastion of classical traditions, would most probably not have been received as positively. In this play, Schnitzler's irony, with all its convolutions and complexity, comes into full realization. In this work, even the subtitle, *Der Familientag,* is an example of the extent to which some characters sense, but others have no idea, that they are related to each other. The conservative reviewers of the time found fault with the fact that it had to do with the illegitimate children of a prince and a count, because the nobility were supposed to be above such middle-class lapses.

In this year, Schnitzler writes *Das Tagebuch der Redegonda,* a mysterious short story about a late-night conversation on a park bench. In this tale, a peculiar individual tells about a love affair in his garrison, and also about the duel he had to fight afterwards in which he was killed. It is impossible for the reader to determine what is real and what is not. Schnitzler plays here, as in *Traumnovelle* and *Fräulein Else*, with the credibility of the narrative voice.

One month after the *Tagebuch*, Schnitzler finishes *Das weite Land*, on which he has worked since the past June. True, it does not particularly appeal to Otto Brahm, but as Schnitzler reads it to Olga, in the fifth act, she bursts into tears. The tragicomedy, which focuses on the industrialist Friedrich Hofreiter – based on Schnitzler's friend from his youth, Louis Friedmann – and his wife Genia, is one of Schnitzler's most successful works. In his own words: "If I feel about so much of my work that I am somewhat less than that, which I myself call an artist: here I am somewhat more."[202]

Nevertheless, it will be two more years until the premiere. Schnitzler, who often moves several projects forward at the same time, is working

202 TB 1913–16, 14.6.1915.

in parallel on *Der junge Medardus.* The drama is completed in June. With this work, he continues in the tradition of Grillparzer's historical dramas, which interest Schnitzler not only as far as the Renaissance pieces *Die Frau mit dem Dolche* und *Der Schleier der Beatrice.* Over the next few years, he considers, on and off, writing a play about Joseph II. With Grillparzer in the back of his mind, there finally arises the possibility, with this material, of enrolling in the canon of the greatest Austrian writers. Although this place is, regardless, already secured for him. Regrettably, he never actually writes the work.

On September 13, 1909, his daughter Lili is born. With this second child, the relationship with Olga is further cemented. On the very same day, he continues with his work on *Professor Bernhardi* and on the story *Die Hirtenflöte.*

In the fall, an opera version of *Der tapfere Cassian* is performed at the Neues Stadttheater in Leipzig with the music of Oscar Straus. The following January, his pantomime, *Der Schleier der Pierrette,* is staged with music by Ernst von Dohnányi, at the Royal Opera House in Dresden.

Schnitzler finds the musical accompaniment to his plays not uninteresting, but is not as taken with it as with their film adaptations – and with the movie theater in general. That also goes for the premiere of the *Liebelei* as an opera, which takes place in Frankfurt am Main on October 18, 1910. With regard to finances, which Schnitzler is forced to take into consideration, these productions are not as rewarding as his plays.

In the beginning of November, Schnitzler reads *Der junge Medardus* to his circle of friends. Hofmannsthal, Beer-Hofmann, Salten and Schwarzkopf agree that the play is too long, that a staging would be too problematic, and that therefore it is not suitable for a performance. Schnitzler, nevertheless, believes in the play and does not let himself be put off.

In the spring of 1910, Schnitzler is discontent with his apartment. There are petty disputes with the landlord and with the neighbors. Besides, his bigger family needs more space. Then he discovers that a Burgtheater actress, Hedwig Bleibtreu, wants to sell her villa in the Sternwartestrasse. The Schnitzlers look over the villa and sign a sales contract on April 7.[203]

203 TB 1909–12, 7.4.1910.

Arthur's brother Julius makes available to him part of the necessary sum. The move is only accomplished in July.

On September 20, the Burgtheater actor Josef Kainz dies from cancer at the age of 52. He was one of the very few friends with whom Schnitzler was on the more intimate familiar basis of addressing one another. Julius had operated on him, but could no longer save him. Schnitzler experiences this death as particularly tragic, not only because Kainz would have been the best performer for the character Hofreiter – but also because of the loss of an understanding confidant and an incomparable actor.[204]

The negotiations with Brahm and Reinhardt over *Das weite Land* and *Der junge Medardus* are underway. It is Schnitzler's tremendous luck that Paul Schlenther would be replaced as Director of the Burgtheater in March by Alfred von Berger. Von Berger had already presented several of Schnitzler's plays in the Deutsches Schauspielhaus in Hamburg, and is much more favourably disposed toward him than Schlenther. When the negotiations with the two Berlin directors bring no results, in February, Berger accepts *Medardus*. It does not take long until the rehearsals begin.

Two Successful Years: *Der junge Medardus* and *Das weite Land*

For Schnitzler, 1910 is a year of triumph. A real-life model for the character of Medardus was the Nuremberg bookseller Johann Philipp Palm, who, on 26th August, 1806, was executed on the order of the French Emperor at Braunau. His crime was the publication of a pamphlet in the same year, *Germany in its Deep Humiliation*, which was a call to resistance against Napoleon.[205] In contrast to Palm, however, Medardus is no martyr to the national cause. To be precise, he puts his individualism above his loyalty to the state: "As a citizen of this land, I may be a traitor. But first and foremost, I am indeed Medardus Klähr." These ideas return in more effective form in *Professor Bernhardi,* where they express steadfastness

204 Ibid., 20.–22.9.1910.

205 One of the latest publications on this: Bernd Thure von zur Mühlen: *Napoleons Justizmord am deutschen Buchhändler Johann Philipp Palm*, Frankfurt / Main: Bramann 2003.

against anti-Semitism.

A further parallel to Bernhardi are the characteristics of Medardus as an anti-hero. He despises Napoleon to an extreme, but instead of killing the Emperor, he does, in fact, spoil an attack on him. In prison he then chooses not the easy way to freedom, but rather insists on his guilt as a consequence of his convictions, and thereby condemns himself to death. Admittedly, this posture is characterised by courage and integrity. But is it really heroism? In its personal form, perhaps, which produces no effect on historical events or the environment. This is also discernible in Bernhardi's opinion that his battle is a purely personal affair, and his rejecting every form of support.

Der junge Medardus premieres on November 24 at the Burgtheater. It is a monumental production in terms of costumes, scenery and effects, as well as its cost of an unbelievable 60,000 Gulden. Hedwig Bleibtreu, whose former villa Schnitzler occupies with his family, plays Helen Klähr. The play is sold out even before the premiere. Enthusiastic applause already breaks out after the prologue. At the end of the evening, Schnitzler is called on stage no fewer than thirty times to bow before a cheering, exuberant audience. It is the high point of his life, and he celebrates into the early morning hours with friends, actors, and Olga at the Hotel Sacher.[206] By 1914, the "Dramatic History in a Prologue and Five Acts" has been performed a further 47 times.

To this, Schnitzler's greatest success to date, is added the almost euphoric reception of the *Anatol* cycle, which has never before been presented as a coherent whole. Now, Otto Brahm takes on this task in the Lessingtheater, where the series of scenes was presented in December at the same time as at the Volkstheater in Vienna. Schnitzler finds, in fact, some of the *Anatol* scenes to be less successful, but is very happy in view of the positive reviews and the substantial income brought in by these performances. *Anatol* is performed 75 times at the Vienna Volkstheater and 50 times in Berlin. In the remaining season, thirteen further German theaters include the cycle in their program. In 1911, *Anatol* manages to be successfully performed in translation in Hungary and in England.

In March, 1911, while Schnitzler makes progress on the short story

206 TB 1909–12, 24.11.1910.

Doctor Gräsler and the journalistic piece *Fink and Fliederbusch*, he determines that *Professor Bernhardi* needs a fifth act, to take place after Bernhardi's arrest. Among other elements, it includes a discussion between minister Flint and the Hofrat.

The two prose works that are published in this year are called *Die dreifache Warnung* and *Die Hirtenflöte.* Both narratives take place in a fairy-tale atmosphere without a specific historical background. *Der Mörder* also appears in this year. Just as in *Sterben*, the theme is developed of being bound to a dying individual. As always with Schnitzler, the emotions are not all unequivocal, but are distinguished by too human internal contradictions. A beloved person has shown himself to be untrue, and the long-desired common future dissolves, unexpectedly, into nothing.

On September 9, Schnitzler's mother, who the previous year had celebrated her 70th birthday, succumbs to periostitis. Besides the suffering induced by the disease, her death is preceded by a period of mental confusion that is interspersed with lucid intervals.[207]

Schnitzler barely ever mentioned his mother, neither in his work nor in his diary, although he had lived with her until he was more than 40 years old. Her presence and care were as much taken for granted as was the complete subordination of her interests, indeed, her whole personality, to that of her husband. The Schnitzler siblings are united in sorrow at Christmas and cannot believe that their mother is gone forever.

The premiere of *Das weite Land* constitutes a major theatrical event. It takes place on October 14, 1911 on eight stages at once: at the Burgtheater, Berlin's Lessingtheater, the Lobe-Theater in Breslau, the Munich Residenztheater, the German Landestheater in Prague, the Altes Stadttheater in Leipzig, the Schaubühne Hannover and the Bochum Stadttheater.

The character Hofreiter is an older version of Schnitzler's Don Juan from *Märchen* and *Liebelei.* He has affair after affair, one of which results in the death of a friend. Hofreiter's wife, Genia, suffers greatly from his infidelity. As Genia, in her isolation, is driven into the arms of a young naval cadet, Hofreiter challenges him to a duel and shoots him. The fifth

207 Ibid., 9.9.1911.

act ends with the arrival of their child from England.

The crass egoism that Hofreiter has in common with Julius Fichtner and Stephan von Sala from *Der einsame Weg* is shown blatantly, with all its devastating consequences. *Das weite Land* affects a public of the 21st century just as powerfully as that of 1911, because here timeless human emotions play a primary role. The self-destructive tendencies that not only a marriage, but rather each relationship between husband and wife can bring with it, affect Genia much more strongly than they do her husband. This brings to mind certain schemes, which, according to the diary, must have played out between Schnitzler and his own wife.

With the character of Erna Wahl, Schnitzler left the "demonic" woman of his early prose behind him and reached a new level of reality in the representation of the female psyche. Erna well knows that the thoroughly upright, reliable Dr. Mauer, who is devoid of all bourgeois pretensions, can offer her security. But she herself says, "Only I don't really know if this feeling of security is such a desirable thing. At least for me." In the third act she falls in love, to Mauer's great disappointment, with Hofreiter.

This independent-minded young woman, who sleeps naked on an alpine meadow, covered only with Hofreiter's coat, breaks the bounds of the literary female stereotypes of the 19th century. Naturally, this "new woman," who knows her own mind and lives out her sexuality, is a threat to the established order of society. The disturbing effect of these strong women, notably the power of female sexuality, is just as potent today as it was in 1911.

The public is impressed, even if not as overwhelmed as by the scale and effects of *Medardus*. Berger receives anonymous insulting letters for having produced a play by Schnitzler the Jew.[208] The reviews also show the author that the play was not understood in the way he had intended. Still, the next performance and those at the Burgtheater are sold out, as well as those in German theaters the following year. *Das weite Land* remains on the theatrical programme, and brings in a high income for Schnitzler. He travels from one performance to another, giving well attended readings, and is honored for his work. In the year of his 50th birthday, Schnitzler finds

208 Ibid., 20.9.1911.

himself at the height of his fame.

Samuel Fischer plans to honor Schnitzler's birthday with a celebration, since Schnitzler is, after all, one of his most famous authors. Instead, Schnitzler proposes a complete edition of his works. This is in the bookstore already in the same year, and sells very well. By 1918, the print run has risen to 33,000 for the volumes of prose and to 18,000 for the dramatic works.[209] This successful undertaking relieves Schnitzler of his financial worries.

Against the backdrop of these major successes, 1912 brings the loss of three dear friends. Max Burckhard, who staged the first of Schnitzler's plays at the Burgtheater, dies on March 16. Alfred von Berger, his tireless champion at the same venerable institution, dies on August 24. The heaviest blow is, nevertheless, the death of his close friend Otto Brahm on November 28. It is very likely that Schnitzler's gradual withdrawal from the theater and increasing focus on prose works in the course of the following years stems from the loss of these great friends and supporters.

Stephi Bachrach enters into Schnitzler's circle of acquaintances this year. Her uncle advises the author in financial affairs. Schnitzler falls in love with the intelligent young girl, but refrains from beginning an affair with her. Olga befriends her as well. Jakob Wassermann, on the other hand, makes no attempt to conceal his passion for the 24-year-old. This, understandably, is very offensive to Wassermann's wife, Julie. The difficult situation that results from this, which becomes even more complicated through the attentions of Rudolf Urbantschitsch, drives the sensitive young woman to suicide five years later. It is possible that she was the inspiration for *Fräulein Else* and other female characters.

At the end of 1912, the Bachrach family, which is very close to Schnitzler, is in a desolate situation. The father loses a fortune of several million crowns on the stock market, and commits suicide in November. His wife and two daughters live on his meagre pension, which barely suffices. Their social downfall from the upper middle classes hits them very hard. They spend Christmas with the Schnitzlers.[210]

---

209 Wagner, pp. 247, 253.

210 TB 1909–12, 31.12.1912.

Professor Bernhardi — Anti-Semitism on the Stage and in Reality

Professor Bernhardi is, next to *Der Weg ins Freie,* the only work in which Schnitzler seriously come to terms with anti-Semitism. The play grew out of the draft of a drama with the title *Die Egoisten.* Already in April, 1903, Schnitzler decided to divide the "young bachelor-and-doctor play" into two separate dramas. The first part was soon renamed *Der einsame Weg.*[211] The second was to be finished only in May of 1912.

In November of this same year, *Professor Bernhardi* was banned by the Viennese censors. It succeeded in being premiered only toward the end of the month at the Kleines Theater in Berlin. Contrary to the fears of the authorities, the play was a great success, with no form of theatrical scandal or other "disturbance of the public order." In spite of this, the ban remained in place in Austria until the end of the Monarchy in 1918. *Professor Bernhardi* did achieve staging on Austro-Hungarian territory by the ensemble from the Kleines Theater in Berlin and was a great success. But an attempt to produce it only a few weeks later in Pressburg (present-day Bratislava), was foiled by the authorities.[212]

The only demonstrations against the play took place in Wiener Neustadt in 1919, when nationalist-minded students noisily disturbed the performance, and afterwards even assaulted a few of the audience.[213] All in all, however, *Professor Bernhardi* proved to be one of Schnitzler's most lasting successes. It was continually produced throughout his lifetime.

Following the first performances in Germany, the Liberal and Social Democrat press in Austria took up the play's cause, demanding a repeal of the ban, whereas the Christian Social and Nationalist papers argued in favour of the censors' decision. The situation was, ironically, amazingly similar to Professor Bernhardi's own predicament in the play.

The play opens with a fatally ill patient at the stage of euphoria just before death. Bernhardi, the Jewish director of the clinic, forbids the

211 TB 1903-1908, 18.4.1903.

212 More detail on this in Beier, pp. 459-67, 472.

213 Ibid., pp. 479-80.

priest to enter for the last rites, since he wants to ensure that his patient's final moments are free of distress. This occurrence, as soon as it becomes public, is blown up into a scandal and is vigorously debated in parliament. Intrigues among Bernhardi's colleagues lead to his voluntary resignation. Nevertheless, he is prosecuted and sentenced to two months imprisonment for "Religionsstörung" [religious disturbance]. Bernhardi's sentence is revoked following the confession of the key witnesses to false testimony. In the end, Bernhardi, in conversation with a friendly, high-ranking official, confides that he would act exactly the same way a second time. He adheres unshakably to his principles, and to what he feels is right.

"How It Could Have Happened" — Schnitzler's Father, Director of the Vienna Allgemeine Poliklinik

Among other sources, Schnitzler was inspired by his father's experiences as director of the Wiener Allgemeine Poliklinik, where he had to deal with anti-Semitic tendencies among the doctors. Schnitzler was his father's assistant in the clinic, and also treated patients in his private practice, as does the character of Oskar Bernhardi. Like Oskar, Schnitzler chaired the polyclinic's ball committee in 1889.

His years as an assistant, from 1885 to 1893, provided Schnitzler with insights into the daily routine of medicine and administration, as well as into the internal politics of the clinic. As described in *Jugend in Wien,* "an anti-Semitic wing" had formed among the assistant doctors in the late 1880's.[214] Writing to Georg Brandes in 1913, Schnitzler attributed a decline in his father's reputation and in the number of patients, especially from the higher social circles, not only to the rise of a new generation of specialists, but also to the increasing spread of anti-Semitic tendencies.[215]

Georg Brandes, in any case, assumed that the model for Bernhardi was Schnitzler's father. Schnitzler's reply is dated February 27, 1913:

214 Ibid., pp. 199, 307.

215 Briefe 1913–1931, p. 12.

> The comedy does not deal with, basically, a "life the way my father experienced it." The content is, rather, imagined. My father had, indeed, together with friends, founded a hospital in the style of the Elisabethinum, and had brought it to full bloom, against all sorts of hostility, with the full array of his talents and ability, and naturally, not without the help of work- and battle-comrades. Especially toward the end of his life, he experienced ingratitude and insults from some quarters; – but if his departure from the institute that he had founded was possibly not unpleasant for one or another individual, it was in no way part of an intrigue against him. In fact, he was even still director of the institute when he died on 2nd May, 1893. By the way, the hero of the title, "Professor Bernhardi," has borrowed only a few traits from my father, and the other characters of my play are, admittedly with the unavoidable use of real characteristics, so freely imagined that only Philistines, of whom there is naturally no lack, could refer to this as a "roman à clef." My play has no other truth than that the plot, exactly as I imagined it, could have happened like this – at least in Vienna at the end of the previous century.[216]

If one looks more closely at the internal situation in the polyclinic in the early 1890's, it appears that Schnitzler worked more of it into his drama than he admitted to Brandes. In January 1893, the doctors of the clinic voted to replace the head of accounting, a Jewish specialist for venereal diseases, with the non-Jewish dermatologist Prof. Hans von Hebra.[217] The doctors were accused of acting out of anti-Semitic motives. The parallels to the question in the play, whether Dr. Hell or Dr. Wenger should take over dermatology, are obvious.

Nine of these doctors sent a rather curt letter to Schnitzler's father, in which they asked him to confirm that the decision was not made on the basis of party, but rather, purely in the interests of efficient administration. If Schnitzler's father had accommodated them, he would have, in his

---

216 CUL, Briefe Brandes an Schnitzler, 27.2.1913, Folder B17b.

217 William Rey: *Arthur Schnitzler – Professor Bernhardi*, München: Fink 1971, p. 90.

function as director, denied the anti-Semitic component of a clearly anti-Semitic intrigue.[218]

Twelve days before his death, Johann Schnitzler composed a detailed reply, in which he stated his displeasure with the corrupting influence of political interests among the doctors – as well as with the unnecessarily formal tone of their letter:

> Is this from now on the tone which is supposed to dominate in the polyclinic?! So *this* is the tone that you, sirs, adopt against the one who helped found and create the institute; this is the language that one uses against the one who, throughout the years, defended the polyclinic against all attacks [...].[219]

This message could have just as well come from Bernhardi during the discussion scene in the third act. However, whereas the term "anti-Semitism" is never used in that scene, Johann Schnitzler speaks it without hesitation:

> [...] if, indeed, one or another possibly had been previously inclined to anti-Semitism, as soon as they became active in the polyclinic, certainly they would change their previous attitude, because they knew only too well that the polyclinic is exclusively of Jewish origin – in that solely and exclusively Jewish doctors participated in the consultation planning for the founding of the institute; because, further, everyone knew that also in regard to the means to set up the facility, then to buy the land and later to construct the new building, it was in large part Jews who donated the money.[220]

The situation of the "Elisabethinum" is identical, as Dr. Löwenstein also comments in the play that 80 percent of the money for the clinic came from Jewish donors. In any case, Johann Schnitzler did not want to publicly

218 Ibid.
219 Ibid., p. 93.
220 Ibid., p. 96.

admit the anti-Semitic currents in his clinic.

> On the contrary, I have constantly protested against the presence of those kinds of tendencies, at least, within the polyclinic. [...] This was the standpoint, that I [...] took against the whole world, [...] when, according, to the rumours being spread by *your* own friends, the talk was, one would endeavour to make the polyclinic free of Jews now.[221]

His son oriented the circumstances of the "Elisabethinum" very much toward the situation in the polyclinic. *Professor Bernhardi* shows clearly the individualistic, anti-political tendencies of the author, who highly valued consistency and steadfastness of conviction. The play certainly casts a bright light on Schnitzler's conception of his own Jewish identity, as well as on his position on the Jewish Question – which makes this a critical document.

Institutional Anti-Semitism and Other Sources of Inspiration

During Karl Lueger's term of office as mayor of Vienna, his Christian Social Party, through its organs, repeatedly attacked the Jewish press, Jewish teachers, and Jewish doctors. When the budget for Vienna's hospitals was up for debate in Parliament in October, 1903, a friend of Lueger's, Leopold Steiner, accused the Jewish doctors of conducting experiments with vivisection, which ostensibly proved that they were less cognizant of their patients' suffering than were Christian doctors.[222] The Christian Social Party immediately launched a campaign to ban vivisection in Vienna's hospitals. The medical faculty of the University of Vienna protested against this interference in their affairs on the part of politicians. In the Reichsrat, Lueger justified himself: "The college of professors should rather look to themselves and make an effort to eradicate certain elements in the medical

221 Ibid.

222 Richard Geehr: *Karl Lueger — Mayor of Fin de Siècle Vienna*. Detroit: Wayne State University Press 1990, p. 185.

profession that only damage them, so that finally a Christian sensibility can re-enter these circles."[223] But, by a few weeks later, in December, the furore had died down. The Christian Socials had embarrassed themselves over and over again by their inadequate medical knowledge, for which they were repeatedly lampooned in the liberal press.[224]

In a file stored in Cambridge, which holds the drafts for *Professor Bernhardi*, there is a newspaper clipping from May 7, 1910, that describes an anti-Semitic incident in the Kaiser-Jubiläums-Spital. This clipping was previously unknown to research, and it is reproduced here, because it is an important indicator of the political atmosphere at that time. The item appeared only a few weeks after Lueger's death. Unfortunately, there is no indication of which newspaper it could have been taken from:

> Dr. Oskar Hein refers, in an interpellation, to a statement of the Vice-Mayor Hierhammer made, according to the reports of the Christian Social papers, in a gathering of the voters of the first voting district of Josefstadt, and the tenor of it was that at the Kaiserjubiläumsspital only "doctors of Aryan origin" should be hired, and asks: Is the mayor inclined, firstly, to express his disapproval of the cited statement of Vice-Mayor Hierhammer, which stands in clear contradiction to his sworn oath of service, secondly, to take action such that, in the future, in keeping with Article 3 of the Constitution of 21st December 1867, [...] on the general rights of citizens, the offices of the Viennese municipality are to be equally accessible to all citizens?[225]

This article proves that tension persisted between the officials and the hospitals. The openly anti-Semitic Vice-Mayor involved himself without any lawful right in the internal affairs of a clinic, upon which Dr. Hein protested that this was in contradiction to the constitutionally guaranteed rights of the Jews. The question whether from now on only doctors of Aryan origin should be employed reminds us of the problem of Dr. Tugendvetter's

223 cited in: Geehr, p. 186.

224 Ibid., p. 188.

225 CUL, MS Entwürfe zu Professor Bernhardi, Folder A 118, Nr. 3–4.

succession in *Professor Bernhardi.* Furthermore, the above item illustrates Lueger's heritage: a high-ranking member of the city administration seeing no reason to hold back his anti-Semitic leanings.

An anonymous letter that appeared in January 1913 in the *Illustriertes Wiener Extrablatt*, underlines that the "issue" of which Dr. Cyprian speaks in the play, which relates to the admission of priests to hospitals, was at the time a hotly disputed theme in Vienna.

> Many years ago, when Hofrat Professor Theodor Meynert led the psychiatric clinic, he gave the staff the order only to call the priests if the patient on his deathbed had lost consciousness. Otherwise not. One had heard nothing about any opposition to this order. Hofrat Meynert [...] delegated his first assistant to stand in for him, a Jew. While the head was absent, the director of the Allgemeines Krankenhaus came and asked if it was true that priests [...] were not allowed access to the patients. "And what do you think about such an order?" probed the hospital director further. "It would be tactless of me if I wanted to criticize decrees of my superior and teacher." stated the assistant. They waited for Hofrat Meynert's return. What happened then is beyond my knowledge.[226]

The performance of the last rites in hospitals was criticised especially by the Social Democratic press, whereas the Christian Social press was in favour of it. Schnitzler himself had worked as a doctor in Meynerts' psychiatric department and could draw on experiences like the one described above for his play.

Although it does not have any direct political implications, it is worthwhile at this point to bring in a further newspaper article. This article can be seen as the immediate inspiration for the controversial starting point in the first act of the play, in which the core of the whole Bernhardi scandal lies. The excerpt is in the same Cambridge file, and is dated 1910. Among other things, it addresses the childhood experience of a well-known

---

226 cited in: Beier, p. 440.

dramatist of the Liberal Era, Franz Nissel (1831-1893), is addressed. Nissel received the Berlin Schiller Prize for his play, *Agnes von Meran* (1877), in which the battle of an individual against the overwhelming power of the Church ends tragically.

> He had a brother whom he loved very tenderly. The brother was in Linz […] mortally ill [...]. Now the father gave the directive to send for the priest. The lamenting mother objected [...]. The father, however, of a pedantic and fearful nature, worried that the neglect of such a tenet of obligatory belief could damage his position in the city, insisted, and the priest was called in. When the priest entered […] the sick youth rose up on his bed in wild fury and gave out a cry of terror: "Must I *die*?" – and sank back into bed, unconscious. After that, the crisis developed quickly. The end effect of this deplorable scene on the other, younger brother remained ineradicable – it had made him a heretic.[227]

This short excerpt offers an invaluable insight into the nearly ten-year long genesis of *Professor Bernhardi.* It can stand as the key text of the creative process of the play.

To turn back to daily events, Schnitzler had recorded in his diary in April of 1908: "The Wahrmund and Feilbogen affairs bring the Bernhardi material very close to me again."[228] The "Feilbogen Scandal" had occurred in the same month. A Jewish university lecturer named Feilbogen traveled with his family to Rome in order to take part in the papal Easter mass in the Sistine Chapel. Because his wife was not initiated into the Catholic liturgy, Feilbogen's sister-in-law received the Eucharist (communion) whereupon she, when she grasped what she had done, took the host out of her mouth and wrapped it in a handkerchief. For fully two long weeks, the *Deutsches Volksblatt* railed against "Jewish insolence" and "blasphemy." It was repeatedly maintained that this occurrence offended the religious sensibilities of the Christian population. Thus, the event was considered a

227 CUL, MS Entwürfe zu Professor Bernhardi, Folder A 118, Nr. 3–4.
228 TB 1903–1908, 30.4.1908.

religious disturbance. On April 30, anti-Semitic deputies introduced the affair into Parliament and demanded preventive measures, in order to keep something similar from happening in the future. Although it did not come to a court case, Feilbogen was required to give up his teaching position and retire from his profession at the end of the semester.[229]

Dr. Ludwig Wahrmund, professor for ecclesiastical law at the University of Innsbruck, was one of Schnitzler's closer friends. He had repeatedly criticised religious instruction in the schools and criticised Catholic dogma. He had also spoken out for a reform of marital law. He had laid out his opinions in *Katholische Weltanschauung und Freie Wissenschaft* (1908), where he argued that the basics of scientific research were not compatible with religious orthodoxy.[230] Clerical parties demanded his resignation. Violent student demonstrations in Graz and Innsbruck reached such dimensions that the universities had to be closed for the summer months. In the end, Wahrmund was transferred to Prague while receiving an annual research grant in the amount of 10,000 crowns for two years' duration. In case he were to decide to retire early, a pension of 2,000 crowns was offered to him. When these details became known, Wahrmund lost all academic credibility, although he had already rejected the pension.[231]

The slanderous press campaign that was launched by the clerical and nationalist parties only reinforced Schnitzler's decision, instead of merely observing the situation, as in *Der Weg ins Freie,* to now practice marked criticism. After he had once determined on a course, Bernhardi's individualism allowed no compromise. In view of the Christian Social harassment campaign against Jewish doctors, the corruption of the city officials and the anti-Semitic agitation, Schnitzler himself came to a very similar position.

---

229 Gaisbauer, pp. 153–56. Cf. Matthias Höttinger: Der Fall Wahrmund. Diss. Univ. of Vienna 1950.

230 See Ludwig Wahrmund: *Katholische Weltanschauung und freie Wissenschaft*. Munich: Lehmann 1908.

231 Geehr, pp. 189–90.

"Every [...] Austrian has Experienced his Individual Case of Bernhardi" — the Play's Reception

After he had discussed the play with Gustav Schwarzkopf and other friends, Schnitzler did not believe that *Professor Bernhardi* could be performed at the Burgtheater. He was right. Neither Alfred von Berger, Director of the Burgtheater, nor Otto Brahm of the Berlin Lessing Theater wanted to stage the play, although both had worked in the past with the author very successfully. Schnitzler sent his work on June 17 to Berger with the words: "[...] if I also have to consider it completely out of the question, that the theme of discussion dealt with here could be permitted on the k. and k. court stage."[232]

Berger's rejection was less surprising for Schnitzler than that of his friend Brahm, who had always taken the part of such controversial contemporary authors as Ibsen and Hauptmann. Brahm mentions "the, to us, alien milieu" as well as "the difficulty of the north-German audience in relating to the circumstances." He continues:

> The Jewish doctors in Berlin are not persecuted, they dominate; we are not Catholic [...] and so the point of departure of the play and its progression are less compelling for us than in the land of the Eucharist-Congress. [...] So I must, with the deepest regret, come to the conclusion to do without the performance – at least until by the effects on that soil in which the play is rooted it has proven itself strong enough to overcome my doubts.[233]

Finally, Viktor Barnowsky of the Kleines Theater Unter den Linden takes the play on. The premiere on November 28, 1912, is a complete success. The reviews are also predominantly positive. The conservative and clerical papers provide, naturally, the exception. The following three performances are sold out. By March, 1913, *Professor Bernhardi* will be staged more than a hundred times. The drama is also taken on with great success in

232 Briefe 1875–1912, p. 698.

233 DLA, Briefe Brahm an Schnitzler. Fodler B0016d, 19.9.1912.

Stuttgart, Köln and Karlsruhe, where it remains part of the programme in the following year. After the Munich performance on February 8, 1913, with Schnitzler present, he is given standing ovations.

The Bavarian censors had allowed *Professor Bernhardi* without hesitation, and the demonstrations that the Austrian officials had feared did not take place. Nevertheless, the ban in Austria remained. On April 16, 1913, the play was performed in Budapest, which did not lie within the administrative area of the imperial-royal Interior Ministry. Schnitzler was present at this performance. His work had become so famous by now that critics and theater-goers travel from Austria to Budapest to see the performance. The *Wiener Wochenschrift* cites the following statement by Schnitzler: "We are, after all, neighbors, Austria and Hungary. In Berlin the play had a lucky break, but it was as though there were a veil between stage and audience. Here, they understand everything, every reference and every joke."[234] Further advantageous commentary is printed in *Der Morgen*: "Every Austrian who is not completely oblivious has experienced his individual case of Bernhardi."[235]

The ban remained in place, in spite of all the peaceful enthusiasm with which the play was received. This fact only proves that, for the Austrian officials, other factors were decisive besides the maintenance of public order. Nor was the anti-Semitism limited to the imperial officials of Vienna. After the Budapest success, Schnitzler had planned another performance with the ensemble of the Kleines Theater in Pressburg, which also lay within the Hungarian administrative sphere. On April 29, 1913, Schnitzler's friend Heller received a communication from the Pressburg City Council, the contents of which stated that one could not perform the play because it had not been submitted by the deadline. Heller offered to donate 200 crowns to the city garrison if the officials would cooperate. This proposal was voted on and, nevertheless, rejected by seven to five votes. According to the official verdict, a stage play that was forbidden in the Austrian half of the empire because of "derogatory treatment of religious questions" could not be staged

234 NL: Zensurakten: "Professor Bernhardi" in Ungarn. In: *Die Zeit*, 10.4.1913 (Evening Edition).

235 NL: Zensurakten: Der Fall Bernhardi. In: *Der Morgen*, 23.12.1912 (Morning Edition), Zl. 2910/1912.

by a visiting ensemble in Pressburg.[236]

On the following day, Berta Zuckerkandl wrote in the *Wiener Allgemeine Zeitung*:

> As the play appeared, opinion was divided as to dating it. Some thought it was set in the middle of the 1880's, when the seeds of anti-Semitism were sown. Some thought they recognised a later era. Arthur Schnitzler, when asked about it, replied that he had had in mind the period around 1900, which inspired some, including myself, to contradict. Because we thought, with regard to the conditions that lead to dramatic conflict in "Bernhardi," that we were already beyond that. But we were all of us wrong. The time of "Bernhardi" is 1913. The fate of this comedy shows that, the affair in Pressburg shows that. Or, much more, this is what basically every play from a writer's essence should be: it is eternal! [...] And if it is usually claimed for plays: "as though taken from real life," so must one say about the ban of the Bernhardi comedy, that it was the very best theater. Arthur Schnitzler cannot complain. His "Bernhardi" was performed in Pressburg after all. At the city hall![237]

Whereas Budapest, perhaps out of a certain local pride, did not cooperate with the Austrian ministers, the city council of Pressburg, in contrast, was ready to. The officials there and in Vienna were apparently more committed to the interests of the church than to the principle of artistic freedom.

After the end of the First World War and the breakdown of the Dual Monarchy, censorship was abolished. In November, 1918, the preparations for staging *Professor Bernhardi* at the Volkstheater under the leadership of Alfred Bernau were already well underway. Although police officials had warned Schnitzler of possible protests, the Vienna premiere on December 21, 1918, was a resounding success. Even the reviewers were benign. By the end

236 Beier, p. 465.

237 NL Zensurakten: Die Zeit des "Bernhardi" ist 1913. In: *Wiener Allgemeine Zeitung*, 30.4.1913.

of May, 1919, the play had been staged over 50 times.[238]

On October 16, 1919, however, an openly anti-Semitic comment appeared in the *Wiener Neustädter Zeitung*:

> Should, however, the theater direction consider a repetition, the leaders of today's anti-Semites refuse any responsibility. No number of policemen would be able to hold back a second time the deserved reception of this tendentious play.[239]

On October 25, the students at different local high schools organised a protest strike against the play's performance, which was also supported by numerous teachers-[240] Apparently the deprivations of the war, as well as the consequent political instability, had intensified anti-Semitic tendencies in the population. Schnitzler noted in his diary that this was the first scandal that was caused by *Professor Bernhardi*.[241]

Over a decade later, in 1930, Arthur Eloesser wrote: "Schnitzler's modern historical play has remained extraordinarily contemporary, and for us Germans become even more to the point. [...] How wise this play is and in what a shameful way are we obliged to acknowledge that the writer was, indeed, right about us, after this proliferation of class and race hatred."[242]

Bruce Pauley refers to the election success of the National Socialists in the same year, which was based on 6.4 million votes. Through it, the NSDAP became the second largest party after the Social Democrats.[243] In view of this, it is not surprising that on October 21, 1931, *Professor Bernhardi* provided the centerpiece of a memorial event for Schnitzler.[244]

---

238 Beier, p. 477.

239 Wiener Neustädter Zeitung, 82/17 (October 1919), ZAS MF 253.

240 Riedmann, p. 298.

241 TB 1917–19, 25.10., 15.11.1919.

242 cited in Hans-Peter Bayerdörfer: "Österreichische Verhältnisse?" Arthur Schnitzlers Professor Bernhardi auf Berliner Bühnen 1912–1931. In: *Von Franzos zu Canetti – Jüdische Autoren aus Österreich*. ed. by Mark H. Gelber and Hans-Otto Horch. Tübingen: Max Niemeyer 1996, pp. 211–24, p. 223.

243 Pauley, p. 233.

244 Bayerdörfer (1996), p. 224.

Perhaps some of those present suspected it, but none of them knew for certain: that this would be one of the last opportunities for an actual public pronouncement against anti-Semitism in Germany.

A Mirror of Institutional Anti-Semitism: Censorship of the Drama

Nikolaj Beier has performed a very useful service to research in that he introduces, in his study of Schnitzler and anti-Semitism, material from the Niederoesterreichisches Landesarchiv on the censorship of *Professor Bernhardi.* A detailed examination of this material is to be found in *Vor allem bin ich ich.*[245]

What can the censorship of *Professor Bernhardi* tell us about forms of white-collar anti-Semitism in the early years of the twentieth century? The censors themselves never used the term, and found other justifications for the ban. The Emperor insisted on fair treatment of all his subjects, regardless of religious practice, according to the Emancipation of 1867. Therefore, reports by Austrian officials mention that the play targeted specific weaknesses of the Austrian administration and exaggerated them, or that it showed certain Viennese citizens in a negative light.

Of the three censors on the council, only one, Karl Glossy, spoke against a ban. He argued that a press campaign in Austria and abroad would only provide the book with more publicity.[246] Indeed, after its publication in December, 1912, the book sold extremely well both in Germany and Austria, reaching 25,000 copies by 1925.[247]

The notice of the Statthalterei (city government) to the director of the Volkstheater, Adolf Weisse, pronouncing the ban on *Professor Bernhardi,* does not give any reasons. This was, however, customary, usually with a list of the passages in question, when the Censors' Council could not

---

245 Cf. Beier, pp. 445-67.

246 NL Zensurakten: Bericht des Zensurbeiratsmitglieds Glossy (20.10.1912), Zl. 2910/1912-XIV/197a4.

247 Renate Wagner: *Arthur Schnitzler – eine Biographie.* Wien: Molden: 1981, p. 253.

reach a unanimous decision.[248] The Statthalterei explained to the Ministry of the Interior that a full justification of the ban, which was based on "endangerment of the public peace and order," was in principle impossible, because it would have to be as extensive as the play itself. Furthermore, it would lead to unwelcome public discussions.[249]

These discussions would naturally be of a political nature and would be critical of clerical interests. The underlying anxiety, to be read between the lines of the officials' reports, regards a public debate about anti-Semitic tendencies among civil servants, as the quote below indicates. It would raise such questions as why the Jews could only rise to a certain level at university and in the legal profession. Naturally, this would cast an extremely negative light on all public institutions in Austria. Supposedly impartial officials risked being exposed as prejudiced. This was particularly dangerous in the Habsburg Monarchy, where neutrality in questions of ethnicity and religion was one of the ruling principles of the Habsburg dynasty. The equality of the Emperor's Jewish subjects was a subject particularly dear to his heart, and therefore, under no circumstances could it be permitted to be discussed publicly that his administration continually acted in contradiction to this maxim.

The officials of the Ministry of the Interior who dealt with the ban on *Professor Bernhardi* were only too aware of these dangers. A statement of the Vienna Statthalterei to the Ministry of the Interior of January 15, 1913 makes this especially clear:

> Schnitzler's comedy "Professor Bernhardi" is no usual tendentious play in the commonly understood sense of the term- It is not the case that, in it, one particular hostile attitude is promoted against any specific situation. Rather, in a more or less all-embracing fashion, nearly everything that in Austria comes into consideration as an important factor in public life is subjected to an extremely sharp, acerbic criticism and is presented as thoroughly corrupt and fraudulent. The

248 Beier, pp. 452–53.

249 Vienna, Austrian State Archive, MS Informationsschreiben der Statthalterei an das k.k. Ministerium des Innern, 15.1.1913, Zl.1565–913.

> institutions at our universities, namely, the connections of personnel questions with political and other conditions that are far removed from pure science, then these political conditions themselves, parliamentarianism in the form and function it takes in our country, the highest government officials and the functionaries who belong to the Council of the Crown; no less though, the court system, the church officials, even the press – everything, everything appears in the play either to be consumed with shocking internal corruption or riddled with ridiculous backwardness, cowardice and intolerance.[250]

Schnitzler's highly effective criticism struck exactly where imperial officials were most sensitive. None of their institutions were spared. The words of this anonymous communication make clear that the ministry officials knew very well the kind of corruption Schnitzler brought to light with his play. Were the message not intended exclusively for internal use, Schnitzler's implications would never have been put down in such unmistakable words.

More than the Conflict between Faith and Science

The whole affair has its source in the conflict between religious and medical duty, which is carried out between the followers of the priest on the one hand and those of a man of science on the other. The temptation is great to read this antagonism exclusively as a battle between religion and science. But what Bernhardi struggles against in the larger sense is the political concept of anti-individualism. From this perspective, we have, on the one side, the discerning seeker after truth and, on the other, the man of the masses, who willingly accepts the programme of an institution or a party as his own.

As the aristocratic sponsors of the clinic withdraw their support, Dr.

250 Ibid.

Cyprian reproaches Bernhardi for his provocative behaviour during an earlier discussion. He continues:

> There are things on which the Countess dare not even reflect, otherwise she would be an outcast like you, if you did not reflect on these things. We must understand these people, that is our nature, and they are not allowed to understand us at all, that is theirs.

Here Cyprian is referring to nothing less than critical reflection. He seems to be implying that the aristocracy would begin to doubt its own right to exist if it began to think critically. Bernhardi, on the other hand, represents rational skepticism and the scientific drive to know, which, above all, seeks truth – and thus engages to reveal the true nature of an institution or a personage.

Bernhardi and the priest – in whose latter category the Countess Stixenstein also belongs – can, on the basis of their completely opposing worldviews, only talk at cross-purposes. Whereas for the priest, the first rule is "conformity and obedience," the Countess has to submit to the strict behavioural and moral code of the aristocracy. Bernhardi's free will as an individual, which is founded on his scientifically supported doubt, is in fundamental opposition to these institutional and social programs.

To confirm this, there is, in a diary entry of Schnitzler's from December 17, 1912, a reference to the play that makes clear that he did not want to reduce it to the tension between religion and science.

> It is a comedy of character. The theme is not, as superficial journalism would maintain, the conflict between belief and science; rather, it is the fate of a doctor, who, far removed from all political partisanship, simply because in a special case he does what is only natural, is sucked into a political intrigue, and who endeavours to escape this undesired conundrum as soon as possible.

The professor's opponents misuse religion as a cover for their true motive, one that will always be bound up with the history of the 20th century: anti-Semitism. Well before the First World War, these resentments were successfully employed in mass politics. The key of *Professor Bernhardi* lies in the individual itself, which defends itself against absorption by the group, whether the group is of a social, religious, or political nature. The critical thinker stands in opposition to the anti-individualist, the creature of the masses. This basic conflict is what secures Schnitzler's work its continuing relevance.

A Comedy in a Higher Sense?

First, a word regarding terminology: in Austrian usage, "playing comedy" means engaging in a deceptive manoeuvre. In his work, Schnitzler uses the expression more often in this sense; for example, in the *Grosse Szene*, a one-act play from the cycle *Komödie der Worte*. In this cycle, Schnitzler explores words in personal relationships, when, for example, one half of a pair takes words seriously and the other not at all. In the play referred to, Sophie asks of her fiancé Herbot, that, if he were to be unfaithful, to be honest with her: "I could understand everything, forgive everything. I ask only one thing of you. Don't deceive me. Not me. [...spiele keine Komödie. Vor mir spiele keine]."

In the same sense, Schnitzler uses the expression in an aphorism about politicians: "Among politicians themselves there will scarcely be one who would not be aware of the deception (Komödie) that he is professionally obligated to act out [...] before his fatherland, indeed, before the whole human race."[251] The specific Austrian meaning of this word seems to be very appropriate for the efforts of Bernhardi's enemies, who seek to hide the true reasons for their enmity. This definition should also be kept in mind with regard to the question of why Schnitzler labels his work a comedy – by no means the obvious choice of genre.

In literary studies, Bernhardi is repeatedly referred to as "a half-hero" or an "involuntary hero." Robert Weiss proposes that Bernhardi is, in principle,

---

251 Schnitzler: *Ohne Maske*, p. 56.

a passive character, because he repeatedly finds himself in circumstances beyond his control, and only reacts to incidents rather than taking the initiative himself. To a certain extent, he is even "ridiculous" because he "becomes a representative of positions that he never intended to support [...]. A rebel without a cause, a martyr without martyrdom, an avenger incapable of revenge. This way he becomes a popular hero, without having done anything heroic, or even having intended to."[252] That is why Bernhardi is a kind of "comic figure." According to Weiss, it is primarily the irony of the situation of its main character that makes *Professor Bernhardi* a comedy.

A more subtle element of the "comedy" is that it lies in Bernhardi's hands to avoid, or at least alleviate, the more serious consequences of the affair. One opportunity would have been the letter of apology to the priest that he, however, tears up after Dr. Ebenwald's visit. An apology would have, at any time, taken that wind out of the sails of his opponents. Aside from that, the Professor could have mobilised the political organs of liberalism to launch a public campaign to his advantage, as the journalist Kulka offers. But he turns this down, just as Bernhardi does not apologize, out of personal principle. Integrity of character is, it appears, Bernhardi's highest law.

William Rey writes that Bernhardi, because he unites several Christian virtues in his person, "paradoxically presents one of the few true Christians in a corrupted Christian society." Analogous to the twelve apostles, there are twelve doctors in the play. In this "Passion" grouping, Heinrich Kaulen recognizes a Judas, a Pilate and other figures out of the Passion of Christ. For Kaulen, the fundamental comedy of the play is that the messiah is a Jew who is persecuted by Christians, contrary to the events depicted in the New Testament.

It is possible that Schnitzler intended this confrontation. In a draft from 1910, Dr. Pflugfelder says: "Bernhardi had acted out of the purest motives, out of true humaneness, out of charity, that you, sirs, for reasons unknown to me, choose to label with the epithet "Christian."

The biblical quotations that Bernhardi cites provide further proof of Rey's and Kaulen's thesis. Without exception, they come out of the New

252 Robert Weiss: The "Hero" in Schnitzler's Comedy Professor Bernhardi. In: *Modern Austrian Literature*, Heft 2, Nr. 4 (1969), 30–34, pp. 32–33.

Testament. For example, after the incident with the priest, the following exchange takes place:

> Hochroitzpointner: Director, we live in a Christian country.
> Bernhardi: Yes. *gives him a long look* May the Lord forgive you – – You know damned well what you are doing.

This is, clearly, a paraphrase of the cry of Christ, before he was nailed to the cross: "Forgive them, father, for they know not what they do." As Dr. Adler votes against Bernhardi, nonetheless, he expresses his admiration for the professor. Bernhardi merely replies: "Whoever is not for me, is against me." In the end, Adler does testify in court on Bernhardi's behalf, whereupon Bernhardi salutes him with these words: "A repentant sinner is more pleasing to my eyes than ten just men."

These parallels between Jesus and Bernhardi were not only provocative for the clerics. The bitter irony of this Christian-Jewish confrontation lends Schnitzler's criticism an even sharper edge. The author does, in fact, succeed in using humour to illustrate the fundamental injustice of anti-Semitism.

THE WORLD IN RUINS 1913–1918

The only publication of 1913 is the story *Frau Beate und ihr Sohn,* in which a widowed woman commits incest with her son. Schnitzler had already addressed the mother-son relationship in *Der Sohn*, which he later develops into his second and last novel, *Therese*. *Therese* is the socio-critical depiction of the misfortunes of an unmarried woman from the lower social spectrum. *Frau Beate und ihr Sohn,* in contrast, focuses on the suppression of female sexuality by the religious and social mores of the era. The influence of psychoanalytical theories of suppressed sexual urges is clearly recognisable here.

Neither Beate nor her son are libertines like the Baroness Fortunata. It is exactly for this reason that they are shaken to the core by the power of their own sexuality. This is intensified by a fundamental bourgeois sense of propriety, which is why they both know that, after this incident, they can never go back either to shore – or rejoin society. Schnitzler traces Beate's psychological development minutely, in order to render understandable to the reader why she is driven to commit the apparently perverse act of incest. In the course of the story, the dualism is brought out that recurs throughout Schnitzler's work between people who do and those who do not take things seriously. It is a question of two opposite types of human being, and whenever they come together in a relationship, it can end tragically. This, for the deeply rooted reason that neither "he" nor "she" can help themselves. In the novel, the careless individual is represented by Beate's dead husband and the Baroness, the more serious one by herself and her son. In *Der einsame Weg*, Sala and Fichtner are men, who, in their younger years, took every human relationship lightly. In *Das weite Land,* as in the cycle *Komödie der Worte*, there are also examples of the grave consequences that result from a love between these two different types of human being.

On December 12, 1913, Schnitzler experiences a surprise during a visit with Berta Zuckerkandl: a comedy by Tristan Bernard, *Les deux canards,* premiered on February, 28 1913, at the Berlin Trianon Theater as *Er und der Andere*.[253] The material is nearly the same as in *Fink und Fliederbusch*: a journalist writes, (under duress, however, from the complications of a love affair) for a politically left-wing as well as a politically right-wing newspaper.

Schnitzler stresses to his friends that his first inspiration for it lay nine years back – in reality, the first recorded idea for it dates as early as 1901 – and that he had hastily resumed working with the material four years before. In the next few days, Schnitzler completes copies of all that he has composed to date, and commits the drafts to three trusted individuals: his secretary, Frieda Pollak, Berta Zuckerkandl herself, and the artistic secretary of the Hofburg Theater, Richard Rosenbaum. Schnitzler fears, above all because of his anti-clerical leanings, that his enemies could somehow harm him, using this completely independent parallel work conceived in French.[254]

The Schnitzlers' marriage during this period is not stable. Olga singing career is not progressing. Rather the opposite: her teachers are giving her all-too-frank verdicts on her talent, and, after her public performances, the reviews are unfavourable. This makes for considerable tension in her relationship with her husband. During a particularly intense argument in May, they even consider separation.[255]

In December, Schnitzler reads the just-published book about him by Theodor Reik, *Arthur Schnitzler as a Psychologist,* "with really strong interest, not at all infrequently with agreement in substance, naturally, in no way without lively objection." Reik is a student of Freud's, and Schnitzler's letter of thanks to him contains an interesting indication of difference between Schnitzler's and Freud's conception of the human psyche.

> About my subconscious, my half-conscious, we should rather say – , I still know more than you and toward the darkness of the soul lead more paths, I feel it ever more strongly, than the psychoanalysts allow themselves to dream of (and interpret).

---

253 CUL, MS Fink und Fliederbusch – Skizzen, Folder A 115,5.

254 Ibid., Folder A 114,2. It is worth mentioning here a study by Wolfgang Lukas comparing both of these works: Arthur Schnitzler und Tristan Bernard: Anmerkungen zu einem singulären Fall von *Doppelgängerschaft* in Germanica 52 (2013), pp. 85-99.

255 TB 1913-16, 28.5.1913.

> And very often a path leads right through the middle of the illuminated inner world, where they – and you – believe one must turn all-too-early into the shadow world.[256]

In contrast to Freud, Schnitzler holds firmly to the notion of an "in-between region" between the conscious and the unconscious, that he calls the half- or middle-conscious [Mittelbewusstsein]. In a letter to the psychiatrist Dr. Hans Hemming, he writes at the beginning of April, 1914, about the book by Reik:

> That here, namely, which on the part of a certain professional critic so rarely happens, that reference is made to my representation of non-erotic relationships such as those between siblings, between parents and children, between friends and to all kinds of deeper psychological connections [...]. I also have, from conversations with Reik [...] the conviction (he himself however not yet) that later the Freudian method of interpretation [...] will mean to him not the one-and-only sanctified approach, but rather one among others, into the secret of poetic creativity, sometimes, however, also heading past into vagueness or error.[257]

A comprehensive study that compares Schnitzler's and Freud's conception of psychoanalysis and the human psyche remains an academic desideratum. There are several articles in psychoanalytic and German studies periodicals, however, that shed light on aspects of both approaches.[258]

In March 1914, Schnitzler receives the Raimund Prize for *Der junge Medardus.* He is very happy about this and so financially secure in the meantime, that he considers donating the 2,000-crown prize money to the

---

256 Briefe 1913-31, pp. 35–36.

257 Ibid., pp. 37–38.

258 More detail in Eric R. Kandel: *Das Zeitalter der Erkenntnis : die Erforschung des Unbewussten in Kunst, Geist und Gehirn von der Wiener Moderne bis heute.* Munich: Pantheon 2014. Two unpublished dissertations from the University of Vienna also treat this topic: Birgit Illner: Psychoanalytische Diagnostik – Sigmund Freud und Arthur Schnitzler im Spannungsfeld von Wissenschaft, Kunst und Psychoanalyse. Eine Bestandsaufnahme. Diss. Univ. Vienna 1991. Erika Seierl: Arthur Schnitzler und die Psychoanalyse. Diss. Univ. Vienna 1987.

Kleist Foundation.[259]

Already in February, the Danish film version of *Liebelei* is shown in Vienna. It is the first film based on a Schnitzler drama. Although he is interested in the new medium and goes to the cinema regularly, in this particular case, he is irritated by the text subtitles and the musical accompaniment. Granted, he has written the script, but he does not find the film convincing.

Outbreak of the First World War

On June 28, Julius calls and tells his brother the news of the assassination of the successor to the throne, Franz Ferdinand, during a visit to Sarajevo. A Serbian nationalist, Gavrilo Princip, has shot the Archduke and his wife. Ferdinand was not very popular among his Austrian subjects, but his assassination aggravates the already precarious situation in the Balkans. Exactly one month later, the Austrian government sends an ultimatum to Belgrade, so designed that it is almost impossible to fulfil its demands. Austria-Hungary issues its declaration of war on Serbia on the same day. Russia, Serbia's ally, orders mobilization, and the alliance system of the European powers is set in motion like a row of dominoes. Inevitably, Germany's declaration of war on August 1 is followed by that of France on August 3 and that of Great Britain on August 4. By mid-month, the nations of the Triple Entente, France, Britain and Russia, stand opposed to the Central Powers, Germany and Austria-Hungary.

Schnitzler and his family had been vacationing in Switzerland since July 17. Not until September 2 do they manage to return to Vienna, with many detours and without being able to access their accounts abroad.

Schnitzler is one of the few intellectuals who does not greet the outbreak of the war with enthusiasm. Hermann Bahr and Hugo von Hofmannsthal as well as Gerhard Hauptmann and Thomas Mann, all join the general patriotic enthusiasm. Even Stefan Zweig cannot restrain himself, contrary to his later assertions, as the most recent research proves.[260] Olga is

259 TB 1913-16, 27.3.1914.

260 Ibid., 7.9.1914. Schnitzler records Zweigs statement, that Zweig would volunteer if

embarrassed by Schnitzler's silence as a public figure, whereas he forbids her to sign up for volunteer work at the Red Cross.[261] In a time in which other writers profit financially from the war, Schnitzler's resolute silence leads to a considerable decline in his income, as his bank manager determines with anxiety.[262] His son Heinrich, born in 1902, is fortunately still too young to serve in the Austro-Hungarian army.

Anti-Semitic outbursts are bruited about, such as that Jews should be placed in the front lines, in order to be shot. Schnitzler comments in his diary: "Is this country still sane?"[263] Nevertheless, he finds the composure to work on the novella *Wahn*, one of his most sinister works, the final title of which will be *Flucht in die Finsternis*. He also works on the comedy *Fink und Fliederbusch*.

The new attitude on German and Austrian stages is that good plays should deal with the war, and should feature uniforms. Schnitzler's *Ruf des Lebens* is therefore performed in October 1914, at the Volkstheater to great acclaim. *Medardus,* for now, disappears from the programmes. Under the circumstances, nobody wants to see French soldiers outside the walls of Vienna. The performance of Schnitzler's plays suffers under the one-sided atmosphere of war. Even if war plays a background role in some of his works, he sees no reason why he should conceive a literary monument to the First World War.

In May of 1915, Schnitzler finishes *Fink und Fliederbusch*. He immerses himself in volumes on and by Casanova. In the course of the next two years, this reading bears fruit in the form of a drama and a novella. He also begins work on his autobiography, for which he re-reads the letters and diaries of his younger years.

During the summer months, he becomes aware of his feelings for

---

he were a German citizen. See also the following essay, which underlines Zweig's patriotic views: Pawel Zajas: Bellizismus eines Pazifisten. Stefan Zweig und der Insel Verlag im Ersten Weltkrieg. http://www.academia.edu/9263419/Bellizismus_eines_Pazifisten_Stefan_Zweig_und_der_Insel-Verlag_im_Ersten_Weltkrieg_Bellicism_of_a_pacifist._Stefan_Zweig_and_Insel-Verlag_during_the_First_World_War (14.3.2019).

261 Ibid., 8.9.1914.

262 Edward Timms: *Karl Kraus – Apocalyptic Satirist*. New Haven, CT: Yale University Press 1989, p. 300.

263 TB 1913–16, 14.9.1914.

Stephi Bachrach, and he confesses his love to her in a letter. Even though his marriage has reached a low point, he does not betray his wife. After Olga Waissnix, this is Schnitzler's second platonic relationship. He and Stephi are very close, but their relationship does not become physical, out of mutual consideration for others.[264]

In September, *Das weite Land* is staged in German in New York. One month later, the cycle of one-act plays, *Komödie der Worte,* appears at the Burgtheater, at the Frankfurter Neues Theater and at the Hoftheater in Darmstadt.

1916 is a disheartening year for Schnitzler. There are no new publications, and the only premiere is *Denksteine,* performed at a charity event for soldiers. The novella *Wahn* is complete, as is *Fink und Fliederbusch.* Both Olga and Gustav Schwarzkopf advise him not to have this journalistic drama staged, with the argument that, during this propaganda-inflamed period, he will only make himself enemies. Even though Schnitzler believes the play would have the desired effect on stage, he hesitates to send in the manuscript. He also withholds *Wahn* from publication until the last year of his life. It is a very personal work that reflects his intimate fears and obsessions.

In the second year of the war, the so-called "Judenzählung" [count of Jews] is carried out in the Prussian Army, in order to prove that the Jewish soldiers do not perform at the same fighting level as their Christian comrades. The opposite, is, in fact, revealed: It is rather proven that, as measured against their population, a disproportionately high number of Jewish soldiers serves at the front.[265]

The Two Faces of the Political Press: *Fink and Fliederbusch*

Along with *Professor Bernhardi*, *Fink and Fliederbusch* is the only other play in which women do not play a major role. Both plays are, to an extent, political. Whereas the former deals extensively with the issue of anti-

264 Wagner., pp. 286–87.

265 David Brenner: *Marketing Identities – The Invention of Jewish Ethnicity in 'Ost und West'.* Detroit: Wayne State UP 1998, p. 151.

Semitism, the latter ridicules political allegiance in the press. When *Das Wort* is included, these three plays make up the trilogy *O du mein Österreich,* as Schnitzler had already speculated about in July of 1906.[266] It should come as no surprise that Schnitzler was working on *Fink and Fliederbusch* during the First World War, when propaganda lies on the part of all participating countries were rampant. Nor could one really believe the official news about victories and defeats. The protagonist of the play is a journalist who writes for a conservative paper under the pen name "Fink," and for a liberal paper under the name "Fliederbusch." His relentless attacks on his counterpart escalate to the point where a challenge to a duel is unavoidable.

The Bloody Suppression of a Strike at Reichenberg

Even in studies on Schnitzler's Jewish identity, it has, until now, been ignored that the drafts of the comedy *Fink und Fliederbusch*, stored in the Cambridge University Library, have strong references to anti-Semitic discrimination and the Jewish dilemma. In the final draft, these elements are completely purged. Only the recently published work of Verena Vortisch has shed light on this subject.[267] In the very first notes for the "journalistic play," (as it was called then), that date from August of 1901, the son of the editor-in-chief fights a duel for his father's convictions, which are, however, completely mutable and therefore lacking in substance. Schnitzler raises the question of whether someone who holds clerical interests should be running a liberal paper.[268]

Two years later, Schnitzler commits to paper the idea that the newspaper should publish an article opposing the pro-clerical Count, after he has publicly made an anti-Semitic remark. It is not clear whether the Count, as in the final version, will continue to support the paper financially. Besides this development, the early version also deals with the bloody suppression of a strike that ultimately, after a parliamentary investigation, is intended

266 TB 1903–8, 16.7.1906.

267 Verena Vortisch: An der Grenze des Poesielands. Arthur Schnitzlers Komödie Fink und Fliederbusch. Würzburg: Ergon Verlag 2014.

268 CUL, MS Fink und Fliederbusch – Skizzen, Folder A 115, 1–3.

to lead to the fall of the conservative government. A progressive editor-in-chief, who had repeatedly written articles opposing the earlier government, also becomes disillusioned by the new liberal one and sells his paper.[269]

As his point of departure, Schnitzler had used an incident near Bohemian Reichenberg (Liberec) on May 21, 1896. The relevant Parliamentary documents are contained in the folders with the drafts of the play. Because of a low weekly salary, several hundred workers of the factory "Lederer und Wolf" had gathered on the Reichenberger Landstrasse. They were confronted by six gendarmes. As the people refused to break up after the repeated warnings of the superior officer, and instead responded with whistles, jeers, and stone-throwing, he ordered an attack with sheathed bayonets. Because the demonstrators soon regrouped, he finally had his soldiers shoot into the crowd. The result was three dead and three wounded.

In May of 1910, Schnitzler noted in the current draft that he was working on another possible background to the strike, that, namely, both government and people had greeted with enthusiasm the state visit of a Minister from Russia or the Balkans who had encouraged a pogrom. The editorial staff is nevertheless divided, as the editorialist Voll wants to write an article about the "murderer," whereas the young editor-in-chief, Markus, who is himself a Jew, wants to forbid this for diplomatic and political reasons. Although the pogrom, in fact, took place, Markus considers it a rumour. After a toast in which the journalist Silberstein attacks Markus, the editor-in-chief challenges the journalist to a duel, which leads to a major argument between father and son. In this version, the journalist Ruben steps up, here depicted as a "good-natured giant, a Zionist with grease spots." Markus embraces him, beaming with joy, after Ruben has beaten up the clerically-minded Count.[270]

The drafts between 1906 and 1907 concentrate primarily on the relationship between father and son, which is much more thoroughly developed here. The convictions of the father, which the son pretends to represent, and which in reality do not exist, negatively affect the son, who fights a duel for his father's sake. After the duel, there is a long discussion

269 Ibid.

270 Ibid., Nr. 3.

about the direction of the paper, the different views of the journalists and editors, about political vacillation and corruption and also about the background of the strike. The conflict with the son, who stands for the pro-Jewish position that one would expect from the father, ends in reconciliation.

Anti-Semitic Commentary in the Drafts 1903–1916

In 1903, Fliederbusch is still called Silberstein, the Count is called Werburg, and about him is determined: "1. Baron, 2. Christian, 3. Anti-Semite." A line below that, there is written a verbal expression for later use: "These liberal Jewish pigs would love it." In this connection, it is worthwhile to cast a glance at the anti-Semitic allusions that are particularly plentiful in the draft of 1903. Here Obendorfer, whose name, in contrast to those of all the other characters, remains the same through all revisions, makes no secret of his anti-Semitic inclinations. Here, he is still responsible for the "Vienna Sketches" in the print version for the "Feuilleton." He makes such statements as the following: "The ministry is still relatively – as we say – free of Jews."[271]

Later, the following dialogue occurs:

> Obendorfer: Now, between us, I've never sought intimacy with people with spinach spots on their vest... but I still liked him. Between us, they are above certain things. If all these Israelites were as undemanding as Epstein, we wouldn't have any anti-Semitism in Vienna.
>
> Kohnberger: *with cutting humour* You, Obendorfer, take heed. I'm not above anything, and there are certain things I don't joke about.
>
> Ob.: But...but...
>
> Kb.: *indicating his forehead* That comes from a certain German-nationalist student, who had apparently thought I was above it

271 This and the following excerpts in: CUL, MS Flink und Fliederbusch – Skizzen, Folder A 115.

> all. Do me the favour of keeping that in mind, and indulge in your anti-Semitic leanings with other people.
> Obendorfer: But Kohnberger, I know that you're a Maccabee. Now listen. You know what I think about these things. Proof enough: I sit in this newspaper's office and – please – – (He indicates that Markus is coming in.)

Here we are reminded again that the editor-in-chief is of Jewish origin, although he himself strives for "objectivity" with regard to anti-Semitism. In a talk with Silberstein, who is responsible for theatrical criticism, and who, in another context, describes himself as a "little Bohemian Jew," Kohnberger states, "We are a liberal paper, Jewish liberal, as opponents say, and Werburg is a Christian, nearly an anti-Semite: That alone would be reason enough for our chief to crawl on his belly before him."

Other scenes in which Jewish identity is addressed are introduced as follows:

> Fialla: Oh, I see... Yes, yes... But you don't really want to change to another paper, do you?
> Obendorfer: What an idea! I wouldn't even consider it. They are for the most part astute – gifted people. Certain qualities ... naturally, but you get used to that. – After all, when one comes from a very good old Vienna family, and when destiny wills that one spends practically one's whole life among a crowd of Israelites, – I assure you, Herr Fialla, sometimes one thinks one is a Jew oneself.

As the editorial staff grows, Obendorfer reacts in the following way:

> Obendorfer: Oh, what an honor! Now, Miss Loser, how are you? Nice day – isn't it? You'd almost think you were in Israel. – By the way, I've heard, Miss Loser, is it true? – that you are joining our office.
> Adele: O that is still a big secret! However, it wouldn't be impossible.

Obendorfer: Oh, That would be great! Then we would already be three.
Adele: What do you mean?
Obendorfer: Three of another faith. [Christians]
Adele: Herr Obendorfer, I must point out that my husband is a Jew.
Obendorfer: But, really, dear lady, if all Israelites were like your husband –!

By those "of another belief" is meant Christians, in a reversal of the usual usage of the time. It is a play on the Jewish majority among the liberal newspaper editors. Whereas here only a latent anti-Semitism is apparent, the following "joke" is more clearly stamped with it. Two Jewish employees converse at the beginning of the third act over the impending duel:

Kö.: They will shoot each other.
Ru: Shoot?
(Obendorfer comes in here.)
Ob: With Scholet balls.
Ko: You, Obendorfer, I'm telling you for once and for all. With the next anti-Semitic remark, I'm going to throw you out the window.

Still in 1913, the editorial writer (now with the name Voll) is supposed to utter this sentence about Count Niederhof. "He will one day rule Austria. Then the Jews will be completely chased out of the country." Markus replies to that, true to the principles of the liberal press: "I am a-Jewish. Whatever we do not write about, does not exist."

The Count speculates about the title of the paper meanwhile:

It is supposed to be called "The Elegant World," "The Christian World." Maybe even "The Catholic World." [...] One could, perhaps, misunderstand such a title, and the public would assume that our organ wanted to promote a kind of Christian mildness, and so would be certain to wonder whether the title itself should

> not express the energy, assertiveness, and inflexibility of our principles.

Still, two further examples should, because of their unmistakable language, be mentioned here:

> Silberstein: You anti-Semite!
> Obendorfer: I'm not one at all. I'm against anti-Semitism, but because it's going to continue as long as the Jews exist, one has to exterminate the Jews, and then anti-Semitism will stop by itself.

The first quote dates from September 20, 1913, the later comes from the time between 1913 and 1916. Below, the cancellations are indicated:

> Füllmann: (about Count Niederhof) I assure you, gentlemen, in a decade we will have the Inquisition again. (Obendorfer and Frühbeck laugh)
> Füllmann: Well, I guarantee that Jews will be driven out. [...]
> Frühbeck (You are indeed a fool,) Füllmann. You're suffering from a persecution complex. Nobody in the world pays any attention to what Count Niederhof says. ~~We only embarrass ourselves when we give a serious reply~~. Even the "Arbeit" contented itself with a few ironic remarks.
> Füllmann: That's just it. That's our misfortune. We keep our mouths shut, we, his opponents. But his friends, his entourage, they talk. What am I saying, talk. They raise their voices, they blow ~~the attack call, they join the fanfare.~~

In the draft from September, 1913, the following sentence is the direct occasion for a challenge to a duel. Fink writes: "In it, aristocracy and racial purity were played against the masses, yes, even against the working population." Here Fliederbusch is shown to be much angrier than in the final version and wants to shoot down his opponent like a "rabid dog." In general, here the question of duelling and honor is developed in more detail.

For a better overview, following is a quick summary of the theme's development: In the drafts, Schnitzler had introduced an anti-Semitic character, the editor Obendorfer, whose provocations are significantly more radical than anything that the reader had been exposed to in *Der Weg ins Freie* or *Professor Bernhardi.* The point was to satirically target the presumed Jewish "penetration" of the liberal press. Why has Schnitzler then completely left out these very strong references to anti-Semitism in the final version? One can think of several different reasons. First of all, he certainly wanted to avoid again being categorised as a "Jewish author," as he was after the publication of *Der Weg ins Freie.* From his own experience, he knew that his play would be exclusively read as a "Jewish play" if there were too many such allusions. Or perhaps it did not seem to him to be an opportune time, in the precarious situation that Austria found itself in in 1917, to pour more oil on the fires of the still-burning "Jewish Question." It is also entirely possible that he left out these provocative lines simply because they were not essential to the plot, in contrast to *Professor Bernhardi.* Schnitzler wanted to focus, first of all, on the question of the unreliability of political convictions, and he granted to the Fliederbusch character – unlike Minister Flint in *Bernhardi,* whom he sharply condemned for the same thing – that perhaps both positions can be justified on their own merits. This way he could express his own struggle with the effort to be objective, which preoccupied him his entire life, not only in his work but also in his private life, and which he suffered over repeatedly.

Encounters with Casanova and *Dr. Gräsler Badearzt*

Because of the war, Schnitzler cannot spend the summer abroad, so he travels to Aussee, where Jakob Wassermann lives. Wassermann's overflowing self-confidence irritates Schnitzler just as much as do Hofmannsthal's sympathies for Catholicism.

Schnitzler puts the finishing touches on *Casanova's Heimfahrt* and also wants to dedicate a play to Casanova, with whom he had much in common during the first 40 years of his life. This is *Die Schwestern oder Casanova in Spa*. For this comedy, Schnitzler takes up an idea from *Der Schleier der Beatrice*, in fact one that he will bring to full effect in *Traumnovelle*: the confession of a young woman, Anina, to her lover, Andrea, that she has spent the night with another man – and the utter disarray into which the young man is thrown as a result. In this case, there was a nocturnal confusion. A mature Casanova, who has his flight from the prisons of Venice behind him, believed himself to be lying in the arms of Flaminia, the wife of Baron Santis. He resolves the story by stating: "Betrayed are all three: The youth twofold/ Once, the ladies, each in her own way/ Thus all is even, and I declare this whole adventure invalid."[272]

The prose work *Casanova's Heimfahrt* also centers on an older Casanova, but one who decidedly has his best years behind him. He is 53 and "no longer chased through the world by a youthful lust for adventure, but by the unrest of impending old age."[273] In the latter Casanova work, his character is more fully developed. He sees himself in the mirror and sticks his tongue out at his own reflection, a clear sign of how revolted by himself he has become. In contrast to the dashing philosopher of *Die Schwestern*, who is still fully capable of seducing a beautiful woman, in *Casanova's Heimfahrt*, he appears cynical and dishonest. The murder of Lorenzi is a completely unnecessary crime after he has already destroyed his relationship. Marcolina realises full well that Lorenzi, in the end, sold her to Casanova. Rather than accept responsibility and explain the situation to his hosts, who have sheltered him in their house for days on end, he leaves without a word of farewell.

While Schnitzler is revising *Fink und Fliederbusch* for the stage, the Emperor Franz Joseph dies on November 21, 1916. He had ascended the throne in 1848, at the age of 18, and witnessed the change from a rural Europe dominated by royal dynasties to a continent of industrialised nation-states. His multi-ethnic empire, held together mainly by the Habsburg dynasty, already appeared to contemporaries, in the early 20th century, to be anachronistic and destined to fall apart. If, in the meantime, drawing on statistics for infrastructure and economic development, historians can make a convincing case that Austria-Hungary was in the

272 DW II, p. 722.
273 ES II, p. 231.

process of becoming a modern European state,[274] the military defeat made the end and dismemberment of the Danube Monarchy inevitable. For the time being, however, in 1916, the 600-year-old Habsburg Monarchy is still intact, and the successor of the dead Emperor is Karl I.

Schnitzler's health takes a turn for the worse. The otosclerosis is increasing, and he has to struggle with nausea, fatigue, and permanent headaches. In addition, his marriage has reached a stage where it can no longer be salvaged. After Olga's concerts, neither the audience nor her teacher is satisfied. She blames her failed career not the least on her husband, claiming he did not support her enough, and that his name was a burden for her. Without her husband, however, she would certainly never have made the acquaintance of Bruno Walter and Gustav Mahler. The crisis with Olga has reached such an extent that it distracts Schnitzler seriously from his work.

One of the new works Schnitzler decides to publish is *Doctor Gräsler, Spa Physician*. Before it appears in book form from the Fischer Verlag, the *Berliner Tageblatt* publishes it in spring of 1917 in serial form against an advance.

Gräsler is an unusual character in Schnitzler's prose works. He is a bachelor, and, like Schnitzler's Casanova, in the "decline of his youth."[275] Like other male characters in his later works, notably Casanova, Gräsler has misanthropic tendencies. He is disillusioned and confused by the world around him, and wanders restlessly from town to town, unable to settle down. Schnitzler's own insecurities are reflected in this: not just the problems of aging, but also the uprooting event of his divorce and his degree of dissatisfaction with the war era.

One day after his 55th birthday, Schnitzler hears terrible news. Stephi Bachrach, torn between two men, Rudi Olden and Rudolf Urbantschitsch, committed suicide with an overdose of veronal and morphine. Schnitzler saw this tragedy coming, and is desolate at the loss of this good friend. With this event fresh in his mind, Schnitzler must have thought back frequently

---

274 Held, among others, by Alan Sked: The Decline and Fall of the Habsburg Empire 1815–1915. London: Longman 2001.
275 ES II, p. 115.

to the death of another young woman he loved, Marie Reinhard. He works on a story entitled *Der letzte Brief eines Literaten,* that is only published in 1932, one year after his death. The theme is very similar to the story *Sterben.* Here, however, it is developed from a "masculine" perspective. The title of the novel is not chosen without intent, because in the philosophical work, *Der Geist im Wort und der Geist in der Tat,* Schnitzler contrasts the word "Dichter" or poet, with its positive connotations, with the term "Literat." The latter denotes rather a journalist than a real artist, who, in dealing with words, can be not only superficial, but an out-and-out falsifier.

On November 14, the journalistic comedy *Fink und Fliederbusch* premieres at the Volkstheater. The audience receives it well, but, as was to be expected, the newspaper critics do not. In view of the usual "barking of the anti-Semitic rabble,"[276] the press club "Concordia" considers legal proceedings, but holds back in the end. Schnitzler's friend Raoul Auernheimer is one of the few journalists who does not feel attacked and insulted by the play.

In December 1917, Schnitzler is content with the lucrative sales of *Doctor Gräsler*, and regrets that, in all likelihood, he will not be able to finish his autobiography. On Christmas Day, he writes in his diary: "I am very much preoccupied with thoughts of posterity – but without any trace of vanity. As if I had to speak to friends who are not yet born."[277]

The End of the War

In the last year of the war, paper is scarce. Schnitzler's correspondence with Fischer testifies to this serious concern of his, because his income is directly dependent on the number of printed and sold copies of his books. His literary colleagues are in the same predicament, and complain to Fischer whenever another author's book is published as opposed to their own. It speaks not only for Schnitzler's reputation, but also for Fischer's appreciation of him, that the publisher gives in to his Austrian author's insistence and founds a Viennese branch of his publishing house – which

276 TB 1917–19, 13.12.1917.
277 Ibid., 25.12.1917.

then publishes primarily Schnitzler's work. The print run of *Casanova's Heimfahrt,* which is published in this year, continues to increase beyond his lifetime.[278]

In the meantime, his relationship with Olga deteriorates further. There is no chance of real reconciliation, only a temporary ceasefire. Schnitzler's nerves are stretched to the breaking-point, and Olga's accusations border on the hysterical. On 6 May, 1918, the diary reads:

> The discussion [she would receive no invitations without his permission, likewise for him, "limitations on freedom"] escalates quickly – although I at first refuse and remind her that she has to sing today and tomorrow.
>
> […] I take my sorrowful morning walk and, as I return, I find her more incensed than ever; she can't stand it anymore – I torment her – not this last matter, no, for years, my probing, etc.; – I remind her – it has been a long time since there could be any talk of probing into the soul; and that the bad moods of the last months have regularly resulted from her song-and-career calamities. By the way, she's simply standing by the word that she gave me ten years ago: if she didn't make progress as an artist, there would be catastrophe. – The discussion intensifies – we should, she finally says, only live side-by-side in the same house. I should find that enough, that she should be the mother of my children etc., and not stop her, by the way […], otherwise she'll leave. I reply that I can't possibly obligate myself in advance to approve of everything it occurs to her to do – and, naturally, would not hold her back if she wanted to leave. Then she became completely furious – and declared that she hated me. Whereupon I left the room without a word.

Barely a week later, one day before his birthday, Schnitzler writes:

> What is actually going on here –? What I have already experienced at times – the agony of love – this time particularly

278 Wagner, pp. 302–3.

> long and painful – because the relationship was so extremely strong, – and because of the attending circumstances. – For manifold reasons we aren't succeeding – as is the case in so many marriages – in letting it end: – not to make too many demands. In addition, her basic error – and mine, too; – I see no hope; except to summon all one's strength to kill what's left of erotic feeling – to withdraw completely into oneself. – It didn't have to come to this, if discontent didn't fester in her like a disease, and in me, that which she calls my "possessiveness addiction" were not so highly developed... It's only that without the latter – we would have long ago separated. – Tomorrow is my birthday – I'm almost afraid of the deceptive mood of reconciliation; – because it's a lost cause. – and another injection of camphor will change nothing.[279]

As Olga has learned of her husband's feelings for Stephi Bachrach, she confides more and more of her side of the story in the pianist Wilhelm Gross, whom she regularly meets for practice sessions in the Sternwartestrasse. It is also because Schnitzler suspects an affair that he begins to prepare himself for a divorce.

On November 11, the armistice is agreed on. Peace brings with it grave economic and social instability. What began as an uprising of sailors in Kiel spreads throughout Germany as a revolution. Revolutionary currents eventually reach Austria. There, Emperor Karl I abdicates on November 11, bringing to an end the centuries-old Habsburg monarchy that ruled Austria without interruption since 1282, and, in the 16th and 17th centuries, governed over a large portion of Europe.

The collapse of the old government also means the end of censorship. The director of the Volkstheater, Alfred Bernau, immediately begins preparations to perform *Professor Bernhardi* on a Vienna stage for the first time. The premiere takes place on December 20. Schnitzler notes in his diary that it was, probably, the most successful performance he ever saw.[280] Returning home from the theater, however, he is confronted with sober

279 TB 1917–19, 6. & 14.5.1918.

280 Ibid., 22.12.1918.

reality: both food and coal are in short supply, as are many other goods that were everyday staples before the war. The political situation is highly unstable, and there are the first signs of inflation. Schnitzler is suffering from the constant buzzing in his ears, and he thinks back to the years of safety and stability before 1914.[281]

281 Ibid., 31.12.1918.

A NEW AGE 1919–1922

During the first months of 1920, Schnitzler goes through his diaries after 1911 again, weighing the height of his literary reputation against the instability and dangers of the present.[282] During this period, he would rather read Theodor Fontane than contemporary authors.[283]

The war is completely overlooked in Schnitzler's work, with the exception of the *Komödie der Verführung* from 1924. Here Schnitzler does without the usual stage direction "Vienna – Present." Instead, he specifies that the three acts play out respectively on May 1, the middle of June, and August 1, 1914. Aside from the occasional reference to the deteriorating political situation, the war itself is not mentioned. Possibly, the year was chosen to emphasize a certain decadence in the aristocratic milieu, which is the setting for the three primary relationships of the play. The coming defeat in the war is prefigured by the tragic destiny of the heroine. In the third act, shortly before her death, the declaration of war is posted on the hotel's bulletin board.

Schnitzler's preoccupation with historical material during the war years appears to justify his critics when they label him a "poet of a sunken world." Furthermore, Schnitzler feels strongly repelled by Expressionism. To his friends, he protests against the "hateful atmosphere" of the contemporary literature.[284] And yet, it offends him to be dismissed as an author of a vanished epoch. In the following years, he creates two masterworks of literary modernism, *Fräulein Else* (1924) and *Traumnovelle* (1925). Furthermore, Schnitzler is an avid movie-goer and repeatedly collaborates on scripts for film versions of his works. The last project before his death is a script for a "crime film." Why did Schnitzler not publicly defend himself against the accusations of being, to a certain extent, passé? One reason is certainly his convictions: "My position is to rise above the times – not to go

282 TB 1920–1922. 22. & 30.5.1920.

283 Ibid., Stine 21.2., Poggenpuhls 20.4., Effi Briest 25.4., Kriegsgefangen 4.6.1920.

284 Ibid., 31.7.1920.

along with them (at the rate of journalists, politicians and speculators.)[285]

"Statements of Justice and Peace among Peoples"—Schnitzler's Views on the Armistice of 1918

> The Emperor's abdication. Hohenzollern and Habsburg within three days. – The awful, nonsensical terms of the armistice with Germany. The Entente is overstretching their bounds. Supposedly, the workers' and soldiers' councils are fraternizing at the front.

Thus runs Schnitzler's diary entry for November 11, 1918, on the day when the weapons were finally silenced in the bloodiest war in world history until that time. Although Schnitzler had not made any political statements during the war, he was not neutral. In a letter to his publisher, Samuel Fischer, he defends the Austrian cause, when Fischer maintains that the Austrian army did not fight with as great a determination as the German army. Schnitzler mentions the "readiness for sacrifice and the impulse to help" among the Austrian population, as well as the army's military achievements.[286] This is an expression of Schnitzler's attachment to his native country, or "Heimat" – which he carefully distinguishes from the political construct of the state. Two days before the proclamation of the republic, he notes laconically:

> About the upheavals. – I see no grounds for rejoicing yet. – Forms of state mean nothing, show me the one or several persons I can stake my hopes upon, – in Germany – or even in our country ... The same people who still cheered the Emperor 4 years ago, – 1 year ago, and who shout today: Long live the republic.

When the republic is actually declared, Schnitzler remains true to his fundamental skepticism of all political doings. On that day, he records

285 Briefe 1913-1931, p. 561.
286 Ibid., p. 46.

in his diary shootings provoked by the "Red Guard," and a profusion of contradictory news in the papers and by telephone. He concludes: "An important day in world history is over. Up close, it doesn't seem all that grand."

In the beginning of November, Schnitzler notes in his diary an incident that occurs on the Schwarzenbergplatz, which an acquaintance recounted:

> Schwarzenbergplatz: [Schmutzer reported an experience of Engelhart (painter)] A citizen came out of the public lavatories on Schwarzenbergplatz still occupied with putting his clothes in order – at that moment, a troop with red banners comes past. The citizen ... completely at a loss – "Well, what's going on–? Another says to him: Well, don't you see it. It's a coup! – The first (still buttoning up): What do you mean? A coup? The other, Well, yes. A coup. The first: What kind of coup? – The other: Just a coup – Dunno anymore. Schönherr deduces from this that in Vienna there's no soil for Bolshevism!

But the reality is, however, less funny than brutal: Alone in the fall of 1918, Schnitzler records three pogroms, one in Posen and two in Galicia, one of them particularly cruel.[287] On October 13, he hears from his friend Leo Van-Jung that houses are also being marked for a pogrom in Vienna. One week later, Schnitzler admits that he is harbouring "the worst expectations." In the beginning of November, he writes that one should, especially as a Jew, "be calm – but prepared for anything."[288] During this period, Schnitzler's packed suitcases are always ready, so that the family can flee in case of a pogrom. He had already ordered a passport in August.

Why had the situation deteriorated to this extent? There was a lack of everything in Vienna, as the British blockade, in spite of the end of hostilities, still remained in place for months until March of 1918.[289] Most pressing was the shortage of food, which remained acute until late 1919. Schnitzler records a visit to his brother-in-law's clinic, where the

---

287 TB 1917-1919, 27. & 18.11., 31.12.1918.

288 see also Ibid., 13.10., 21.10. & 3.11.1918.

289 Ibid., 8.3.1919.

tracheotomy patients, unable to speak, are pleading for food with gestures. All they receive is a sheep's milk cheese.

Christian Social and Pan-German activists blamed the inflation of the immediate post-war years as well as the defeat in general on Jewish war profiteers.[290] George Berkley points out that this was, at least partially, the result of the break-up of the Habsburg monarchy. Whereas the German Austrians were used to blaming their problems on the Jews, Czechs and Hungarians, now the Jews were the only scapegoats left. As such, they came to bear the full brunt of the frustration and desperation of the lost war.[291]

And yet, in 1914, the Jews of Vienna had hoped that it would be exactly the war that would put an end to anti-Semitism. Here, at last, was the opportunity to prove that they could defend their fatherland just as well as their Christian countrymen. The Austrian-Israelite Union, while advocating loyalty to the state, and at the same time trying to sustain a unique Jewish identity, issued a statement when the war broke out:

> With the blood of our children [...] we want to prove to this state, that we are its loyal citizens, as good as any other. [...] After this war, with all its terrors, there must be no more anti-Semitic harassment in Austria. [...]
>
> We will fight for our full, unlimited equality, for the unconditional acknowledgment of our rights as citizens.[292]

These aspirations were not fulfilled. Throughout the war, both in Germany and Austria, there was an unofficial understanding between the political parties known as the "Burgfriede," invoking the image of peace within a beleaguered fortress. In the first months of the war, this meant a noticeable cutback on anti-Semitic attacks in the press. But already in December 1914, Schnitzler had to defend himself against accusations

290 Pauley, pp. 71, 80.

291 George Berkley: *Vienna and Its Jews: The Tragedy of Success 1880–1980*. Cambridge, MA: Madison 1988, p. 149.

292 Monatsschrift der Österreichisch-Israelitischen Union. Vienna, July–August 1914, p. 2. Cited in Pauley, p. 61.

in Russian propaganda that he had issued derogatory statements not only against Tolstoy, but also against Maeterlinck, Anatole France, and Shakespeare.[293] Schnitzler's public denial of this was taken by the anti-Semitic press as solidarity with the enemy, and interpreted as a lack of patriotism. The *Reichspost* named Schnitzler as well as the Zionist Max Nordau as "internal enemies" and as "wolves in sheep's clothing." According to the *Deutsche Tageszeitung.* "Schnitzler & Co." were German only in the "geographical-political sense."[294] The brief period of calm for the Jewish community of Vienna was over. By January, 1915, Schnitzler had determined that the anti-Semitic attacks had reached pre-war levels, and he remarked on the hollowness of the phrase "Burgfriede."[295]

In the context of intensified post-war anti-Semitism, the Galician refugees from the east of the failed monarchy constituted a major problem. Even before the war, the orthodox, Yiddish-speaking Eastern Jews had made up a visibly foreign element in the city. Because their homeland Galicia had been the scene of repeated Russian invasions up to 1917, the number of Jewish refugees in Vienna steadily increased since 1914. The Russian army occupied Galicia until late 1915, during which time the area was subject to extensive pogroms against Jewish "spies," who were allegedly spying for Austria. During this period alone, 125,000 mostly penniless refugees streamed into Vienna.[296] The increasing aversion to this human misery on the part of a large portion of the Viennese population was aggravated by the lack of food.

This situation had gone so far that charitable associations ran collections nominally for Galician, not for Jewish refugees, although the terms were, in this case, synonymous. In a letter to the journalist Adolf Gelber at the end of 1915, Schnitzler mentions that, as the committee explained to him, this was done "out of consideration for the feelings and opinions in certain influential and official circles," since otherwise "the practical success of the

293 Briefe 1913–31, p. 60.

294 Reichspost (24.1.1915), p. 9. Cited in: Richard Miklin: Untersuchungen zu Arthur Schnitzlers Tagebuch der Kriegsjahre 1914–1918. Diss. Univ. Vienna 1987, p. 41. Deutsche Tageszeitung cited in Briefe 1913–31, p. 860. See also Schnitzlers letters to Paul Block: Briefe 1913–31, p. 76.

295 Briefe 1913–31, p. 77.

296 Riedmann, p. 45.

entire scheme could be called into question."[297]

Even after the war, Galicia remained the scene of bloody conflict, as both Poland and Russia claimed the border region. This meant that the refugees could not return. By 1923, the Jewish population of Vienna reached a record high of 200,000, or 10% of the population.[298] This increase was visible in the city and fuelled the population's anxiety about a perceived "Jewish Flood." Anti-Semitic groups escalated the situation by claiming there were between 500,000 and 600,000 Jewish refugees in Vienna, and by making them responsible for the city's serious housing problem. Such demagogues as Walter Riehl, the founder of the Austrian Nazi Party, openly called for the expulsion of Eastern Jews. That anti-Semitic rallies managed to attract thousands of spectators led the *Ostdeutsche Rundschau* to comment that the citizens of Vienna were "much more anti-Semitic now" than they had been in the 1890's.[299]

It was not exactly an advantage that the deputies of the Social Democrats – which, under Karl Renner, was perceived by many to be a "Jewish Party" – signed the Peace Treaty of St. Germain. Otto Bauer was a prominent Jewish party member who occupied the post of foreign minister and, in this function, had participated in the Versailles conference. He refused, however, to put his signature to the peace treaty, since the Allies denied Austria the option of uniting with Germany. So it happened that the humiliating document, which sealed Austria's defeat and division, was signed by the Chancellor, Karl Renner, who was, in fact, not Jewish.[300] In public opinion, however, that counted for very little. The humiliation and hardship of the lost war was too great for such fine distinctions.

On June 3, 1919, Schnitzler records in his diary:

> The Entente's conditions of peace for us. – Words cannot express it. – Not what is happening here is the outrageous thing, in my opinion – a triumph is there to be exploited. But these phrases of justice and peace we keep hearing [...] they are what is new.

---

297 Briefe 1913–1931, p. 111.

298 Berkley, p. 150.

299 Pauley, pp. 80–81.

300 Ibid., pp. 81–82.

> Cruelty, power madness, crime and idiocy – these things repeat themselves in all "great periods in history" [...], but lies [...] without purpose, without wit, without meaning or greatness, – these we are experiencing for the first time.

What Schnitzler meant was the exception made for Austria, as a defeated power, from Wilson's programme of national self-determination. Predominantly German-speaking lands were given to Czechoslovakia and Yugoslavia, while South Tyrol, with 250,000 Austrians, was ceded to Italy.[301] Schnitzler was disgusted with what he considered the blatant injustice practiced by the victorious powers in the name of peace, humanity, and national self-determination.[302]

Schnitzler felt that there was a certain deception behind Wilson's ostentatious honesty. In his diary, he mentions Wilson's "mendacity" and his "deceptiveness," in spite of Wilson's pose as the liberator of oppressed ethnic groups, and as the honest "broker of peace in Europe." To Clemenceau's public statement that Austria deserved the misery that it was experiencing, Schnitzler replies, on November 28, 1919: "The full, shameless mendacity of the pur sang politician; the tremendous unscrupulousness of this breed shows itself in these official statements."

The "Anschluss" as a Feasible Option?

Many Austrians did not believe that the leftover rump state of German Austria would survive alone economically. One month before the calling into being of the Republic, Schnitzler writes: "Grim situation in the world, in Austria in particular. A federal state that nobody wants. Less than a month later, on November 12, the provisional National Assembly votes 164 to 165 for annexation by Germany. The Allies have, however, specifically forbidden a union of the two lands.[303]

Bound to his homeland as Schnitzler is, and as a decided opponent

301 Berkley, pp. 142–43.

302 TB 1917–1919, 4.11.1918, 3.6, 11.6., 25.6.1919.

303 Berkley, pp. 142–43.

of this pan-German propaganda, Schnitzler cannot drum up enthusiasm for unification plans. On January 6, 1919, he writes about the stupidity of annexation by Germany at this moment." Only five days later, he admits, however, "I ask what G. Aust. [German Austria] should do, which economically can't manage alone, since [...] the Czechs are irreconcilable in their hatred?" In addition, he mentions a possible "Swissification" of Austria, and also interjects a note of humour, that the country would then really be "a realm of artists and waiters."

In spite of his considerable fear of a Bolshevist uprising, Schnitzler does not see the country's salvation in an "Annexation" to Germany. The neighboring country has, after all, its own problems in this regard, as both Berlin and Munich, in the immediate post-war years, become showcases for different coup attempts, from the right as well as from the left. There is the proclamation of the "Räterepublik" in Bavaria in 1919; the Kapp-Putsch in Berlin in 1920; and, naturally, also the Hitler Putsch in the inflation year of 1923.

More than once, Schnitzler acknowledges a generally negative attitude toward a possible "Anschluss": "The annexation question. Basically, opinion is everywhere against it – even among those who propagate it for reasons of party politics."[304] In regard to the developments in Germany, he writes on May 20, 1919: "Nationalism – ? Bolshevism – ? German-Austria dragged into it –? The end of the world –?" Although Schnitzler was perhaps still undecided in January, by May, he had apparently arrived at the opinion that Austria would be better off solving its problems alone.

The fact is, that for all his skepticism of Expressionism and also of contemporary political developments, it becomes clear that Schnitzler is more invested in the new era than his critics would have us believe. He embraces the latest technological developments: He is greatly enthused by his first flight from Venice to Vienna. He is an avid cinema-goer, and is very interested in the artistic potential of film. In fact, throughout the 1920's, he must rely more and more heavily on his income from film rights as his literary income dwindles.[305] *The Affairs of Anatol* is already filmed by Cecil B. DeMille in 1921. *Der junge Medardus* finds its way to the screen

304 see also: TB 1917–1919, 24.4.1919.

305 Briefe 1913–31, p. 217–18.

in 1922. After a Danish production in 1914, *Liebelei* is filmed again in 1927. *Freiwild* is filmed in 1928, and *Fräulein Else* in 1929. In 1931, MGM studios creates *Daybreak*, starring Gloria Swanson, which is based on the novella *Spiel im Morgengrauen.*

In Berlin, in January, 1919, the Spartakus uprising is violently put down by the conservative Freikorps militias, groups of former military soldiers that continue to remain active. Two of the worker-leaders, Karl Liebknecht and Rosa Luxemburg, are murdered. In Vienna, the times are no less chaotic. In these days, during the ongoing crisis of Schnitzler's marriage with Olga, two new women come into his life. The first is Hedy Kempny, a 24-year-old girl who is well-read, vivacious and who, in February, asks him by letter for a meeting. The other is Vilma Lichtenstern, a doctor's wife, whom he met in Reichenau. She is six years older than Hedy and for Schnitzler an important confidante – one whom he can entrust with his marital dilemma. After Schnitzler's divorce two years later, the public counts on his marrying Vilma. But in spite of their affection for each other and all of their mutual support in these difficult years, the two cannot bring themselves to take this decisive step.

From a literary point of view, 1919 is not a good year for Schnitzler. *Die Schwestern* is published in the Fischer Verlag to moderate success. In addition to *Professor Bernhardi,* for which, in October, Schnitzler receives the Volkstheater Prize, a few Viennese theaters stage *Ruf des Lebens* and *Freiwild.* However, because of his continual conflict with Olga and the resulting psychological stress, he can hardly concentrate on his work. In a diary entry from August, he compares the present situation with Olga to the nadirs of earlier relationships: the farewell from Olga Waissnix in Reichenau; the letter of Mizi Glümer in which she justifies taking up an engagement in Wiesbaden – where she consoled herself with someone else; the morning after the death of Marie Reinhard, when he realised that she was gone forever. "How thoroughly, how all-too-thoroughly, I understand all this!" he concludes. "And yet – it is the end […]"[306]

At the beginning of the following year, Schnitzler discusses the

306 TB 1917–19, 22.8.1919

performance of *Die Schwestern oder Casanova in Spa* with the director and the actors of the Burgtheater. Interestingly, Hugo von Hofmannsthal has also written a play about Casanova, which shows a parallel with Schnitzler's idea at least in the title – in the novella *Casanovas Heimfahrt: Cristinas Heimreise*. At the premiere on March 26, Schnitzler is called to take a curtain call several times. Although not all the critics are impressed, the play is popular with the audience, and stays on the programme for a further three years, with 24 performances.

In the same month, Schnitzler signs a contract for the filming of *Der junge Medardus*. This brings in much-needed financial relief in difficult times, but the news that Olga's sister Liesl is very ill casts a shadow over this fortunate turn of events. Despite his longing for Olga – "rather for her who she once was for me, and who she will never, never, never be again" – he is relieved that she will spend a few days with her sister.[307]

Even if, already in the autumn of 1919, anti-Semitic demonstrations with several thousand people are conducted, the largest gathering of anti-Semites in terms of numbers takes place from March 11 to 13, 1921. Forty-thousand participants travel from Germany, Czechoslovakia, and Hungary. Austria is represented by delegates from 62 anti-Semitic associations, which number 400,000 members altogether. The event is organised by the Austrian "Antisemitenbund" (Anti-Semitic Union) under its leader, Dr. Anton Jerzabek. Among other demands, they ask for the withdrawal of citizenship for Jews, and the reduction of the number of Jewish university and high-school students, as well as the deportation of all Jews who immigrated to Vienna after April 1, 1921.[308]

After a decline in numbers in 1922, the year 1923 again brings out a massive contingent of 20,000 to 100,000 in a march organised by the "Völkisch-antisemitischer Kampfausschuss" (Popular Antisemitic Fighting Committee) between the city hall and the Burgtheater. Several paramilitary organizations make an appearance, among them the Austrian National Socialists. The speakers demand that the government classify the Jews as a separate, non-German people, and also the institution of a quota system

307 TB 1920–22, 16.3.1920.

308 Pauley, pp. 82–83.

not only for the universities, but for all public offices.[309]

In light of the worsening inflation, Schnitzler is very grateful for the $4,000 that the film rights for *The Affairs of Anatol* bring him. This silent movie by Cecil B. DeMille takes considerable liberties with both characters and plot, but an income in foreign currency is much more secure than in Austrian crowns. Compared to book sales and stage rights, in the economic turmoil of the post-war period, only film rights are actually lucrative. Nevertheless, one particular work will relieve him of all financial trouble, even if it is torn to shreds by the critics, and its performance results in legal proceedings against him: the *Reigen.*

Scandals and Court Cases Surrounding the *Reigen* — The Berlin Trial

Already in April of 1919, Max Reinhardt proposes to Schnitzler in a letter: "I consider the performance of your work not only opportune, but completely desirable." Fischer also makes the cautious suggestion, "Maybe you shouldn't maintain your standoffish attitude toward the performance. In our liberated times, doubt and hesitation are not as determinant as before [...]. Schnitzler had still resisted having *Reigen* performed in 1917, but after being approached by these two individuals, he changes his attitude. Reinhardt, however, gives up the leadership of the group of Berlin Theaters to Felix Holländer, with whom Schnitzler considers a staging in the Kleines Schauspielhaus.[310]

The premiere of *Reigen,* which he had written over twenty years before, takes place on December 23 at the Kleines Schauspielhaus. The play had already been published before the First World War, but it never before shown on the stage – with the exception of a Hungarian performance in Budapest in 1912, which was not approved by Schnitzler. Just before the premiere, the Prussian Ministry of Education and the Arts prohibits the staging,

309 Ibid.

310 Gerd K. Schneider: Die Rezeption von Arthur Schnitzlers Reigen 1897–1994. Riverside, CA: Ariadne, 1995, pp. 92–93.

since the play is considered obscene. A temporary injunction on behalf of the Hochschule für Musik, which owns the Kleines Schauspielhaus, forbids the performance of *Reigen* on pain of imprisonment. Because this interdiction only occurs on the scheduled day of the performance, whereas the actors are rehearsed and the house is sold out, the Directress of the theater goes in front of the curtain, informs the public of the situation, and nevertheless, lets the play be performed. The play is a success, and the critics are also positive, aside from the usual anti-Semitic attacks. Besides the sexual license of the plot, the critics are also offended by the ban. As so often in the history of theater, it is the ban itself along with the spiciness of the plot that ensures the popularity of this ten-scene sequence. In Berlin, the ban is provisionally lifted on December 25, in all likelihood due to pressure from the reviewers.[311]

But in the *Deutschvölkische Blätter*, the organ of the "Deutscher Schutz- und Trutzbund" (German Protective and Defensive League) it says that the leader of the political department of the Berlin Police, Bernhard Weiss, had "facilitated the commercial greed of Jewish sexual speculators," as well as the "systematic destruction of the German soul in Jewish theaters." The demonstrators in Berlin are "martyrs for German morals and respectability," and it is now up to the national government to legally ensure that art, through the rapid exclusion of Jews, is cleansed from Jewish amorality and the green of mammon." To name only one further example out of many, it is noted that the *Tägliche Rundschau* of February 25, 1921, which is close to the German National People's Party, claims that, through the performance of *Reigen,* the celebration of Jesus' birthday was desecrated in a Satanic fashion.[312]

In January of the same year, the well-known publicist Maximilian Harden, who became famous in the days of the Empire for his critical posture toward William II, launches, in his magazine *Die Zukunft*, vicious attacks on Schnitzler's "coital conversations." He states that Schnitzler's artistic development has gone wrong and is angry about the unveiling of the secret "of the highest sexual communion."[313] Beginning in February, it

311 Farese, p. 216.

312 cited in Beier, pp. 535–36.

313 Schneider, p. 108.

becomes obvious that Harden's criticism does not hold water, as Schnitzler makes clear that it was not he who tried to persuade Max Reinhardt to stage *Reigen* but the other way around. Reinhardt had approached him in order "to be the first to shake my own opinion as to the un-stageability of *Reigen*.[314] On July 3, 1922, Harden is himself attacked with an iron bar by members of the radical right-wing "Organisation Consul," most likely because of his support for the Republic and the Russian Revolution, and barely escapes with his life. This is the same group that had carried out the assassination of Walther Rathenau nine days previously.

But Schnitzler has in no way put the turbulence around *Reigen* behind him. In Berlin, he has to fight in the courts. The basic trial only lasts three days, January 3 to January 6, 1921. The critic Alfred Kerr is summoned as an expert witness. The court proceedings end with the temporary injunction being lifted.

In Leipzig, everyone who wants to buy a ticket for the performance on January 22, 1921, must sign a statement, "to raise no objections to the content of the scenes," and to use the tickets "only for himself or to pass them on only to a like-minded person who is not under eighteen."[315]

In Berlin, on February 22, it comes to a proper theater scandal, if not to the same degree as will occur when the play is staged in Vienna. Stink bombs are thrown, but the police are able to arrest the activists. The play is interrupted for the theater to be aired out, but then continues.[316]

In November of the same year, *Reigen*, does in fact, come before the court again. Even though actors were acquitted of amoral behaviour in January, the play itself was found to be "objectively amoral."[317] The trial lasts from November 5 to 18, and this case also ends with the acquittal of all participants. The councillor Prof. Dr. Karl Brunner, who worked in the "Central Office for Combatting Improper Performances and Writing," had pushed for the second trial. He now had, in addition to a public defeat, the

---

314 Arthur Schnitzler: Berichtigung. In: Neues Wiener Journal, 30.1.1921 (Morgenausgabe), cited in: Schneider p. 109.

315 Schneider, pp. 231–32.

316 TB 1920–22, 23.2.1921.

317 Schneider, p. 194.

court costs to pay for.[318] After these second proceedings, the Berlin public gradually loses interest in the *Reigen.*

The Viennese Scandal

The Viennese premiere scheduled for February 1, 1921, is completely sold out. At the beginning of the year, the latest news on the legal difficulties surrounding *Reigen* is still fresh. In fact, the premiere at the Vienna Volkstheater is a success. In the course of this year, because of the high demand, an extra night-time performance must be added on, in addition to the evening performance.[319] Admittedly, the Christian Social papers complain about the piece, most loudly among them the *Reichspost.* It claims that the theater, through Schnitzler's newest work, is becoming a "brothel" and a "whorehouse."[320] How little these journalists understand of the author's actual intentions is shown by a letter to Schnitzler's Berlin friend Dora Speyer, in which he speaks of the "tremendous alienation between men and women" that he tried to portray, and suggests *Der einsame Weg* as a subtitle for *Reigen.*[321]

The shows on February 7 and 8 are disturbed by an anti-Semitic "paid rabble." In addition, the clerical papers agitate vigorously against the play, and on February 11, this leads to the desired ban by the federal government, "for reasons of peace, order and morality."[322] These reasons are exactly the same as those given for the ban on *Professor Bernhardi.* However, the mayor of the city of Vienna, Jakob Reumann, does not, in fact, enforce the ban on the theater. In addition to the personal attitude of the mayor toward *Reigen,* these different approaches are explained by a Christian Social majority in the federal government, versus a Social Democratic majority in the city council.[323] The play's performance plunges the young Austrian state into a

318 Ibid., pp. 193–97.

319 Ibid., pp. 328, 333.

320 Reichspost, 1.2.1921, cited in: Schneider, p. 126.

321 Ibid.

322 "Illustriertes Wiener Extrablatt," 10.2.1921. In: Schneider p. 136.

323 Wagner, p. 334.

short-term conflict between the city and the federal government regarding their division of political authority.

In this connection, an article in the morning edition of the *Illustriertes Wiener Extrablatt* of February 19, 1921, is of interest. Not only is it pointed out that the Vienna Police President Johann Schober, although he himself is against the staging of the play, will not enforce the ban. Furthermore, the differences among the performances in Berlin, Munich and Vienna are discussed:

> In Berlin, there were, because of the *Reigen*, also conflicts and partisanship. But it is the case in Germany's capital city that the courts have recognised: Schnitzler's *Reigen* does not appear capable of harming the sensibilities of the audience. In Berlin, the play is repeatedly performed without any trouble. One has yet to hear of any disturbances. As opposed to Munich, where it has come to excesses, as our readers are already aware. In Munich, a ban was passed and the Munich example now seems to be what the Austrian minister has in mind.[324]

Also, on February 11, Social Democrat deputies in parliament lodge a protest against the ban. The progressive parties and their conservative opponents whip up such a fury, that they begin to assault each other physically. The Christian Social deputies revile the Social Democrats as "Jews, Jewish pigs, Jewish baggage."[325] One day later, the federal government sues Mayor Reumann before the constitutional court.[326] The *Reichspost* writes, on February 14: "Schnitzler is a Jew, Bernau is a Jew – social democracy has once more [...] proven itself to be the protector of Jewry."[327] Even worse, on February 16, the *Obersteirerblatt* opines: "The Social Democrats (or rather, their circumcised and uncircumcised leaders) for racial reasons give official protection to indecency as the pleasure of rich smugglers and wastrels."[328]

---

324 Schneider, p. 136.
325 Ibid., p. 143.
326 Wagner, p. 332.
327 cited in: Wagner and Vacha, p. 119.
328 Schneider, p. 164.

Protesters march through Vienna shouting anti-Semitic slogans such as "Pfui, Jewish vermin." The later Chancellor, Ignaz Seipel, states at a meeting of the "Volksbundes der Katholiken Österreichs" (People's Union of Austrian Catholics), that the "moral feeling of the native Christian population [...] has been most gravely offended by the performance of a dirty play from the pen of a Jewish author."[329] The director of the Volkstheater, Alfred Bernau, receives anonymous letters threatening riots at his theater and threatening him with violence, even death.

On February 12, Schnitzler is asked in an interview with the *Illustrierte Wiener Extrablatt,* if he could finally make some changes to *Reigen.* To which he replies: "After I have finally decided on a performance, nothing will be stricken. No scene will be left out and there's no question of going back. However, I have no objection to changes in the stage direction."[330]

Just as with *Professor Bernhardi,* it is not only the parliament, but the liberal and clerical press that are divided into two enemy camps. German nationalist groups protest in front of theaters against the *Reigen*, impeding the ticket sales so that the police have to restrain them.[331] As before, the theaters in both Germany and Vienna are overflowing at performances.

On the evening of February 16, visitors to the Volkstheater are attacked by protesters. The next day, the *Arbeiter-Zeitung* reports that women had clothes torn from their bodies and that the men who tried to defend them were beaten bloody. According to the *Neues Wiener Journal*, stink bombs and tar-filled eggs were thrown.[332] The police arrested twenty people and had to use fire hoses to disperse the crowd. Because of these disturbances, the police institute a performance ban the next day. The anti-Semitic press rejoices. Schnitzler calls the incidents around the *Reigen* performances a "unique event in the history of theater."[333]

Shortly thereafter, Bernau files an appeal, after which the decision about a continuation of the performances reverts to the mayor. Schnitzler supports Bernau, who does not want to give up in the fight against the

329 Wagner, p. 332.
330 cited in: Schneider, pp. 151–52.
331 Wagner, p. 333.
332 cited in: Schneider, p. 165.
333 TB 1920-22, 16.2.1921.

clerical parties. Yet Police President Schober advises exactly that, in order to avoid a conflict of power between the federal and city governments.

The administrative court has acquitted Reumann of having ignored the instructions of the minister of education. However, he must still appear before the constitutional court in April. The question is whether the instruction to stop the performance of *Reigen* was merely personal advice, or an actual administrative directive. In the end, on April 29, Reumann is acquitted by the constitutional court as well, on the grounds that the minister had not signed his letter to the mayor himself.[334]

It is painful for Schnitzler that his long-time publisher Samuel Fischer, with whom he had worked so often successfully, and in whose publishing house he is a profitable author, does not want to print the *Reigen.* Fischer is afraid that the government will confiscate it, but Schnitzler considers that very unlikely. In a long letter to his publisher toward the end of his life, he again gives his opinion on this matter:

> You have, after long hesitation and vacillating, ultimately missed the opportunity, and I must, unfortunately, suppose that I, at the bottom of my heart, more deeply regret this lost chance – not a business opportunity, above all, a human one, than you, dear friend, have the right to do.
>
> Because, let me say it freely – already the consciousness that I personally, whether rightly or wrongly, seemed to lay a special value on seeing that *Reigen*, especially *Reigen,* finally takes its deserved place beside my other works in my life-long publishing house, – this alone might have, should have, must have been enough for you to further expedite an affair that obviously lay so close to my heart, and steadfastly to bring it to fulfilment than was, sadly, the case [...].[335]

In March 1922, Schnitzler has had enough of the uproar about *Reigen.* He also fears for the security of his audiences and lets the Fischer Verlag

334 Wagner, p. 335.

335 Letter dated 5. 4. 1930, in: Briefe 1913–1931, p. 677

know that he does not want to permit any further performances.[336] Only in 1981, nearly 60 years later, does his son Heinrich permit the play to be staged again. Since then, it has been regularly staged in Germany and Austria, and remains controversial.

Once more, in the run-up to the performance of a Schnitzler play, occurred what the author in *Professor Bernhardi* has dealt with on the stage: a major political scandal that only claims to be about morals and decency. Here manifests in reality what Schnitzler has already often enough put on record in his aphorisms. In this situation, friends and enemies are equally repugnant. In his diary, he notes on February 10, 1921: "The papers are full of *Reigen*. What deception. Politics. Enemy and friend both insincere. – Alone, alone, alone. –"[337]

336 Wagner, p. 337.
337 TB 1920–22, 10.2.1921.

PERSONAL AND NATIONAL CRISES

In the middle of the *Reigen* scandal, Schnitzler's marital situation deteriorates to an irreparable state. Already in September of 1920, Olga writes to him:

> What sense does it make for you and me to continue living side-by-side in such an agonizing way. When I am away, I always feel it most intensely, how oppressed and deeply tormented I am with you, how this perpetual mistrust undermines me and leaves me shaken in my whole being and essence. I am too old to be able to put up with this in the long run.[338]

From Schnitzler's perspective, as follows:

> [...] and you must see that this incorrectness [?] escalated to the grotesque because it had, earlier, repeatedly, and still does until now, leave the decision in <u>your</u> hands, – and [you] never, out of your own free will, had come to the decision to leave husband, home, and children.[339]

Meanwhile, the preparations for Schnitzler's divorce are in full swing. It takes place on June 22, 1921, in Munich, before the Rabbi David Feuchtwang. Olga would have been content with a civil divorce, but Schnitzler wants the assurance that she can never live with him again. In spite of many tears, and a scene in which his wife, a few weeks before the event, throws herself at his feet, Schnitzler sees his decision through.

However deeply affected Schnitzler is, for all his dismay, he is relieved that the divorce is now official. In the summer, which he spends at Altaussee near the Wassermanns, he has the inspiration for *Fraulein Else*. In autumn, he finds himself capable of working again, and continues with

338 DLA, Briefe Olga an Arthur Schnitzler, Folder 1223, 10.9.1920.
339 DLA, Briefe Arthur an Olga Schnitzler, Folder 530, 13.3.1921.

the *Doppelnovelle* and the *Verführer*.

All the while, the *Reigen* affair goes on. In early November, Berlin's public prosecutor opens proceedings against the director of the Kleines Schauspielhaus. After barely two weeks, as noted in the previous chapter, it ends with the acquittal of all accused.

On Schnitzler's 60th birthday, in May, in addition to performances of his dramas in Vienna and Berlin, there is a celebration in Tokyo. Japanese translators pay 40,000 Marks for the rights to his work. By the end of the year, he already receives the Japanese translations. Apart from this, the American publisher Scofield Thayer is interested in Schnitzler's novellas. He has them translated into English and printed in his journal *The Dial*. In April, Schnitzler goes on a financially very successful reading tour of the Netherlands. The Fischer Verlag publishes his collected works, with the prose and the dramatic works now each expanded by a second volume. Thus, at the beginning of his 61st year, Schnitzler sees the approval and admiration of his audience extend beyond the German-speaking countries, with not only a European, but a truly global readership. His popularity reaches to the far shores of the Atlantic and to the other end of the world, Japan.

On his 60th birthday, Sigmund Freud also congratulates him, paying him a tribute: "Yes, at the bottom of your soul, you are a seeker in the psychological depths, as honest, non-partisan and unafraid as anyone ever was." It is in the same letter that the famous Freud, "makes the private confession," that he had avoided Schnitzler until now "out of a kind of fear of his Doppelgänger."[340]

Already in May of 1906, Schnitzler congratulated Freud on his 50th birthday, saying that he was thankful for the "manifold powerful and deep stimulation of his writings."[341] In his letter of reply, Freud explains:

> For years, I've been aware of a far-reaching concordance that exists between your and my conceptions of certain psychological and erotic problems [...]. I have often wonderingly asked

340 Sigmund Freud: Briefe an Arthur Schnitzler. ed. by Heinrich Schnitzler. In: Die neue Rundschau 66 (1955), pp. 95–106, p. 97.

341 CUL, Briefe Schnitzler an Freud. Folder B 030, 6.5.1906.

> myself from whence you could have taken this or that intimate knowledge, which I attained through laborious research of the subject […]. Now, you can guess how happy and uplifting your lines were for me, in which you tell me that you have also been stimulated by my work. It is almost insulting that I had to become 50 years old in order to experience something that so honors me.[342]

On June 16, 1922, Schnitzler is a dinner guest in the Bergasse. He and Freud talk about their medical student days and the senior doctors with whom they did their internships. Charcot's works on hypnosis, which Schnitzler had reviewed in the *Internationale Klinische Rundschau* in 1892, are also to be found in Freud's library, which he shows Schnitzler after the meal. Freud gives Schnitzler the volume *Über Psychoanalyse,* which contains five lectures. He decides, in addition, to accompany Schnitzler the considerable distance to the Sternwartestrasse. Age and death are the themes of the two psychologists' personal conversation.

On August 16, Schnitzler visits Freud, who is just then vacationing at the Obersalzberg. They talk, among other things, about Gustav Mahler, who asked Freud for help in his difficult marital crisis. Mahler's last year of life was peaceful. After his conversation with Alma Mahler-Werfel, Schnitzler assumes this was owing to Freud's influence. The sentence that Schnitzler writes in his diary is noteworthy: "In his whole being, he attracted me again, and I experience a certain desire to converse with him over all sorts of low points in my work (and existence) – which I, however, would really rather not do."[343] After this visit, the contact became more tenuous. Very likely, the inhibition between the two spiritual brothers again won the upper hand.

Meanwhile, the political events of 1922 allow one to anticipate the coming dangers in Europe. In June, the German foreign minister, Walther Rathenau, is assassinated by nationalists. Rathenau embodied the inner conflict of a German-speaking Jew in that, in spite of his background, he published such critical essays as *Höre, Israel* (1897), which was directed

---

342 CUL, Briefe Freud an Schnitzler. Folder B 031, 8.5.1906.
343 TB 1920-22, 16.8.1922.

against Jewish nationalism and Zionism. For Rathenau, the cultural and political interests of Germany were paramount, and he fought for them as Foreign Minister in the chaotic post-war period. The tragedy that a man of such patriotic convictions should fall victim to radical right-wing assassins testifies to the increasing danger of blind anti-Semitism. By now, it must be taken seriously as a political force. Its members are apparently incapable of reflection or of making any distinctions between individual Jews.

In October, Mussolini marches on Rome. Soon after, Italy becomes the first fascist dictatorship in Europe. Thus, it becomes the role model for extreme right-wing movements in numerous European countries, such as Hungary, Spain, Austria, and, of course, Germany.

In early November, Schnitzler is confronted face-to-face with this new political force while on a reading tour. In Teplitz (today Teplice), in Czechoslovakia, "Swastikites," as he calls them in his diary, disturb a reading of his. They ask him loudly to read *Reigen,* and they cough continually or stomp their feet. When attendants and other members of the audience try to eject them from the room, the situation escalates into shouting and scuffles.[344] The main exits are blocked by numerous protesters, but the organizers manage to get Schnitzler out through a side exit. Then, something happens that could have been straight out of one of his own early stories: Two ladies step up to hook arms with him and, chattering away in Czech, lead him out of danger. The author himself remains quite calm and is able to see the humorous side of his narrow escape. Nevertheless, the protesters, who belong to the anti-Semitic association "Die Eiche" (The German Oak), had been waiting for him in front of the theater. The reading could have had a very different ending.[345]

As 1923 begins, the works with which Schnitzler is occupied are: *Der Gang zum Weiher, Doppelnovelle, Fraülein Else* und *Die Frau des Richters.* In Germany and Austria, hyperinflation has set in. The Mark is so devalued that it exceeds even the worst prognoses.

In all respects, the year 1923 is a destabilizing one for Germany. On October 3, Schnitzler writes to his now ex-wife: "The shouting, the yelling from the parties right and left, is so out-of-tune and loud that one is barely

344 Ibid., 3.11.1922.
345 Ibid., 4.11.1922.

capable of hearing the fine melody of Germany any longer." In November, Hitler, supported by the authoritative General Ludendorff, calls out a national revolution in Munich. The SA exchanges gunfire with the police. The name "Hitler," by the way, rarely occurs in the diaries. Schnitzler saw in him nothing more than just another nationalistically-minded agitator. The "Swastika-ism" [Hakenkreuzlerei] is, indeed, mentioned repeatedly in passing. But it is obvious that Schnitzler's greatest fear is a threatening Bolshevik revolution in the immediate post-war years, since such a revolution has been achieved in Russia as well as in neighboring Hungary.

With respect to literature, the year proves to be a relatively unproductive one. There are no new publications, even if the silent film, *Der junge Medardus,* premieres in Vienna on October 5. In autumn, Schnitzler resumes work on his play, *Der Verführer*, and on the short story, *Spiel im Morgengrauen,* which still carries the title, *Bezahlt.*

The women in his life at this time are Clara Pollaczek, with whom, since August, he has embarked on a liaison; Hedy Kempny, his much younger, somewhat eccentric friend, with whom he goes to the cinema; and the unhappily married Vilma Lichtenstern, who Schnitzler sees as an intellectual equal and companion.

The economic misery, aggravated by the catalyst of hyperinflation, causes a full-blown "hunger pogrom" from November 5 to 8 in Berlin – the first of its kind to take place in 20th-century Germany. A hungry, rebellious mob of 10,000 people enters the Jewish Scheunenviertel, where the residents are robbed and beaten. The plundering of local businesses can only be stopped by a massive police presence. Popular outbreaks against Jews also take place in Nuremberg and Königsberg. In some Bavarian cities, Eastern Jews are driven out, as in the Middle Ages.[346]

346 Aschheim, pp. 242–44.

THE LATE MASTERPIECES 1924–1928

Fräulein Else

The next year shows unmistakably that Schnitzler, in spite of the ailments of old age and ongoing personal problems, is capable of producing outstanding literary work. In June 1924, he completes *Fräulein Else*, the first sketches of which he had already drafted in December, 1922. Toward the end of the year, the novella is published by Fischer in book form. In this narrative in the form of an interior monologue, the character of Else emerges as the feminine counterpart of Leutnant Gustl. It is one of Schnitzler's best-known works, up to this day. By 1929, 70,000 copies have been sold.[347]

Fräulein Else is proof that, in the post-war years, Schnitzler did more than produce simple variations on his early characters, as some of his critics claimed. The use of the modern technique of the interior monologue to probe the female psyche is one innovation he introduced into the literature of the time. Furthermore, the realization that individual freedom of action or "free will" could be an illusion is the experience of a new, more merciless age. This realization is so devastating that it ultimately costs Else her life. It does not for a moment enter the head of her masculine counterpart, Lieutenant Gustl, because of his limitations. Else's fall illuminates just how vulnerable she – and the new age – is to economic and social pressures.

In *Fräulein Else,* the varied possibilities of the interior monologue are more fully exploited than in *Leutnant Gustl.* This narrative approach permits a dense plot concentrated over only a few hours. Towards the end, thanks to this narrative technique, the inner conflict of the protagonist is revealed, which results in two narrative voices: Else's words and actions on the one hand, and her thoughts on the other. Ultimately, a gap opens up between the reader and the narrator, in spite of the immediacy of the character's thought-world. The reason is exactly this proximity to Else's mental associative processes, which become increasingly strange as a function of

347 Wagner, pp. 353, 357.

the faster pace of the narrative and Else's growing confusion. Else no longer appears as a reliable narrator. Schnitzler uses the stream-of-consciousness initially to reinforce Else's credibility through direct glimpses into her psyche. Then, on the final pages, he destroys her credibility completely.

Another interesting technique is the insertion of staves of music on the last pages. From the first to the third insertion, the number of natural signs increases, which strip a note of its sharp or flat, as they reflect Else's descent into insanity. Furthermore, the alternation of these tones, taken from Schumann's *Carnaval*, mirrors Else's inner turbulence. Three crescendo signs in the last staff point up the plot's dramatic climax.[348]

Else is a modern woman in that she is not only fully aware of her physical attractions, but also of her sexual magnetism. She has a more natural relationship to her body than Schnitzler's female characters from earlier works. Both Berta Garlan and Beate Heinold were aware of their effect upon men, especially the latter, but neither of them stood in front of the mirror, like Else, and said, "Am I really as beautiful as in the mirror? Come closer, pretty young lady. I want to kiss your blood-red lips. I want to press your breasts against mine."

As a writer, Schnitzler is not interested in the emancipated actresses and artists, the bohemians enjoying their freedom on the fringes of society, but rather, in women like Miss Else who were firmly bound by middle-class conventions. Schnitzler shows Else's conflict with great clarity, and these stem partly from her own sexual drive. By having Else break down under Dorsday's desire to "see" her, he exposes the unjust and deceitful aspects of middle-class morality.

But Else's conflict is not, first and foremost, between libido and middle-class conceptions of decency, as it is for Berta Garlan and Beate Heinold. Else has two options for sexual fulfilment: the voluntary, with a man of her choice, and the imposed, in order to save her family. The dilemma no longer centers on the fear of being ostracised as the "fallen woman," as in the pre-war novels, but rather on her self-image and her sense of honor. For it is her feminine sense of honor, and not her pride, that drives her to suicide. She has no serious problem with showing herself to the hotel guests; she

348 Antonia Maria Caputo: Arthur Schnitzlers späte Werke. Munich: Uni-Druck 1983, pp. 118–21.

plays with the thought repeatedly. She is indifferent to her reputation in society. The key factor is her sense of shame. She does not want to show herself to this particular man, who is repulsive to her, and this aversion is irreconcilable with her sense of commitment to her family as a daughter.

Else is by no means a "süßes Mädel," but rather the child of a new, unstable era that has yet to find its bearings, but which offers decidedly more freedom than pre-war society. For exactly that reason it can provide no moral guidelines. This novella is a testimonial to the amorality of the post-war period, its financial insecurity, the demise of the old European order, and the general lack of orientation in society.

In September, rehearsals for the *Komödie der Verführing* begin at the Burgtheater. In this play, one of his last, Schnitzler conjures up a whole colorful series of representatives of the era before 1914: Lieutenant Leindorf and his fiancée Elisabeth; the banker Westerhaus, corrupt behind his respectable facade; Elegius Fenz, a singer who lives with his daughter Seraphine in modest circumstances; Prinz Arduin; and the painter Gysar. All are brought together in a comedy, in which they both spin intrigues against and fall in love with each other. We see situations borrowed from earlier Schnitzler works: from *Fräulein Else,* the well-regarded businessman involved in embezzlement, and from *Das Wort*, the painter who seduces his model, to name just two. For the first time, Schnitzler sets a play against the impending collapse of the Habsburg Monarchy. Whereas the first act is set in peacetime, on May 1, 1914, by the second act, it is mid-June – shortly before the assassination of Archduke Franz Ferdinand in Sarajevo on May 28. The last act is set on August 1, the day of the French mobilization and the German declaration of war on Russia.

Traumnovelle

The two publications of 1925 are *Die Frau des Richters* and *Traumnovelle,* Schnitzler's last prose masterpiece. Increasingly, there are differences with Fischer on the subject of royalties, so that Schnitzler enters into negotiations with the publisher Ullstein in addition to the publisher Zsolnay. *Die Frau des Richters* is, in the end, published by the former. Whereas this book does not exceed a print run of 10,000, one year later, Fischer reports sales of 30,000 for *Traumnovelle*.[349]

Recently, much has been written about the parallels between Stanley Kubrick's *Eyes Wide Shut* (1999) and the book on which it is based, *Traumnovelle*. Whereas there are obvious similarities in their plots, each remains an independent work, and the film can stand on its own merits. The haziness of the narrative perspective and the unreliability of the narrator's voice of the *Traumnovelle* are not reproduced in *Eyes Wide Shut*, where all events are depicted as real. In Schnitzler's novella, the reader is much less certain of what is actually happening and what is merely the product of Fridolin's overwrought nerves. In fact, the same dreamlike quality as in the final pages of *Fräulein Else* is extended over large sections of the narrative. This reflects both the modern literary phenomenon of calling into question the narrator's authority, and Schnitzler's own personal preoccupation with dreams. They have the power to throw a relationship, even a marriage, into crisis.

Schnitzler is less fortunate on the stage. *Der Gang zum Weiher*, which he completed in the summer, appeals neither to the director of the Burgtheater, Franz Herterich, nor to the directors of the Berlin theaters. Once more, Schnitzler has imposed verse on himself, in spite of the great effort and serious difficulties he encountered years earlier while working on *Der Schleier der Beatrice*. Once more, the credibility of the main characters suffers from the rules of the metric scheme, which hinder him from delineating the psychological motives behind their actions. Schnitzler is an author who, through his very precise reflection of Beate Heinold's psyche, is capable of making even incest comprehensible. In *Der Gang zum Weiher*, however, he fails to make either Leonilda's drive for independence or Thorn's suicide convincing. In contrast to the monologue novellas, *Fräulein Else* and *Leutnant Gustl*, in which the reader is brought as close to the characters as possible, the audience here is kept distant from them. Neither the characters nor their motives are depicted in detail, and therefore believably.

This is not because Schnitzler was not capable of doing so, for he had proven his abilities countless times. The fault lies in the use of verse rather than the everyday language that makes many of his other plays and

349 Wagner, p. 362.

prose so accessible. The play appears to be a later vestige of historicism, in particular of the interest in the Renaissance around the turn of the century. Granted, imposing 20th-century idiom on a play set 200 years previously would have been an anachronism. But both characters and plot would have been rendered much more credible if he had merely chosen to use historic language, as he did in *Der blinde Geronimo und sein Bruder* or in *Der grüne Kakadu*, which were not in verse.

Spiel im Morgengrauen and Lili's Love

A shocking indication of how drastically the situation in Europe in the post-war years has been radicalised is the death of the popular author Hugo Bettauer, who converted to protestantism. On March 10, 1925, he is shot to death in the editorial offices of his own journal. Bettauer's *Stadt ohne Juden* of 1922 is the dystopia of a city brought to its knees culturally by the Jews' expulsion. At the end of the novel, the mayor, who is strongly reminiscent of Lueger, asks the Jews to come back.[350]

Schnitzler's son Heinrich has been in Berlin for some time. He is active on several stages, while training to be an actor. He lives for the stage, both professionally and in his free time. In April, 1926, during a visit to Venice with her mother, Schnitzler's daughter Lili becomes infatuated with an officer of the fascist militia, Arnoldo Cappellini. She had already noticed him on a previous trip. Now she sees him again, entirely by chance, and follows him. When the military man turns around, they start to chat. They get to know each other better in the course of the visit. Cappellini reciprocates her feelings, and soon it is clear that their relationship is serious. Olga writes to her ex-husband:

> He is really an exemplary human being, and our child is in love for the first time, really in love, it seems to me. He is quite captivated, full of tact and very tender with her. – and it seems

350 Pauley, p. 102.

> that something very beautiful can develop out of this. We'll have to wait. We are together daily, and, observing him very closely, I like him extraordinarily. He is intelligent, interesting, a real man, – also with all the dark depths, but full of refined liveliness and of real nobility.[351]

In January 1927, Schnitzler meets his future son-in-law, and is also very favourably impressed. He approves of Cappellini's "unaffected manner," and his lack of vanity. He also appreciates that, out of personal conviction, Cappellini wants to stay with the militia in spite of his low income and meager prospects. At this juncture, it should be noted that although Mussolini had strong anti-Semitic leanings personally, the official governmental programme remained untouched by his prejudice. This situation changed only in the late 1930's, due to increasing cooperation with Hitler's Germany.

Schnitzler works on his aphorisms, which appear one year later in the *Buch der Sprüche und Bedenken.* Furthermore, he begins a philosophical project of human character types, which he entitles, *Der Geist im Wort und der Geist in der Tat.* It is based on the Sefiroth-Tree from the Book of Sohar. He also continues his second novel, *Therese* – working under time pressure, since he is dependent on the fees he expects from it.

The as-yet-to-be-performed *Gang zum Weiher* is published by Fischer at the beginning of 1926. At the end of the year, *Spiel im Morgengrauen* appears serialised in the *Berliner Illustrierte Zeitung* of the Ullstein Verlag, and in January in book form with Fischer.

Spiel im Morgengrauen takes us back to the years of imperial Austria, in the world of army officers, duels, and debts of honor. The protagonist, Lieutenant Wilhelm Kasda, tries to win at cards in order to pay the debts of a friend, Otto Bogner. As in *Der Sekundant*, where Schnitzler seems to evoke a certain sympathy for duelling, an institution that he frequently criticised, here, he sets the entire plot among a class he often ridiculed, whether in *Leutnant Gustl* or *Freiwild.* Perhaps he merely wants, in his old age, to understand more fully the characters and institutions of the pre-war

351 DLA, Briefe Olga an Arthur Schnitzler. Folder 1229, 22.9.1926.

era that he disapproved of. This would be in keeping with his continual, to some extent self-torturing, efforts at objectivity. Once more, the question of honor is central to Schnitzler's novella. According to the military code of honor, an officer was not allowed to incur debt. The options open to an officer who violated this code were already made clear in *Leutnant Gustl.*

The veil of nostalgia that enshrouds *Spiel im Morgengrauen* creates an atmosphere similar to Joseph Roth's *Radetzkymarsch.* However, in Schnitzler's narrative, by contrast, an acute sense of crisis dominates the plot. Schnitzler himself had a weakness for card games, billiards and horse races in his student days, and he would often lose considerable amounts of money. He was, therefore, able to draw on his own first-hand experience when describing the addictive qualities of gambling: the rush of winning and the enduring hope during an unlucky streak that the next round would change his fortunes. He had already once, in the early story *Reichtum*, dealt with a gambling addiction and its consequences. The exactness with which human emotions are depicted comes into full expression as Kasda visits Leopoldine. In his desperate situation, every expression of her lips and her eyes seems to impart hope.

After the weaker prose works of *Die Frau der Richter*, and *Der letzte Brief eines Literaten*, Schnitzler returns to his usual form with *Spiel im Morgengrauen.* This is a compelling drama in prose, stylistically excellent, with a well-structured, gradually unfolding plot that makes it a late masterpiece.

The premiere of the silent movie *Liebelei* takes place in March 1927, in Berlin. The cinema is significant for Schnitzler in several respects. In addition to his genuine interest in the new medium, the sale of film rights to his work in the 1920's is his primary source of income. Time and time again, he suggests such plays as the *Große Szene*, or such novels as *Fräulein Else,* for filming. With Schnitzler's openness to a new medium, he demonstrates that he is by no means the "author of yesterday" that some critics would have him be.

In February 1927, Schnitzler hears the news that Georg Brandes has passed away. The loss of his good friend, on whose honest and understanding verdict he could always rely, pains him greatly. Shortly before Vilma Lichtenstern's wedding, this good friend and kindred spirit is also taken from him, as she dies in a car accident.

Lili and Arnoldo marry on June 30. Schnitzler, who loves his daughter very much, has already rented a house for her in April. It is located, incidentally, right in Alma Mahler-Werfel's neighborhood. Schnitzler has declared himself ready to support the two financially.

The Palace of Justice in Flames

On July 14, 1927, the members of the "Frontkämpfervereinigung" (Front Fighters Association), are acquitted, although they had shot two people in an earlier clash with Social Democratic demonstrators. As the ruling becomes known on the following day, a furious crowd assembles before the Palace of Justice. The protest escalates to the extreme that the building is set on fire and the fire-fighting seriously hindered. The Police President Johann Schober has his men shoot first into the air and then into the crowd. Many contemporaries experience the incident, in view of the large number of wounded, as civil war-like conditions. In the following days, it comes to anti-socialistic acts of vengeance on the part of the Heimwehr-Vereinigungen (Home Guard Associations), as well as to violent anti-Semitic attacks at the university.[352] Schnitzler's version of this in his diary:

> Around 11 by tel. CP. From Cobenzl: Disturbances […] occupation of the Justice Palace, arson, gunfire, torching of the (anti-Sem.) "Reichspost," the streetcar isn't – running – I continue work meanwhile undisturbed (novel files; letters) – At 1:30 a.m. tel. Benedikt, who was supposed to have dinner with me: Revolution; he can't come, dead, wounded […] quiet all around; that one can still telephone is deceptively calming ... From the ground floor I can see the Justice Palace burning... , shooting in the distance. [...] barricades Ringstr., crimes?, – etc. – from now on no more telephone connection. I walk

352 Pauley, p. 124.

> outside a little. The atmosphere also stormy, distant thunder; – to the park, – the streets with empty tram tracks; very few cars that were ordered; – the park nearly empty; – a few people on benches; – very few couples. Meet Director Stern, we chat on the corner; – politics as usual – with not fully justified good cheer; – the peculiar mood on the fringe of a revolution […] not fundamentally disturbed; – but once again disgusted by the [...] agitators "on this side" and "on that side."[353]

353 TB 1927-1930, 15.7.1927.

THE FINAL YEARS 1928–1931

The Last Novel

At the beginning of 1928, Schnitzler is working on several projects: the "theater novel"; several plays, including *Zug der Schatten*, *Das Wort*, and *Im Spiel der Sommerlüfte;* as well as the novella *Der Sekundant.* He will complete only the last two.

Schnitzler's health is declining. Clara Pollaczek subjects him to frequent scenes of jealousy, after which he has heart pains. The otosclerosis has worsened his hearing considerably. In his condition, he supports not only his own household, but also that of Olga and his daughter. Without income from his films, he would not have enough money to live on.

The film version of *Freiwild,* which is first shown in Berlin cinemas in March, provides some financial relief. Also, *Therese*, his only other novel besides *Der Weg ins Freie*, is published in April by S. Fischer and alleviates his financial strain. In Schnitzler's entire work, this novel is unique in that it follows the life of a simple au pair, or governess, who has not had the advantage of any particular education. One did not discuss servants among the upper classes of the period. In Schnitzler's other works, their presence is taken for granted as a necessary guarantee of the smooth running of the bourgeois lifestyle. Otherwise, one did not waste a moment's thought on them. Here, Schnitzler dedicates an entire novel to one such young woman, which, perhaps, because it is his last, may be taken as a kind of testament.

Therese Fabiani is no kind of "süßes Mädel." Like some of Schnitzler's masculine characters, she seems, rather than being able to take her life in hand, to be buffeted about by the negative forces of fate, as she desperately grasps at whatever happiness she can find. Not infrequently, she must pay dearly for even this small token.

Here and there, Therese's latent anti-Semitism is indicated. She accuses Albert of being comfortably off as the son of a middle-class household, who "naturally feels solidarity with Jewish bank directors." Once, she enters the service of a "well-off factory owner":

> [The mother] herself, as well as the children, spoke an ugly Jewish jargon, against which, as against the Jews themselves, Therese has since felt an aversion. Although in some Jewish homes, she had not felt any worse off than in non-Jewish homes. That the Eppichs, even if baptised, belonged to another race against which she was not entirely free of prejudice, she only experienced, to her amazement, just before she quit.

Is Therese, however, really "unhappy," as her brother later has engraved on her tombstone? Here, it seems to be meant, first and foremost, in the sense of a tragic fate. Therese could indulge in her freedom, since she was not bound by a relationship. She had a number of adventures, and was not obliged to consider middle-class conventions. But could she fulfil herself emotionally? Her longings – here Schnitzler's psychological realism again is in evidence – never run in a straight line, but are often contradictory. When she sees Alfred again after a long time, it is in this vein: "She wished him to be more assertive, more of a daredevil than he was. Nevertheless, as soon as he became somewhat more bold, she felt fearful, almost repelled, as though the most beautiful thing that she had experienced until now, exactly through the fact that it had become even more beautiful, was condemned to end all too soon."

A psychoanalyst would interpret the behaviour of her son Franz as a cry for love, or at least attention. This interpretation can apply to Therese herself, because she strives basically, not only for middle-class security and social status, but, rather, like every human being, for emotional security. Her character, however, is not made for that, as becomes clear in the moments that she thinks about Thilda. And therein lies her tragedy:

> She knew also that this 16-year-old, and not only thanks to the favourable circumstances of her life, belonged to another type of being than she did. To the intelligent, cool, self-protective type, who can never encounter anything very serious and difficult, because they always hold themselves back, and know how to take from everyone who comes near them or under their influence or in their magic circle as it seems necessary or merely diverting.

Therese is not this kind of person, not one who is able to be distant or cold to people. She is emotionally vulnerable to them. For this reason, she cannot control her own life. She relies, in love, on the mercy of men, as in work she is dependent on the arbitrariness of her employers. This at first might seem like feminine egoism – Schnitzler has often enough criticised the male variety – and her brother Karl certainly seems like a masculine example of this. But it is nothing more than a great, desperate dependency with respect to her lovers, her son, and with respect to people who are able to conduct their lives toward a single goal. For these latter, she can never, for societal reasons, be more than a fleeting episode – with the exception of Herr Wohlschein.

Her end is not so directly presented as murder as in the novella *Der Sohn*; because the possibility is hinted at that she could still be allotted “decades of existence," and she dies only on the following day, suddenly and surprisingly. Here, Schnitzler's perpetual interest in the inevitability of fate shines through. Still, in her last hours, it seems to Therese, “that she had found again the son who was lost to her for so long. In that moment that he became the executor of an eternal justice.”

Der Sekundant is not published until after Schnitzler's death, in fact: in the January edition of the *Vossisiche Zeitung* of 1932. The narrative deals with the institution of the duel, but, in this case, primarily with its after-effects. The narrator begins with a justification of the duel to the modern reader. He is fully aware that it is an anachronism. This roots the book firmly in the new, post-war era, even though it is set before 1914. Although Schnitzler criticizes the duel repeatedly in his work, here he observes that it gives or gave “life in society a certain dignity, or at least a certain style.”

Lili's Dramatic Death

On 26th July, 1928, Schnitzler receives a letter from his son-in-law, asking him to come to see Lili right away. She is not gravely ill, he explains, but desires her father's presence. The next morning, he and Olga fly to Venice. Olga has received a telephone call from a friend of the family, Dora Michaelis, in which she mentions a serious illness of Lili's. She, in turn, has received a telegram from Lili's neighbor, Alma Mahler-Werfel.

Cappellini picks them up from the airport and explains the situation. The previous evening, after an insignificant quarrel, Lili shot herself in the chest. When the housekeeper called her to ask her what she had done, she replied, "Un momento di nervosismo."

In the hospital, Lily is confident that she will recover soon. The bullet did not hit any essential organs. Her operation takes place at 6 a.m. on the 26th. In the afternoon, however, her condition worsens rapidly, since the bullet is rusty. Between 10 and 11 p.m. she dies of blood poisoning. It is a cruel irony of fate that the pistol that Lily shot herself with was the weapon of a soldier of the Austrian Mountain Division. Cappellini had taken it from him in the First World War.[354]

Schnitzler has not only lost his daughter, but also the only person in whom he could fully confide during these years. He writes in his diary: "The word pain has become ridiculous, for now I know that, for the first time, I am experiencing what God meant by that. She is gone – with her 18 years, out of this world – this heavenly, unique, creature – never, never will she come again – and there is no chance of rising out of the depths of this despair."[355] He is united with Lili's mother in this pain. Olga writes in September, 1928:

> Why didn't I know more, – sense – why did she hide from me? And writes: I am so longing for you, – too late, too late, most horrifying word in the world.[356]

In order to understand how she could take this drastic step, Schnitzler reads Lili's diary. Two months after her wedding, in August, 1927, it breaks off with the words, "Vorrei morir." She continues it in January, though, and Schnitzler finds no sign of depression on the following pages, but, instead, an almost uncontrollable joy of life.[357]

With regard to Cappellini's request to send him Lili's diaries, Olga

354 TB 1927–30, 30.7.1928.

355 Briefe 1913–31, p. 563.

356 DLA, Briefe Olga an Arthur Schnitzler. Folder 1231, 10.9.1928.

357 Farese, p. 305.

writes to Schnitzler:

> I have to make clear to you that no power in the world will conduce me to give up these diaries. Least of all to Arnoldo – because the passionate lover is worlds away from any understanding, any real compassion, – and he would revenge himself on the dead child as on the living – to his own detriment.
>
> The child did the terrible thing out of fear that he could know something. – and I would feel very unworthy – so far beyond our earthly judgment as she is, if I would now expose her secret. [...]
>
> I want to arrange with Heini, if I don't do it myself by then, to destroy the diaries immediately after my death. These are things that are only the business of us three – nobody else. Our child is no aubject for psychologists, – the beautiful, proud creature should continue to live undeciphered, and pass away with us, only our child. – (and she couldn't even reveal herself completely to us), as long as she made us happy through her living presence.
>
> I am certain, dear one, that you share my view on this. As far as I'm concerned, I have herewith said my last word on the subject of the diary – there's no negotiating about it. I also demand forbearance at last, because to endure this also exceeds my strength.[358]

Lili's diary is, by the way, not destroyed, as her parents had originally intended. Rather, it is located in the German Literary Archive in Marbach, where it is locked away from view until the end of April, 2020, because of testamentary provisions. Even if an evaluation of the document yields new information for research, this step should not be taken without a consultation with the descendants of the family.

In this time of mourning, in November, a glimmer of hope appears: Suzanne Clauser, under the pen name of Dominique Auclères, has translated *Blumen* into French. She asks Schnitzler's permission to translate other works as well.

---

358 DLA, Briefe Olga an Arthur Schnitzler. Folder 1232, 19.2.1929.

In the spring of 1929, Schnitzler sees the film of *Fräulein Else* with Elisabeth Bergner in Berlin. He continues work on the "theater novel," *Zug der Schatten* and *Das Wort.* Until summer, he concentrates on *Spiel der Sommerlüfte,* which is first performed in December at the Volkstheater. It is published by the Fischer Verlag in the following year. *Spiel der Sommerlüfte* is Schnitzler's last completed play. His swan song in three acts is set in the summer countryside around Vienna. The human relationships in the play alternate between love and melancholy.

In the final act of the play, husband and wife find their way back to each other. They both have their flirt with infidelity behind them and have caught a glimpse behind the curtain of the life they would have without each other – although it all may well have been merely imagination. They are both relieved, as are Fridolin and Albertine in *Traumnovelle,* to have overcome all differences and to be together again.

Seriously Ill

Early in 1930, Schnitzler's doctor Ferry Donath, who examines him regularly, diagnoses high blood pressure, but finds no ground for concern. Full of a creative surge, in spite of his weakened condition, Schnitzler divides the first half of the year among the dramas *Zug der Schatten, Der Landesknecht, Die Sängerin,* and *Joseph II,* as well as the one-act play *Heimkehr.* Aside from these, he continues work on the stories *Abenteurernovelle, Der Sekundant,* and the "theater novel." The number of his literary projects is remarkable, considering that Schnitzler is 68.

Abenteurernovella remains a fragment. Even if the genesis of this narrative stretched over two decades, it was completely typical of Schnitzler to work for over a decade on a stage-play or a novella, from the initial idea until its final version. The first sketches date from 1902, when it was still conceived of as a five-act drama in verse. The work was revised in 1909, 1911, and 1913, and not until 1925 was the first draft of the prose version complete. The fragment reproduced in the 1962 edition of the collected works dates from 1928, and was first published in 1937. It is one of Schnitzler's parable-like Renaissance works.

Once more, Schnitzler deals with the idea of human meddling with the powers of fate, illustrated by two strangers gambling at an inn. He takes up an idea from his earlier short stories. The inevitability of fate is also addressed in *Die Weissagung*, *Das Schicksal des Freiherrn von Leisenbogh* and in *Die dreifache Warnung*. In the first and last stories, the protagonist's death is inescapable. In *Das Schicksal des Freiherrn von Leisenbogh,* in contrast, as in the *Abenteurernovelle,* the prophecy turns out to be a fabrication – and yet is fulfiled. At the same time, this novella testifies to turn-of-the-century historicism, the most effective expression of which is presented by *Der Schleier der Beatrice*. The drama, *Der Gang zum Weiher*, can also be considered a late example.

By this time, Schnitzler's plays have disappeared largely from the stage. He is all the more delighted to hear of a performance of *Professor Bernhardi* toward the end of January 1930 in the Komödienhaus in Berlin, where the reception by the audience is overwhelmingly positive.[359] In addition, the current director of the Burgtheater, Anton Wildgans, declares that he is willing to stage *Der Gang zum Weiher*. The rehearsals only begin, however, in January, after Schnitzler has revised the manuscript. After the premiere on February 14, 1931, the reviewers appear to finally concede Schnitzler an overwhelming success, and do not hold back with their praise.[360]

Meanwhile, his relationship with Clara Pollaczek has become more and more difficult. She torments him with all kinds of accusations, quarrels and jealousy, even though she knows that Schnitzler, because of his heart and high blood pressure, needs peace and quiet more than anything else. Her jealousy is not entirely unfounded, however. With Schnitzler, how could it be otherwise, even at his age? The worse he gets along with Clara, the warmer and more trusting his relationship with Suzanne Clauser becomes. In the face of his weak health, the demands made by Clara and Olga – who still has not given up hope to live with Schnitzler again – and the tragedy of Lili's suicide, Suzanne gives him encouragement, strength, even happiness. He is surprised at himself that at his age, he can still have the feelings he does for a young woman. He is visited by memories from the *Anatol* period, and records in his diary that he is happier than he has been for the

359 TB 1927–30, 24.1.1930.
360 TB 1931, 14. & 15.2.1931.

past thirty years, since the first time he met Olga. Suzanne calls him every morning to ask how he is feeling. Her marriage is beginning to show the first cracks. And, after decades, Schnitzler is once more in the position that he has to hide one girlfriend from the other.

Early in December, Schnitzler feels so miserable that he calls his doctor in again. Ferry continues to maintain that his organs are functioning well. Several days later, Clara is concerned by Schnitzler's suffering appearance and asks Ferry how he is. The doctor confesses that his patient's heart is under too great a strain from the high blood pressure, and that Schnitzler has only months left to live. At this stage, therapy would not produce any effect, but Schnitzler should relax as much as possible and avoid any excitement. Despite her good intentions, Clara's jealousy wins the upper hand in the end. She follows Schnitzler, opens Suzanne's letters and, in August, even tries to kill herself – but without success.

In May, *Flucht in die Finsternis* appears in the *Vossische Zeitung* in Berlin, and two months later in the *Neue Wiener Journal.* This is Schnitzler's most sinister work, dealing with the relationship between two brothers, Otto and Robert. The narrative is related in the third person from the point of view of Robert, a hypochondriac who suffers from acute paranoia. He is upset that his left eyelid seems to droop lower than the right. His friend, a doctor whom he consults, simply laughs it off, whereas Robert insists that there is also a strange feeling of fatigue in his entire left side [...].

This is the only work that reflects Schnitzler's own hypochondriac tendencies. These are thoroughly enumerated in his diary. As a medical man, Schnitzler was completely aware of his condition. He knew where his panic attacks came from, why he was torn out of sleep nightly, and how worries and groundless anxieties weakened him. One may also see the novella as a mirror of the competitive, if friendly, relationship with his younger brother, Julius. Although they became closer as they grew older, for a long time, Julius was the son who fulfilled their father's hopes by becoming a successful surgeon. During their father's lifetime, this made for considerable competition between the two, the source of which was the significant pressure put on Arthur by the father's middle-class sensibilities. However, in real life, this tense relationship between the siblings ended in reconciliation, and not with the tragic ending of the fictional work.

Last Plans

Several weeks later, Schnitzler comes across a news article mentioning preparations for an elaborate celebration in his native Vienna for his 70th birthday.[361] Schnitzler is negotiating with the film company Metro Goldwyn Mayer from Hollywood about the filming of *Spiel in Morgengrauen*, with the English title *Daybreak*. On September 19, 1931, it is shown in movie theaters across the USA.

In spite of the aggravations of otosclerosis and chronic nausea, which probably stem from the over-acidification of his stomach, Schnitzler starts to write an original film script for the first time. The provisional title is simply, *Kriminalfilm*.

On October 20, Schnitzler and Clara go to the theater together and then meet friends at a restaurant. Amused and encouraged by the evening, he notes in his diary: "Life is beautiful and interesting – for the sake of its wonderful moments, I want to live it all again."[362]

At night, he cannot sleep because of nausea and trouble with his heart rate. He calls Clara the next morning to inform her. After that, he takes a brief walk to the next mailbox to drop off some letters, already looking forward to his daily talk with Suzanne. In his study, before he can call her, he collapses. When his secretary Frieda Pollak comes in to take dictation, she finds him stretched out on the floor. She immediately calls Ferry Donath and Clara. Schnitzler does not regain consciousness. He dies of cerebral haemorrhage between 6 and 7 p.m., with his head in Clara's hands.

361 Ibid., 23.8.1931.

362 Wienbibliothek: MS Pollaczek, Clara Katharina: Arthur Schnitzler und ich.

AFTERWORD

In the first third of the 20th century, Arthur Schnitzler was one of the most famous personalities in Europe, as is maintained by an American journal.[363] Twenty years before Joyce, he introduced the stream-of-consciousness technique into German literature, and enjoyed the respect of Sigmund Freud, who even designated him his "Doppelgänger." He corresponded with the intellectual greats of his time: Thomas and Heinrich Mann, Rainier Maria Rilke, Hermann Hesse, Stefan Zweig, Hugo von Hofmannsthal, Josef Popper-Lynkeus and Theodor Herzl. Contemporary critics continue to dismiss Schnitzler as a light-hearted writer of erotic stories, bordered in a nostalgia-chased frame of Viennese grace. Let us take, for example, the commentary on the jacket of the "latest" Schnitzler novella, *Später Ruhm* (2014). "Schnitzler evokes the whole Mozartian grace of the Austrian culture [...], the smiling verve and the mild melancholy."

Over a similar airily composed blurb for *Der Weg ins Freie*, Schnitzler writes his publisher in 1907:

> Again the grace and the charm and the spirit. I really can't stand it anymore. I almost have to be happy that I still have the gift of the ironic snigger. [...] But if blowing our own horn has to be done, at least not with the wrong notes.[364]

It is high time that the socio-critical component of Schnitzler's work – in the context of the recently revived interest in Schnitzler's Jewish identity – is definitively acknowledged. This applies naturally to Schnitzler's lifelong confrontation with anti-Semitism, and his own positioning as an Austrian Jew; but equally to his critical evaluation of middle-class morality, with regard to the social position of women. His psychologically precise description of individual female characters extends from his first dramas – *Märchen, Freiwild, Das Vermächtnis, Liebelei* – to his last novel *Therese.*

363 See the interview with James L. Benvenisti for the *American Hebrew & Jewish Messenger*.
364 Briefe 1875–1912, p. 568.

That his works frequently fully contradict the conception of middle-class morality is proven by the fact that each performance of his early plays caused a scandal. But, also, at the height of his fame, Schnitzler felt continually, fundamentally misunderstood by his public. Above all, he felt to some extent, deliberately misinterpreted by the critics.

A good example of this is the "sweet young thing" the young girl from the outskirts, the "süßes Madel." With ger, Schnitzler breathed new life into the feminine literary character types of the end of the 19th century. The cliché has it that what is being described are, uncomplicated erotic dalliances with Viennese-dialect chattering girls from the city outskirts. In fact, the psychologically detailed portraits of the "süßes Mädel," as embodied, for example, in Christine of *Liebelei*, lend themselves to an effective social criticism reminiscent of Theodor Fontane's *Frau Jenny Treibel* or *Effi Briest*.

The sources available on Schnitzler are, in comparison to other authors of the 20th century, enviably good. The Appendix contains letters from his wife to Schnitzler that have been disregarded by research until now. These cast an emotionally laden searchlight on the early years of their relationship, on the conflicts that led to divorce, as well as on the suicide of their daughter Lili. With Olga, Schnitzler conducted an honest exchange with regard to his work, which was not apparent with his literary colleagues. Olga's intelligent insights as to the character and works of Gerhardt Hauptmann, Thomas Mann, and S. Fischer are eminently readable informative.

Accessing both previously unpublished aphorisms and unknown newspaper cuttings of the era, which show the direct inspiration for the point of departure of *Professor Bernhardi*, as well as the only recently rediscovered drafts of *Fink and Fliederbusch*, allows us to locate the origin of the statement "Austrian citizen of German culture confessing to the Jewish race": It was conceived in the time during the creation of *Der Weg ins Freie* and *Professor Bernhardi*.

The difficulty with treating Schnitzler as a Jewish author arises from the fact that he repeatedly defended himself against being understood primarily as such, and instead emphasized that he was a German writer – or, respectively, his Viennese roots. All the while, he was himself well aware that the publication of *Der Weg ins Freie* was considered his public acknowledgment of his background as a member of the Jewish haute-bourgeoisie. All during his lifetime, Schnitzler held fast to his Jewish origin, which he conceived of as a moral duty. His posture is most precisely qualified as enlightened, anti-political and individualist. Enlightened, because he consistently kept his distance from the Jewish orthodoxy, including in raising his own children. Anti-political, because, as is obvious from the many aphorisms and opinions in letters and diaries, he did not think much of self-proclaimed "political people" owing to the fickleness of their views, and his mistrust of the group mentality in general. The differences with Herzl and Zionism resulted not only from Schnitzler's deep attachment to his "Heimat," but also from Herzl's political engagement. Nevertheless, in this regard it was naturally impossible to avoid that the statements of a figure of public life such as Schnitzler were interpreted politically, in spite of all efforts at objectivity. A case in point is his ostentatious silence during the general war euphoria of 1914. In some instances, this might not have been greatly disturbing to Schnitzler. The important thing for him was to abide by his convictions, and not be swayed from them by either the anti-Semites or the nationalists.

As to the third element of his position, Schnitzler was an individualist who sought out his own niche among the various currents in Viennese Jewish intellectualism, and unconditionally held to it. Integrity was a quality that Schnitzler valued very highly, and he would never even have considered converting, as did many of the other middle-class Jewish citizens of his time, for career purposes. As an author, of course, he naturally was not part of a career-determined hierarchy. It is well known that Gustav Mahler felt obliged to be baptised, in order to be named the Court Opera Director. Schnitzler's own position as an enlightened anti-political individualist pushed him, rather, in the direction of Freud and Stefan Zweig.

Schnitzler concerned himself with the Jewish problem in only two works. Aside from the themes of love and death generally associated with him, the masculine ego assumes a prominent role in Schnitzler's work, the consequences of which he always depicts with a sharp, self-critical view. In general, Schnitzler's plays, as well as his prose, are characterised by an out-and-out self-tormenting drive toward objectivity – to the effort to understand the opposing character as well as possible – under which he suffered time and time again. In his later work, loneliness and aging were central themes, but also the contrast between the fundamentally different types of people: those who take things lightly, and those who take things seriously. Hofreiter of *Das weite Land* is an example of the first, whereas Christine of *Liebelei* is an example of the second. Closely bound up with this is Schnitzler's strong interest in the devastating effects of words dishonestly intended, or superficially used. In this regard, he is very aware of the dilemma, as he writes in a letter to Olga dated October 19, 1900: "Incidentally, one can only write *words around* a subject; a word that forces its way to the heart of the matter would shatter it."[365]

Schnitzler's continuing relevance in the 21st century is explained by his clinically precise, meticulous portrayals of masculine and feminine psyches as they are. The alarm over not being master of oneself, i.e., not having one's drives as well as one's feelings under control to the degree that one would like; that a chance meeting or a dream can shake even a serious relationship, even a marriage to its foundations; the distress entailed in colliding with the bourgeois morals of the early 1900's are the reasons why each of Schnitzler's plays caused a scandal. Even if the audience today is not subject to such strict morals as at the turn of the previous century, the fascination and the potential in Schnitzler's work to shake one to the core are still there. In the essential things, human beings have not changed as much since Schnitzler's time as one may think at first.

365 DLA, Briefe Arthur an Olga Schnitzler. Folders 510–5.

APPENDIX

CORRESPONDENCE OF ARTHUR & OLGA SCHNITZLER

Source: Manuscript Collection of the Deutsches Literaturarchiv, Marbach

Dear Doctor!

A few days ago I heard from an autograph collector that, when one asks you politely, you will send a picture or an autograph. Now, I must first mention, to avoid any ugly suspicion, that I never collect signatures under any circumstances. I place no value on an artist's hastily written quote, or something like that, that he is kind enough to send me as a result of a letter full of phrases about "admiration, adoration," etc. He does not know who such a quote is meant for, and his words thus remain words without a soul.

If I think that I got an autograph from you that I framed and was supposed to pass on to my children's children as a relic so that, then, after 200 years, it could contribute to "laundry list literature"| – no, no, I value you too much for that. Yes, if you would know me, and me – understand me well, <u>me</u> – dedicate a thought to me – that would be something else. But this way – !|

Your picture, however – that is what I'm asking you for! Why and wherefore? It seems to me unutterably stupid and tasteless when someone parades his superiority before one's nose. I am always irritated by critics, for example, of "Anatol" – "one must dip the pen into champagne in order to review this book," by means of which the journalist above all wants to show off his cleverness.

But all of that is secondary: if you would only send me your picture, I promise cheerfully that I will not tell anyone else, otherwise you would be overrun with requests. I only want to have it for myself. So please –!

Dina Marius
p./A.H. Rosanis, II. Praterstrasse 15.
Montag, d. 19. Juni 99.

21.6.1899

My very dear young lady,

I am all out of pictures, and so I must ask you to content yourself with this one; if you want, it can be temporary and I will exchange it for you as soon as I have larger pictures again.

To get as kind a letter as yours reconciles one a little with the – others, which are in fact more numerous. I am basically curious as to who you are; a name says relatively little, even a letter betrays, in general, not very much.

Arthur Schnitzler

My very dear Mr. Schnitzler!

Many heartfelt thanks! That was more than I had expected; and you cannot begin to imagine how happy it made me. You are even curious to know who I am? – Quite simply: a girl of 17 years, who wants to have her own life and be herself completely. There were a couple of pathetic shadows that live in a swamp that wanted to prevent me doing so, but I chased them right away and reached out joyfully toward the sun. That is all. –

And my calling – in the truest, most sacred sense! – fulfils me completely. I am glowing – I cannot do otherwise.

Now I still want to tell you what books I particularly like: The Story of Master Heinrich, who brings the sun to humankind and who wanted to free Christ from the cross and who had to die from buried sounds. Then, Peter Altenberg, who looks into the secret crevices of the soul, and in "The Flying Dutchman," portrays the full yearning of a woman." " He is never coming!" –

Then, the only thing I know of from Johannes Schlaf. "In That Old Thing," these beautiful, beautiful stories. And Arthur Schnitzler's "Liebelei," "Die Gefährtin, " the novellas and all the rest, <u>all</u> of it! – Is it then really true, – ? he's looking for a companion? But she is also looking for him! Her whole life long! So there is, after all, hope that they find each other some day?

– Please, what are you thinking of with the so-called temporary picture? I do not at all know when you will get large pictures again; you see, I am not holding back at taking you at your word.

Formerly, I saw you almost daily in the street, but now, no longer for some time; if the next time I see you is very soon, I will greet you. All right?

Dina Marius

Friday, June 23,'99

29.6.1899

My very dear young lady,

I just came back from a little trip and found your amiable words. The pictures must be ordered; I will get them in about 10 days. I am happy that you want to get to know me "very soon" through a greeting on the street – but isn't there an easier way?

Your very devoted,

Arth. Sch.

My very dear Mr. Schnitzler!

You are really very kind; I owe you an apology, because when I received no answer from you, I had all sorts of unworthy thoughts! – You could have misunderstood me, etc. – I had thought myself into such bitterness that I took you for somebody very different from yourself and was very unfair. But I have not misunderstood you, have I? – Now, as to the picture, most joyful thanks.

And an easier way than the greeting? – I would very much like to know you. But the proud words: I play with human souls. – ! And I don't want to be a victim of that.

Dina Marius

2.7.99

6.7.99

Dear young lady,

A picture will be ready. Do you want to pick it up? When?

Your devoted A.S.

Very dear Herr Schnitzler!

I will come Tuesday at 2 p.m. in the afternoon; if you do not expect to be able to see me at this time, please let me know.

Dina Marius

19.10.1900

[…] And the means to the end is also each one for the others. – all human relationships rest upon it. – everything in the future is an end – and everything we use to reach it is a means.

It is always a matter of whether the ends are good and the means pleasant; reasonable people always have good ends – and people with taste always choose good means. Incidentally: one can only write words around a subject; a word that forces its way to the heart of the matter would shatter it.

But when will we see each other again? Good-bye and stay well disposed toward me.

I kiss your eyes. A.

Breslau, 24.11.1900

[...] My window is opposite the Stadttheater, right next to a gigantic parade ground – dreadful. There is a lot of parading with outrageous self-importance; each corporal a little Kaiser Wilhelm, each lieutenant a little god and each general a great cretin – I kiss you. Your A.

Hinterbühl,19.6.1902

I'm missing the walks and you also. Good-bye and I care for you so much.

Olga

Hinterbühl, 23.6.1902

[Olga to Arthur]

(Today a year ago Salzburg – eyes – summer solstice celebration)

And in the afternoon a letter comes from you, in which it says, You had "an unfulfilable, hopeless yearning for me, – the year 1928," (it could also have been '78, but that would make no sense;) it's true that the jealousy or yearning – or whatever is tormenting you – until the year 1928 also makes no sense, because if we experience it, you'll be 68 and I'll be 48, and hopefully you would still love me then, – and should we not live to see 1928, we still have a time together before us, that, as short as it might seem, still harbours much beauty because we are living it through <u>together</u> – Do you understand me? ...

And because of that, life doesn't seem to me short, death not terrible. We <u>have</u> each other, and this feeling gives endless security; at least to me, because it makes me feel so strong to think that I will have you forever. –

Do you understand? Do you understand?… I can't say any more ...

But all of these things only mean anything if you feel them exactly the way I do... And it would be terrible if such things as are written in the letter, – or even more, concealed in it, – you often feel in a momentary mood that is fundamentally false. I see myself immediately then torn away and pushed away from you, and I can't be that way for even a second. I am in you, nestled up close inside you, intertwined with you – and then you <u>write</u> such things, that I have to be dismayed all alone and cry it out all alone instead of being able to throw myself around your neck, which, in this case, would be a great consolation?! (In any case, by the way.) That is almost mean. Luckily, our child consoled me right away, in that he began to kick very hard, and immediately after I found in the garden almost a whole bouquet of 4-leaf clovers. – You know nothing!

9.9.1902

[Arthur to Olga after Heini's birth]

My love beyond words – only a thousand greetings of yearning and tenderness before I walk in the forest […] – Love me, my beloved and feel how I love you, reason, soul, and bliss of my existence. Words ... words, – one always has to feel ashamed.

Thursday, 26 August 09

[Olga to Arthur on Ibsen's *Ghosts*]

Heine: "Is Ibsen still alive? Is he also as famous a writer as my father?"

Ich: "He is more famous than your father."

He: (discontent) "But why?"

Ich: "Because he was already much older and had written much more. When our father is that old, he will be just as famous."

Now he is happy again.

Partenkirchen, 9. Aug. 18

[This and the following letters until 14.5.1921: Olga to Arthur]

Yes, and now I must naturally go on and on about Thomas Mann, who is, unfortunately, in the process of publishing an endlessly gossipy, complicated, indelicate book, but nothing seems to come out of it. The quarrel between the two brothers, carried out this way on the streets, is truly a painful affair. That Heinrich is a little confused does not mean that Thomas must also become unbalanced. Too bad. God bless you that you have kept quiet about all political nonsense. That is what we talk about every day here. – how you are ceaselessly loved, honored, and adored and so, on the quiet, have blown your opposition over, – to me it's a delight to see it. Yes, one must only allow oneself and the others time, – the truth comes out by itself. –

Munich, Thursday, 22. Aug. 18

My dear one, I've just come from Bruno Walter, – haven't sung as well as yesterday, – but it all balances out. He finds the voice very developed, the high register is the best, he said: sparkling, – à la Nickish. And yet he discourages me, – because the voice is a true mezzosoprano in its timbre, and for that the deep register, that is, the deep middle register, is too thin. Most likely, the high notes have become so good at the expense of these registers. I would be a strong expressive talent, a real theater talent, a serious artist. Sensitivity, – but I lack the experience – and if I were 18 years old, he would say yes, – even now, if I really had to earn money. But since that is not the case, he advises me no, – I will only be disappointed. He was terribly kind, and it was clearly difficult for him to tell me all this. But I made it easy for him, was not at all downcast or unhappy. – and said to him that, after all, I had waited to hear a verdict from him, who is the highest authority for me, before I plunged into new artistic adventures.

Shall I tell you that I had basically expected it? I know my strong points, but also my failings, know that some goose has things that are apparently beyond my reach. – and that I, in turn, have some things that others lack. That my whole life story is completely outside the norm, – that is certain. And that I apparently do not seem to have been made for the "practical," and "utilitarian," that Römpler had already made clear to me. Thus, I am a collector's item and not the run-of-the-mill singer.

Now, however, – the effect is, my beloved, that I can cross out the chapter "Public" with a big line and hope I can communicate to my children and maybe still to some growing young people something of the feeling for art that lives in me. Walter spoke of concert singing and teaching if I wanted to earn money.

I ask you urgently to please keep all of this to yourself, – all right? About everything else, I first have to get clear in my mind and talk to you about it.

Friday aftern.

Salzburg, 10. Sept. 20

What sense does it make for you and me to continue living side-by-side in such an agonizing way? When I am away, I always feel it most intensely, how oppressed and deeply tormented I am with you, how this perpetual mistrust undermines me and leaves me shaken in my whole being and essence. I am too old to be able to put up with this in the long run – I must, indeed, stand on stable ground and see what I can make of myself, without being harassed and in perpetual danger.

Thus it is, however, not only what I want that I, – God knows, after a difficult battle – want to leave, – also with regard to you, distance gives me back untroubled feelings, – The strongest and most heartfelt wish in me is to put an end to this destructive drive in you and to get you back to your deserved peace and tranquility, – my very presence alone is an aggravation to you, – and the conversation with the Hofrätin only confirmed that. [...]

We've gotten to the point where I, with the best will in the world, want to do nothing more than stand down.

Here, it's only a question rather of the children, – and I beg you as insistently as I can: Subdue your disinclined being enough so that you don't make them suffer. Heini is so happy here, has become so free through this trip. He is fresh and carefree, just as a young fellow at the beginning of his real life should be. I am happy about him, – and nothing in the world could bring me to speak with him about a troubled relationship between us, his parents.

With the child, who is so much more aware and so much needier of tenderness, it will definitely be more difficult, and it's my most terrifying fear to plunge her into a sadness that could wound her soul with a too-early breath of frost.

Let me make you a proposal: I'll settle my most necessary affairs in Vienna and travel as soon as possible to Lucy, – as though I were going to Liesl, – and I'll come back again to the children, if you want, towards Christmas, – and then we'll see what happens, – if you can put up with it this way or if we need to find a more decisive form of separation.

I know, there are very difficult weeks ahead of me: but anything is better than the ugliness of the past months, and than the poisonous atmosphere, that very soon would have begun affecting the children. [...]

11.2.1921

It has to be enough, dear one, enough, enough. No more reproaches, – they should at least not reach me, and no feeling for you than that of a grieving friend, – and yet still a trace of hope for sometime later.

I cannot fight with you, dear one, believe me – not with you and not with anyone anymore. It's better to give up, do without, there's plenty of that ahead of me [...]

I only know one thing for certain, that the fine house in the Sternwarte-strasse, "the house of the petitioner," it could have been called for me for years, years... that it never again can or will or may be a home for me again.

Maybe it will work yet again, to cobble together from the ruins of my being, – this my so harshly accused, persecuted being, – that it can function again, good and strengthening and conveying blessings.

From you it shrinks fearfully away, there were too many threats, too much hardness. Poor, poor man, how I have to cry for this.

I ask you, from the bottom of my heart, with my voice from before, with the voice of my beloved children, – let it be a gentle, decent solution. No more angry scenes, – it was bitter enough.

I know nothing about my future, – but I would rather be completely alone, than in this Furies-whipped company. Certainly, – the Hofrätin – who wrote me down such a beautiful literary programme for the soul. – She will turn out to be right: I was not strong enough, I was not equal to my task.

But ... no, nothing more. [...]

Don't worry about me, kiss the children, don't think of me unkindly.

From the heart

Tenderly

O

14.5.21

My dear, even if you have forbidden me to telegraph you tomorrow, I have to confess to you that I will be with you in spirit tomorrow with a thousand good and tender wishes and many beautiful memories. Don't be sad, rejoice for your (and my!) precious and beloved children, for your blooming garden, and all the love and homage that is in the world for you. – Be calm and comforted: Everything has a reason, also for you, – and for you the game can only end as "good" or "satisfactory" even if it does not lack dramatic complications. And dear Richard B.-H. is certainly completely and totally wrong: this way, we are forever intertwined with each other, that exactly out of that, out of the all-too-painful precise sensitivity to each emotion of the other, has come this demand for distance. – an extreme in defending one's own limits.

And I have so much hope, and wish it so indescribably that you are able to regard me, in the not-too-distant future, with a calm and friendly heart, – God willing,

Vienna 22.1.1923

[Arthur to Olga]

Munich seems, next to Budapest, to have become the most disgusting city in Central Europe; – as far as harassment of the Jews is concerned, by the way, here we have all sorts of nice things to read. In any case, anti-Semitism is the most ingenious idea that ever occurred to the genius of human spite. One can't really talk about a "siding" – and to vary a well-known expression, – for those who are run over by a speeding locomotive, – it is, in any case, enough of a main track.

Munich, 8 Juni 23

[from J. Schürlein]

Theoretically, I'm basically for boycotting Bavaria (in particular the Tegernsee – Chiemsee area); because the political circumstances are outrageous, criminals run around at large. The innocent are imprisoned, you constantly encounter swastika signs, which has the advantage that you know where you stand right away; with regard to rowdy gatherings and parades in Munich, it has recently become a little quieter. – We don't concern ourselves with anything, but I find the atmosphere nauseating. Nevertheless, I am convinced that you, in all likelihood, will not personally have any unpleasantness and that the spas and also the Tegernsee will be full of Jews.

Vienna, 21.7.1923

[Arthur to Olga about the *Medardus* Film]

The Frenchman – wishes the pardon of Medardus Klaehrs for the greater glory of Napoleon; – America does not care as much about that – on the other hand, Medardus should not kill the princess under the starry banner but marry her – !!!!! How to make that work is unclear. But I think that the dagger that Medardus pulls could be transformed at the last minute, into the Archbishop who conducts the wedding. That wouldn't be much sillier than the *Anatol* film. By the way, I'm increasingly coming to the conviction that it's not the public, and also fundamentally not the directors, who are stupid; – it is the movie magnates, who are <u>at once</u> stupid, cowardly and lacking in conscience and, in their fear about their business, ruin it more often than they realize. –

21.7.1923
[Arthur to Olga]

[…] Yesterday, I spoke to Prof. Redlich ... His indignation is boundless about the doings of the Pan-German clique, whose stupidities and tricks always give nationalist France new pretexts for its infamous actions. He said much that was very intelligent, particularly about anti-Semitism, – and I asked him why he doesn't sometimes write about it or, respectively, publish about it? – I couldn't say he was wrong, when he pointed out to me that in contemporary swastika-ian circumstances, a completely unsupported public presence on this issue would put his life in danger. [...]

Baden-Baden 16. Nov. 23
[Olga to Arthur]

Now there's also anti-Semitic agitation here, – "the Jews have taken the gold-backed loans for themselves, etc." – but it is still paradise compared to Munich. […] [Lucy] has a real fear of Munich.[…] She has a Jew-complex of the worst sort, – and it's so sad for me to see, how this horrible time has also confused the intelligent young *person* and chased her into the extremes.

17.11.1923
[This and the following letter: Arthur to Olga]

I, we, now <u>live</u> from the foreign currencies sold, otherwise, I would have had to sell my papers (to some extent I have anyway done /it/) I still have a few hundred doll. over there, also some franks; – but you have to think about the fact that, since summer, I have certainly not earned a tenth of what we need, – so, understandably, there's no talk of investing... .

Today our manly German students in Vienna want to chase the Jewish readers out of the University Library – which, strangely enough, they do not succeed in. – – "Freedom" ... "Honor – ? Meaningless phrases. – Killing

Jews; that's the single thing that this mob cares about. That's how I've known them to be for more than forty years. It is always the same extras that come creeping out of the alleys; with their bloated beer faces; – God doesn't always take the trouble to create new ones; – the chief of the extras is sometimes called Schönerer, sometimes Hitler. Their enemy, however, is called Einstein, not Poincaré. –

Vienna, 21.7.24

Yesterday evening, I was at Menczel's; they told cruel things from Bolshevik Russia, which are believed by snobbish, evil-minded literary types. Today I dreamed of a fight in the yard of the highschool in the Klostergasse between Communists and Swastika-types; I watched through the window; – a dead girl (black communist Jewess) (as in *Zum grossen Wurstl*) was carried out – I ran desperately around the sports hall and pleaded: Won't you finally be reasonable? –

Sta. Margherita Monday, 22.11.25

[…] I said yesterday to Fritzi: "He is like Peeperkorn! To which she replied: "but didn't you know that he <u>is</u> it?! and he knows that Th. Mann meant him!"

Certain scales fell in loads from my eyes. Yes, I can empathize with Thomas Mann: his measureless amazement at this person – <u>he</u>, who with his feeling of intellectual responsibility always agonizes. – and this comical, wonderful [Gerhardt] Hauptmann, who just <u>does</u> it, in all his naiveté. – and lack of suspicion!! Just think about it, it's a delicious story! […]

But: he would be a match for this good-looking young man, – not, it's true, as Richard III., in 20 minutes, that would be too little time, – but in three days, on the 1st this far, on the 2nd , this much and on the third – !

All left after 12. I had a servant get me a car – as I got in, he said to me, "Madam, the car is paid for." So, he was kind and attentive to the last detail! […]

By the way, Peeperkorn: as I wanted to go around 11:30, Hauptmann said: "No, no, that won't work, – now you must upset your stomach a little!"

And waved to the servant, who brought in a big liver paté in aspic that we all ate from, H. the most heartily. He said to me as he served himself another great helping: "Why not?!" Just like "Peeperkorn. Only that he doesn't say "Perfect." Sometimes he looks like a wonderful old faun, who is banished to Holland and enjoys life there.

Good-bye, my dear. People are a delicious invention, one never tires of them. I have more and more fun each year!

Warmest greeting! O.

Lido, 22.Sept.26

[This and the following letters: Olga to Arthur]

We have just made the acquaintance of "Lili's Fascist." He is Capitano Arnoldo Cappellini, 25 years old, formerly an officer of the Guard, from an old Florentine family. He is really a special kind of person, and our child is in love for the first time, really in love, it seems to me. He is quite captivated, full of tact and very tender with her. – and it seems that something very beautiful can develop out of this. We'll have to wait. We are together daily, and, observing him very closely, I like him extraordinarily. He is intelligent, interesting, a real man, – also with all the dark depths, but full of refined liveliness and of real nobility.

26.9.26

For me it's clear since this summer: she is endangered, if she isn't soon in the hands of a loving and beloved man. [...] Here she is completely captivated, for the first time not egoistically inclined, to give, to do good, to help, to smooth the way – she has become a woman emotionally [...]

He is really an enchanting fellow, and I can sense the security that he gives the child, who has rather bewitched him, this sweet little being, – he looks for her everywhere. He would like me to move to Venice. I said: it's not really worth it anymore.

The child, much as she loves him, even said to me: "But one doesn't join one's life forever to a man whom one met at 17." She is intelligent and unromantic... and unconventional. An astounding little person. (she should call to Vienna, although it is not really necessary.)

Berlin, 10.Sept.28

I'm always hoping that she is coming, is already there, – that by a great detour she comes to me, – to her source... I ask her in all possible ways, with all the tenderness that she needs so badly. But she is already so far away, she doesn't need me anymore. I say to her: I can't yearn for you my whole life long, – I have already had to endure so much yearning. – It's all for nothing. [...]

People want to console me. To say, schizophrenic, or : she would have done it later, – or: she has been spared a great deal of conflict and torment with her divided self. Nonsense. She would battle, she would torment herself. But she would be there. I would always be with her and I could have relieved her of so much disquiet. I don't want anything of this God-given idiotic wisdom, that is nothing more than laziness.

Why didn't I know more, – sense – why did she hide herself from me? And writes: I am so longing for you, – too late, too late, [most] infuriating word in the world.

We all do it like this, over and over again. You're doing it exactly like this. We leave our dear ones alone, even when we know. A lot of mean fools, who have their just desserts. Yes, I'm saying it!

Tuesday, 19.11.29

Yesterday I received a letter from Arnoldo, which caused me a very miserable day of breakdown and a bad night. He is demanding again, as though I had not really meant it, that I send the diary, – he seems in a bad way, incapable of cleaning his little apartment, without belief that he can pass his upcoming military examination, – how much less capable is he of enduring the diary, even after however mild and thoughtful a psychological preparation through a conversation with you.

I must state clearly that no power in the world would be able to bring me to the point of giving up these diaries. They are the least suitable thing for Arnoldo, – because the passionate lover is galaxies away from any understanding, any real charity, – and he would revenge himself on our dead child as [he would have] on the living, – to his own detriment.

The child did the terrible thing out of fear that he could know something.

– and I would feel very unworthy – so far beyond our earthly judgment as she is, – if I would now expose her secret.

Because I still feel a thousand times more bound to my dead child than I do to any still living Arnoldo, – and know that I am favouring her in feeling this way. There is no "right" for me, – above all, no legal right! – that I recognize in this case – and sacrifice unthinkingly also Arnoldo's friendship for this my irreversibly strong instinct.

He has to acknowledge my (our) reasons, and accept them with the same human nobility with which we have spared him and dispensed with that – after reading the last diary – justified accusation. – I can think of parents who would behave differently, very differently indeed. The child is dead, let us let the poor beloved rest in peace! He has to accept it as Fate, what happened, as we must accept all the happiness and all the sorrow that came to us from the most beloved being, – every rooting around for reasons is indelicate, stupid, shallow and criminally indiscreet.

I want to arrange with Heini, if I don't do it myself by then, to destroy the diaries immediately after my death. These are things that are only the business of we three – nobody else. Our child is no project for psychologists, – the beautiful, proud creature should continue to live undeciphered, and pass away with us, only our child. – and she couldn't even reveal herself completely to us, as long as she made us happy through her living presence.

Who can have any idea of my burning longing for her!

I am certain, dear one, that you share my view on this. As far as I'm concerned, I have herewith said my last word on the subject of the diary – there's no negotiating about it. I also demand forbearance at last, because to endure this also, exceeds my strength.

If Arnoldo wants to be together with us in Meran, in order to talk about the diaries, I will, regrettably, avoid this reunion. I will write to Arnoldo, but only after he is back from Venice, so as not to excite him unnecessarily.[...]

Albert's funeral: I don't want to be at any more funerals. For me it was as though my Liserl had died again.

19.10.29

I am in the middle of Bernhardi, – because of a possible performance in the Stadttheater, – and I find, it is an exceptionally good play, of a contemporaneity that can neither age nor pass away, because it is rooted primarily in human-moral rather than transient circumstances.

Only in this sense: the "human in his environment" may demand the place of the trend within art. – Environment as symbol of the countervailing forces there are to overcome, against which the human first has to prove itself.

Berlin, 12. July. 31

The most important event for me I experienced on Monday 13th. – Gundolf is dead, – and you will possibly have some idea of what deep mourning that puts me in. He was one of the most important people in my life, – I respected and loved him very much. So much comes back to me in remembering his wondrous rich presence, – it began with the first meeting in Heidelberg up to the days in Venice that bind him to me still with the beloved child. How much higher force, seriousness, animation, wonderful goodness and humaneness emanated from him, how richly, up to the limits of the expressible, did this man experience the world and reflect it, what a high standard he set for the intellect, how unyielding and close to the pain of living at the same time. I had to write everything down. – so many beautiful, unforgettable words and situations, carefree in the circle of friends, highest, superhuman excitement as he wrote "Caesar," – from which he once read a small excerpt in my house in Baden, – a conversation about the Austrian nature, after reading about Grillparzer, whom he portrayed with an incorruptible vision, – walks – once a word late at night at our door in Vienna: "not what happens to a person, but rather what he perceives of the world, is his destiny," – a very heartrending conversation alone with him about George, over whom he suffered deeply and who he still affirmed above everything... "there is only him;" – and still my heart is on his, the apparently inferior, side, – the last encounter in Vienna, in which I was happy to include you, – over, everything is over, – and still a good that is impossible to lose, that I was permitted to meet him, and that I received so much direction and measure and reaffirmation of my innermost notions of value that I had long before I knew him.

The direction of the world around us? It looks sad, – and if a social order is collapsing that was no longer solid – much time will pass before a new form is found, and we, the victims of a transition, see, because of lots of fighting and struggles of necessity, the magic dwindle, with which our real life and its value first begins.

It's quiet here, – for the moment, – in spite of that, many are losing their nerve.

Very reasonable measures are being taken, something like a business-and-finance dictatorship, which the patient and disciplined people willingly obey. No one knows anything, – how things might develop, – one lives, extremely carefully and sparingly, for the moment, – without being able to make any kind of plans.

Bibliography

Unpublished Primary Sources

Commission for Literary Forms of Use at the Austrian Academy of Sciences, Vienna
[Kommission für literarische Gebrauchsformen der Öst. Akademie der Wissenschaften]

Benvenisti, James L.: Arthur Schnitzler foretells Jewish Renaissance. An exclusive interview with the eminent litterateur. In: The American Hebrew und Jewish Messenger, New York, 29.2.1924, ZAS MF 320.

ZAS stands for "Zeitungsausschnittsammlung," MF for Mikrofiche. The English original text is reproduces in Riedmann, Bettina: Ich bin Jude, Österreicher, Deutscher – Judentum in Arthur Schnitzlers Tagebüchern und Briefen. Tübingen: Max Niemeyer 2002), pp. 396–98.

Wiener Neustädter Zeitung, 82/17 (Oktober 1919), ZAS MF 253.

Austrian State Archive, Vienna

MS Informationsschreiben der Statthalterei an das k. k. Ministerium des Innern, 15.1.1913, Zl. 1565-913.

Zl. stands for "Zulassungsnummer." A detailed evaluation of the censorship documents on *Professor Bernhardi*, kept in the State Archive as well as in the Lower Austrian Regional Archive [Landesarchiv], is to be found in Beier, Nikolaj: "Vor allem bin ich i c h…" – Judentum, Akkulturation und Antisemitismus in Arthur Schnitzlers Leben und Werk. Göttingen: Wallstein 2008.

Lower Austrian Regional Archive (Censorship Files)

Bericht des Zensurbeiratsmitglieds Glossy (20.10.1912), Zl. 2910/1912-XIV/197a4.

Der Fall Bernhardi. In: Der Morgen, 23.12.1912 (Morning Edition), Zl. 2910/1912.

The following three files without "Zl.":

Leserbrief im Illustrierten Wiener Extrablatt (17.1.1913).

"Professor Bernhardi" in Ungarn. In: Die Zeit, 10.4.1913 (Evening Edition).

Die Zeit des "Bernhardi" ist 1913. In: Wiener Allgemeine Zeitung, 30.4.1913.

Wienbibliothek in the Vienna City Hall

Pollaczek, Clara Katharina: Arthur Schnitzler und ich.

Schnitzler Archive, Cambridge University Library

An den Ausschuss zur rituellen Beköstigung der jüdischen Kriegsgefangenen und Zivilgefangenen an den Pessachfeiertagen, March 1915, Folder 60, Nr. 68–72.

Antikritik, Folder A 20 Nr. 10.

Aphorismen, Folder A 5.

Autobiographie, Folder A 173, 34.

Briefe Georg Brandes an Schnitzler, Folder B 17.

Briefe Theodor Herzl an Schnitzler, Folder B 39.

Briefe Schnitzler an Herzl, Folder B 75.

Briefe Hugo von Hofmannsthal an Schnitzler, Folder B 43,2.

Briefe Schnitzler an Hofmannsthal, Folder B 43a.

Briefe Samuel Fischer an Schnitzler, Folder B 121g

Briefe Schnitzler an Samuel Fischer, Folder B 121a & b.

Briefe an Felix Salten, Folder B 089b/2.

Briefe Stefan Zweig an Schnitzler, Folder B 118.

Der Weg ins Freie – Stellen und Einfälle, meist nicht verwendet, Folder A 133,3.

Der Weg ins Freie – Paralipomena, Folder A 134.

Die Entrüsteten, Folder A 132.

Entwürfe zu Professor Bernhardi, Folder A 118.

Gegen Kritik und Fälschung, Folder A 15.

Unabgesandte Briefe, Folder 124 b.

German Literary Archive, Marbach

Briefe Otto Brahm an Schnitzler, Folder B 0016d.

Briefe Arthur an Olga Schnitzler, Folders 518, 530.

Briefe Olga an Arthur Schnitzler, Folders 1223, 1229, 1231, 1232.

Briefe Jakob Wassermann an Schnitzler, Folder B 109.

Charakteristiken aus den Tagebüchern, Folder 187, Nr. 453.

Charakteristik aus den Tagebüchern – Theodor Herzl, Folder 203.

Published Primary Soureces

Bahr, Hermann: Der Antisemitismus. ed. by Claus Pias. Weimar: VDG 2005.

Billroth, Theodor: Über das Lehren und Lernen der medizinischen Wissenschaften an den Universitäten deutscher Nation. Vienna: C. Gerold 1876.

Samuel Fischer und Hedwig Fischer – Briefwechsel mit Autoren. ed. by Dierk Rodewald und Corinna Fiedler. Frankfurt / Main: S. Fischer 1989.

Freud, Sigmund. Eine Schwierigkeit der Psychoanalyse. In: *Imago. Zeitschrift für Anwendung der Psychoanalyse auf die Geisteswissenschaften 5* (1917). 1–7.

Hitler, Adolf: Mein Kampf. Munic: Franz Eher Nachf. 1943.

Kraus, Karl: Wie er Weltanschauungen aufeinanderplatzen läßt. In: Die Fackel, 14 / 370/71, 1912/13, 15-16.

Schnitzler, Arthur: Aphorismen und Betrachtungen. ed. by Robert O. Weiss. Frankfurt/ Main: S. Fischer 1967.

Schnitzler: Briefe 1875-1912. ed. by Therese Nickl und Heinrich Schnitzler. Frankfurt/ Main: S. Fischer 1981.

Schnitzler: Briefe 1913-1931. ed. by Peter Braunwarth et.al. Frankfurt/Main: S. Fischer 1984.

Schnitzler: Buch der Sprüche und Bedenken. ed. by Robert O. Weiss. Frankfurt/Main: S. Fischer 1967.

Schnitzler: Entworfenes und Verworfenes. ed. by Reinhard Urbach. Frankfurt/Main: S. Fischer 1977.

Schnitzler: Gesammelte Werke in vier Bänden. Frankfurt/Main: S. Fischer 1961–62.

Schnitzler: Jugend in Wien. Vienna: Molden 1968.

Schnitzler: Der Weg ins Freie. Frankfurt/Main: S. Fischer 1992).

Schnitzler: Ohne Maske – Aphorismen und Notate. ed. by Manfred Diersch. Leipzig: Kiepenheuer & Witsch 1992.

Schnitzler: Tagebuch. ed. by Peter Braunwarth et.al. Vienna: Verlag der Öst. Akademie der Wissenschaften, 1981–2000.
Vols.: 1893–1902, 1903–1908, 1909–1912, 1913–1916, 1920–1922, 1923–1926, 1927–1930.

Schnitzler, Olga: Spiegelbild der Freundschaft. Salzburg: Residenz 1962.

Arthur Schnitzler – Olga Waissnix. Liebe, die starb vor der Zeit. Ein Briefwechsel. ed. by Therese Nickl und Heinrich Schnitzler. Vienna: Molden 1970.

Wahrmund, Ludwig: Katholische Weltanschauung und freie Wissenschaft. Munich: Lehmann 1908.

Wassermann, Jakob: Die Juden von Zirndorf. Cadolzburg: ars vivendi 1995.

Wassermann, Jakob: Mein Weg als Deutscher und Jude. In: Jakob Wassermann – Deutscher und Jude. ed. by Dierk Rodewald. Heidelberg: Schneider 1984.

Secondary Literature on Schnitzler (Selection)

Aurnhammer, Achim, Beßlich, Barbara und Denk, Rudolf (eds.): Arthur Schnitzler und der Film. Würzburg: Ergon 2010.

Beier, Nikolaj: "Vor allem bin ich i c h…" – Judentum, Akkulturation und Antisemitismus in Arthur Schnitzlers Leben und Werk. Göttingen: Wallstein 2008.

Bellettini, Lorenzo und Hutchinson, Peter (eds.): Schnitzler's Hidden Manuscripts. New York: Peter Lang 2011.

Caputo, Antonia Maria: Arthur Schnitzlers späte Werke. Munich: Uni-Druck 1983.

Farese, Giuseppe: Arthur Schnitzler – Ein Leben in Wien 1862-1931. Munich: C. H. Beck1999.

Fliedl, Konstanze (ed.): Arthur Schnitzler im zwanzigsten Jahrhundert. Vienna: Picus 2003.

Foster, Ian und Krobb, Florian (eds.): Arthur Schnitzler: Zeitgenossenschaften – Contemporaneities. Frankfurt/Main: Peter Lang 2002.

Gaisbauer, Adolf: Der historische Hintergrund von Arthur Schnitzlers "Professor Bernhardi." In: Bulletin des Leo Baeck Instituts 13/50 (1974), 113–63

Herzog, Hillary Hope: Vienna Is Different: Jewish Writers in Austria from the Fin de Siècle to the Present. New York: Berghahn Books 2011.

Kaulen, Heinrich: Antisemitismus und Aufklärung – zum Verständnis von Arthur Schnitzlers Professor Bernhardi. In: Zeitschrift für deutsche Philologie 100 (1981), 177–

Rey, William: Arthur Schnitzler – Professor Bernhardi. Munich: Fink 1971.

Riedmann, Bettina: Ich bin Jude, Österreicher, Deutscher – Judentum in Arthur Schnitzlers Tagebüchern und Briefen. Tübingen: Max Niemeyer 2002.

Scheible, Hartmut: Arthur Schnitzler. Reinbek bei Hamburg: Rowohlt 1976.

Schinnerer, Otto P.: Schnitzler and the Military Censorship. Unpublished Correspondence. In: The Germanic Review, 5/3 (1930), 238–46.

Schinnerer, Otto P.: The Suppression of Schnitzlers *Der grüne Kakadu* by the Burgtheater. Unpublished Correspondence. In: The Germanic Review 6/2 (1931), 183–192.

Schneider, Gerd K.: Die Rezeption von Arthur Schnitzlers Reigen 1897–1994. Riverside, CA: Ariadne, 1995.

Vortisch, Verena: An der Grenze des Poesielands. Arthur Schnitzlers Komödie *Fink und Fliederbusch*. Würzburg: Ergon Verlag 2014.

Wagner, Renate: Arthur Schnitzler: eine Biographie. Vienna: Molden 1981.

Wagner, Renate: Frauen um Arthur Schnitzler. Vienna: Jugend & Volk 1980.

Wagner, Renate und Vacha, Brigitte: Wiener Schnitzler-Aufführungen 1891–1970. Munich: Prestel 1971.

Weiss, Robert: The "Hero" in Schnitzler's Comedy Professor Bernhardi. In: Modern Austrian Literature. 2/4 (1969), 30–34.

Willi, Andrea: Arthur Schnitzlers Roman "Der Weg ins Freie." Eine Untersuchung zur Tageskritik und ihren zeitgenössischen Bezügen. Heidelberg: Carl Winter 1989.

Secondary Literature on the Historical Context (Selection)

Aschheim, Steven: Brothers und Strangers. Madison: University of Wisconsin Press 1982.

Betten, Anne und Fliedl, Konstanze (eds.): Judentum und Antisemitismus: Studien zur Literatur und Germanistik in Deutschland und Österreich. Berlin, E. Schmidt 2003.

Beller, Steven: Vienna and the Jews 1867–1938. A Cultural History. Cambridge: Cambridge University Press 1989.

Berrkley, George: Vienna and Its Jews: The Tragedy of Success 1880-1980. Cambridge, MA: Madison Books 1988.

Brenner, David: Marketing Identities – Invention of Jewish Ethnicity in ‚Ost & West'. Detroit: Wayne State UP 1998.

Fränkel, Josef: The Jews of Austria: Essays on Their Life, History and Destruction. London: Vallentine & Mitchell 1970.

Geehr, Richard: Karl Lueger – Mayor of Fin-de-Siècle Vienna. Detroit: Wayne State UP 1990.

Grimm, Gunter und Bayerdörfer, Hans-Peter (eds.): Im Zeichen Hiobs. Königstein/Ts.: Athenäum 1985.

Hamburger, Ernest: Juden im öffentlichen Leben Deutschlands. Tübingen: Mohr Siebeck, 1968

Hödl, Klaus: Wiener Juden – jüdische Wiener: Identität, Gedächtnis und Performanz im 19. Jahrhundert. Vienna: Studienverlag 2006.

Horch, Hans Otto und Gelber, Mark H. (eds.): Von Franzos zu Canetti – Jüdische Autoren aus Österreich. Tübingen: Max Niemeyer 1996.

Jagow, Kurt und Herre, Paul (eds.): Politisches Handwörterbuch. Leipzig: K. F. Koehler 1923.

Johnston, William M.: The Austrian Mind. An Intellectual und Social History 1848-1938. Berkeley: University of California Press 1972.

Le Rider, Jacques: Modernity und Crises of Identity. Culture und Society in Fin-de-Siècle Vienna. Cambridge: Polity Press 1993.

Mosse, George L.: The Crisis of German Ideology. Intellectual Origins of the Third Reich. New York: Schocken Books 1981.

Palmer, Alan: Twilight of the Habsburgs. The Life and Times of Emperor Francis Joseph. London: Phoenix 2001.

Pauley, Bruce F.: From Prejudice to Persecution. (Chapel Hill: University of North Carolina Press 1992.

Robertson, Ritchie: The "Jewish Question" in German Literature 1749–1939. Emancipation and Its Discontents. Oxford: Oxford University Press 1999.

Rossbacher, Karlheinz: Literatur und Liberalismus. Vienna: Dachs 1992.

Rothaus, Rudolf: Geographischer Atlas zur Vaterlandskunde an den österreichischen Mittelschulen. Vienna: Kartographische Anstalt Freytag und Berndt 1911.

Rothenburg, Gunther E.: The Army of Francis Joseph. West Lafayette: Purdue University Press 1976.

Rozenblit, Marsha L.: The Jews of Wien 1867-1914: Assimilation und Identity. Albany, NY: State of New York University Press 1983.

Rozenblit, Reconstructing a National Identity. The Jews of Habsburg Austria during World War I. Oxford: Oxford University Press 2001.

Shirer, William L.: The Rise and Fall of the Third Reich. London: Bookclub Associates' Edition 1985.

Schorske, Carl E.: Fin-de-Siècle Vienna. London: Weidenfeld & Nicholson 1979.

Schroubek, Georg R.: Der "Ritualmord" von Polná. Traditioneller und moderner Wahnglaube. In: Antisemitismus und jüdische Geschichte. Ed. by Rainer Erb und Michael Schmidt. Berlin: Wiss. Autorenverlag 1987, 149–171.

Sked, Alan: The Decline and Fall of the Habsburg Empire 1815–1918. London: Longman 2001.

Spitzmüller, Alexander: Und hat auch Ursach, es zu leben. Vienna: Frick 1955.

Edward Timms: Karl Kraus, Apocalyptic Satirist. New Haven: Yale University Press 1986.

Volkov, Shulamit: Antisemitismus als kultureller Code. Munich: C. H. Beck 2000.

Whyte, George R.: Die Dreyfus-Affäre – die Macht des Vorurteils. Frankfurt/Main: Peter Lang, 2010.

Wistrich, Robert: The Jews of Vienna in the Age of Francis Joseph. Oxford: Oxford University Press 1989.

Index of Names

Max Haberich was born in Philadelphia in 1984 and grew up in Munich. He studied History, History of Art and German Literature in York, Aix-en-Provence and Tübingen. Haberich completed his PhD on the German-Jewish identity of Arthur Schnitzler and Jakob Wassermann at the University of Cambridge. He has published in various academic and literary journals. One of Haberich's recent publications includes a volume of short stories and satires in German, *Am Abhang der Wind* [*The Wind at the Precipice*] (2019) in the series 'Edition P.E.N.' of the Löcker Verlag.

www.ingramcontent.com/pod-product-compliance
Lightning Source LLC
Chambersburg PA
CBHW070346090426
42733CB00009B/1311

* 9 7 8 1 5 7 2 4 1 2 1 4 9 *